Honoré de Balzac

LA COMÉDIE HUMAINE

The Human Comedy

PROVINCIAL LIFE

VOLUME VIII

IN FINOT'S OFFICE

"*A claim then, no doubt?*" *rejoined Napoléon's former trooper.* "*We were a little hard on Mariette, I admit. But what do you expect! I don't even know why it was as yet. But if you demand satisfaction, I am ready,*" *he added, glancing at a collection of foils and pistols, the modern stand of arms, heaped together in a corner.*

"*Still less do I come for that, monsieur. I desire to speak with the editor in chief.*"

THE NOVELS

OF

HONORÉ DE BALZAC

NOW FOR THE FIRST TIME
COMPLETELY TRANSLATED INTO ENGLISH

LOST ILLUSIONS:
THE TWO POETS
A PROVINCIAL GREAT MAN IN PARIS
THE TRIALS OF AN INVENTOR

BY G. BURNHAM IVES

WITH FIFTEEN ETCHINGS BY ALFRED BOILOT, CHARLES-
THÉODORE DEBLOIS AND FRANÇOIS-XAVIER
LE SUEUR, AFTER PAINTINGS BY
ADRIEN MOREAU

VOLUME I

PRINTED ONLY FOR SUBSCRIBERS BY
GEORGE D. SPROUL, NEW YORK

LOST ILLUSIONS

TO MONSIEUR VICTOR HUGO

You who, by virtue of the privilege accorded the Raphaels and the Pitts, were a great poet at the age when men are usually so puny, have, like Chateaubriand, like all men of genuine talent, been compelled to combat the envious, ambuscaded behind the pillars or crouching in the subterranean caverns of the newspaper.   Therefore do I desire that your victorious name should participate in the victory of this work, which I dedicate to you, and which, in the view of some people, is a manifestation of courage as well as a narrative faithful to the truth. Did not journalists, like marquises, financiers, doctors and lawyers, belong to Molière and his stage?   Why then should the COMEDIE HUMAINE, which *castigat ridendo mores*, omit a single power, when the Parisian press omits none?

I am happy, monsieur, to be able to subscribe myself

Your sincere admirer and friend,

DE BALZAC.

PART FIRST

THE TWO POETS

*

At the time when this narrative begins, the Stanhope press and the ink-distributing cylinders had not yet been adopted in the small provincial printing offices. Despite the special circumstances which establish a direct connection between Angoulême and Parisian printing offices, that town still used the wooden presses to which the language is indebted for the expression, "to make the press groan," an expression which now has no application. The old-fashioned offices there still made use of leather *balls* rubbed over with ink, with which one of the pressmen besmeared the type. The movable plate whereon is placed the form filled with letters, upon which the sheet of paper is laid, was still of stone and justified its name of *marble*. The all-devouring machine presses of to-day have so completely banished all memory of this mechanism, to which we owe, despite its imperfections, the noble volumes of Elzevir, Plantin, Alde and Didot, that it is necessary to mention the old-fashioned tools, for which Jérôme-Nicolas Séchard had a superstitious affection, for they play a part in this great petty narrative.

This Séchard was a former journeyman pressman, one of those whom the workmen whose duty it is to assemble the type, call, in their printers' slang, a *bear*. The constant passing back and forth from ink-well to press and from press to ink-well, not unlike the movements of a bear in his cage, was un-doubtedly responsible for that sobriquet. In re-venge, the *bears* called the compositors *monkeys*, because of the incessant exercise those gentlemen go through in seizing the letters in the hundred and fifty-two little cases in which they are contained.

In the disastrous days of 1793, Séchard, then about fifty years old, was a married man. His age and the fact of his marriage exempted him from the great conscription, which drafted almost all the mechanics into the armies. The old pressman was left alone in the office, the proprietor, otherwise called the *innocent*, having recently died, leaving a childless widow. The establishment seemed to be threatened with immediate destruction: the solitary bear was incapable of transforming himself into a monkey; for, printer though he was, he could neither read nor write. Heedless of his incapacity, a representative of the people, in eager haste to spread broadcast the glorious decrees of the Con-vention, invested the pressman with the commis-sion of master printer, and set his presses at work. Having accepted this perilous commission, Citizen Séchard indemnified his master's widow by paying her for the stock in trade of the office, at about half its value, with his wife's savings. That was nothing. He was required to print the republican decrees without error or delay. At that embarrassing conjuncture, Jérôme-Nicolas Séchard had the good fortune to meet a noble Marseillais, who did not wish to emigrate, or to lose his estates, or to show himself for fear of losing his head, and who could not procure bread to eat unless he turned his hand to some kind of work. So Monsieur le Comte de Maucombe donned the humble jacket of a provincial printer: he, himself, composed, read and corrected the decrees which called for the infliction of the death-penalty upon citizens who harbored nobles; the *bear*, now an *innocent*, struck them off and caused them to be placarded through the town; and they both escaped safe and sound.

In 1795, the hurricane of the Revolution having passed over, Nicolas Séchard was obliged to find another Master Jacques, who could act as compositor and as proof-reader. An abbé, who became a bishop under the Restoration, but who refused at this time to take the oath, replaced the Comte de Maucombe until the day that the First Consul re-established the Catholic religion. The count and the bishop met at a later period on the same bench in the Chamber of Peers. Although in 1802, Jérôme-Nicolas Séchard was no better able to read and write than in 1793, he had laid by sufficient *stuff* to be able to hire a proof-reader. The journeyman with so little thought for the future had become an object of awe to his bears and monkeys. Avarice begins where poverty ends. On the day that the possibility of making his fortune first dawned upon the printer, self-interest developed in him a thorough, but grasping, suspicious and far-sighted understanding of his trade. His method of conducting the business snapped its fingers at theory. He had finally acquired the power of estimating at a glance the price of a page or a sheet according to the style of letters used. He proved to his illiterate customers that it was more expensive to move large letters than small ones; or, if they wanted small ones, he said that they were harder to handle. Composition being a branch of typography of which he had no comprehension, he was so afraid of making mistakes against himself, that he never made any but one-sided bargains. If his compositors worked by the hour he never took his eyes off them. If he knew that a paper manufacturer was in embarrassed circumstances, he would buy his stock at a low price and store it. In 1802 he had saved enough to purchase the house in which the printing office had been located from time immemorial. Fortune smiled upon him in every direction: he lost his wife, and he had only one son; he placed him at the town lyceum, less for the purpose of giving him an education than to prepare a successor to himself; he treated him harshly in order to prolong the duration of his paternal authority; thus, on holidays, he set him at work at the case, bidding him learn to earn his own living so that he could some day reward his poor father who was bleeding himself to give him an education.

At the abbé's departure, Séchard chose for his proof-reader that one of his four compositors who was recommended by the future bishop as being no less honest than intelligent. In this way the good-man prepared for the time when his son should be competent to undertake the management of the establishment, which would expand rapidly in his young and skilful hands.

David Séchard took very high rank in his studies at the lyceum at Angoulême. Although a bear, who had made his own way without knowledge or education, and entertaining a sovereign contempt for science, Père Séchard sent his son to Paris to study scientific typography; but he was so emphatic in his injunctions to him to lay by a handsome sum in a city which he called the paradise of workmen, bidding him not to rely upon the paternal purse, that he must have seen some way of attaining his own ends in this sojourn *in the land of sapience.* While learning his trade, David also completed his education at Paris. The Didots' proof-reader became a *savant.* In the latter part of 1819 David Séchard, whose life in Paris had not cost his father a sou, left the capital at the old man's summons, to return to the province and assume the management of the business. Nicolas Séchard's printing office published at that time the only sheet in the department containing legal announcements, and also did all the printing for the prefecture and the diocese, three sources of revenue upon which an energetic young man might hope to found a handsome fortune.

Just at that time the brothers Cointet, paper manufacturers, purchased the second printer's privilege in the residency of Angoulême, which, up to that time, old Séchard had succeeded in keeping absolutely inactive by favor of the military crises which, under the Empire, held all industrial progress in check; for that reason, he had not deemed it worth his while to purchase it, and his parsimony was one cause of the downfall of the old printing house. When he heard the news, old Séchard reflected with great satisfaction that the contest between his establishment and that of the Cointets would have to be carried on by his son and not by himself.

"I should have gone to the wall," he said to himself; "but a young man brought up by Messieurs Didot will pull through."

The septuagenarian sighed for the time when he could lead a life of leisure. Although he had but little knowledge of scientific typography, he was supposed to be remarkably strong in an art which has been jestingly dubbed by mechanics, *tipsification*; an art much esteemed by the divine creator of *Pantagruel*, but the cultivation of which, under the persecution of so-called temperance societies, is more and more neglected from day to day. Jérôme-Nicolas Séchard, faithful to the destiny his name had created for him, was consumed by an

inextinguishable thirst.   His wife had long kept
within reasonable bounds this passion for the expressed juice of the grape, a passion so natural to
bears, that Monsieur de Chateaubriand observed its
existence in the genuine American bear; but phil-
osophers have remarked that the habits of youth
return with renewed force in old age.   Séchard
afforded a striking testimony to the truth of this
moral law: the older he grew, the more he loved to
drink.   His passion left traces upon his ursine face
that made it quite unique: his nose had assumed
the proportions and the shape of a capital A of triple
canon type, his veined cheeks resembled vine-leaves
covered with violet, purple, often branching protuberances; you would have said it was an enormous
truffle enveloped in autumn vine-branches.   Hidden
beneath huge eyebrows that resembled bushes
laden with snow, his little gray eyes, wherein shone
the crafty gleam of an avarice that killed everything within him, even the impulses of paternity,
preserved their intelligence even in drunkenness.
His bald, shiny head, with its scanty fringe of gray
hair, still curly, reminded one of the cobblers in
La Fontaine's Fables.   He was short and paunchy,
like many of the old styles of lamp that consume
more oil than wick; for excess in everything impels
the body along the path to which it naturally in-
clines.   Drunkenness, like study, makes the fat
man fatter and the thin man thinner.

Jérôme-Nicolas Séchard had worn for thirty years
the famous municipal three-cornered hat, which in

some provinces is still seen on the head of the town
drummer. His waistcoat and his trousers were of
greenish velvet, and he wore an old brown frockcoat, figured cotton stockings and shoes with silver
buckles. This costume, in which the mechanic
could be detected in the bourgeois, harmonized so
well with his vices and his habits, it was so expressive of his life, that it seemed as if the goodman must have come into the world all dressed:
you could no more have imagined him without his
clothes than an onion without its skin. Even if
the old printer had not long before sufficiently manifested his blind greed, the manner of his retirement
would have sufficed to depict his character. Notwithstanding the knowledge and experience his son
was certain to have brought back with him from the
great school of the Didots, he proposed to drive a
profitable bargain with him, upon which he had long
been ruminating. If it was a profitable bargain
for the father, it was likely to be an unprofitable one
for the son. But, so far as the goodman was concerned, there was no father and no son in business.
If he had at first thought of David as his only child,
he eventually saw in him a natural successor in the
business, whose interests were opposed to his: he
wanted to sell at a high price, David would want to
buy cheap; *ergo,* his son became an enemy to
conquer. This transformation of sentiment to personal interest, ordinarily a slow, tortuous and
hypocritical process in well-bred people, was swift
and unswerving in the case of the old *bear,* who

showed how superior a crafty drunkard is to a skilled printer.

When his son arrived, the goodman manifested the commercial affection which clever men bestow upon their dupes: he waited upon him as a lover waits upon his mistress; he offered him his arm, he told him where he must put his feet in order not to soil his boots; he had had his bed warmed, a fire lighted and supper prepared. The next day, after he had tried to make his son tipsy during a bounteous dinner, Jérôme-Nicolas Séchard, thoroughly saturated with wine, turned to his son with a *Let's talk business!* which came out so queerly between two hiccoughs that David begged him to postpone the business until the following day. The old *bear* was too well skilled in turning his drunkenness to his own advantage to abandon a battle for which he had been making ready so long. Furthermore, he said that, after dragging his ball and chain for fifty years, he did not propose to wear it an hour longer. On the morrow, his son would be the innocent.

At this point it will be well perhaps to say a word concerning the Séchard establishment. The printing office, located at the corner of Rue de Beaulieu and Place du Mûrier, was established on that spot toward the close of the reign of Louis XIV. Thus the building had long been arranged to suit the requirements of that branch of industry. The ground floor formed one immense room lighted by an old small-paned window on the street and by a

large window looking on an interior courtyard.
The office of the proprietor could be reached by an
outside passage way. But, in the provinces, the
processes of printing are always the object of such
eager curiosity, that customers preferred to enter by
the glass door in the street front, although they
must descend several steps, the floor of the press-
room being below the level of the sidewalk. Visitors, agape with curiosity, paid no heed to the
inconveniences of the passage through the defiles of
the workshop. While they were gazing at the
cradles formed by the sheets stretched upon cords
hanging from the ceiling, they would stumble
against the rows of cases or knock their hats off
against the iron bars that supported the presses.
If they followed the agile movements of a compositor darting at his letters in the hundred and fifty-
two compartments of his case, reading his copy,
rereading the line in his galley and inserting a
lead, they would run into a ream of damp paper
with heavy weights upon it, or strike their hips
against the corner of a bench; all to the great
amusement of the bears and monkeys. No
one ever arrived without accident at the two great
cages situated at the farther end of this cavern,
forming two dilapidated cells upon the courtyard
side, in one of which the proof-reader, in the other
the master printer, sat in state.

The walls on the courtyard were agreeably embellished with vine-trellises, which, in view of the
master's reputation, had an appetizing local color.

At the rear, supported against the party-wall, was
a dilapidated lean-to, where the paper was soaked
and cut. There too was the sink at which the
forms, commonly called the letter-blocks, were
washed before and after the printing; the waste-
pipe discharged a decoction of ink, which, when
mingled with the waste water from the house, led
the peasants, who came there on market days, to
believe that the devil was in the habit of washing
in the house. The lean-to was flanked on one side
by the kitchen, on the other by a woodpile. The
first floor of the house, above which there were only
two attic chambers, contained three rooms. The
first, which was as long as the passageway, less the
cage of the old wooden stairway, was lighted by a
small oblong window on the street and by a bull's-
eye on the courtyard, and served the double purpose
of a reception-room and a dining-room. The walls
were whitewashed, and the whole room was noticeable by reason of the cynical simplicity of commercial greed; the dirty floor had never been washed;
the furniture consisted of three wretched chairs, a
round table and a sideboard, the latter placed between two doors leading respectively to a bedroom
and a salon; the windows and door were black
with dirt; the room was generally filled with paper,
blank or printed, and not infrequently the dessert,
the bottles and the side dishes of Jérôme-Nicolas
Séchard's dinner were placed upon bales of paper.
The bedroom, which had a window with leaded
panes looking on the courtyard, was hung with the

old-fashioned tapestries that are used in the provinces to decorate the house-fronts on Corpus Christi Day. There was a great four-post bedstead, provided with curtains of coarse cloth, and a coverlid in red serge, two moth-eaten armchairs, two upholstered black walnut chairs, an old secretary and a clock on the mantelpiece. This room, which exhaled an odor of patriarchal simplicity, obscured by sombre coloring, had been arranged by Sieur Rouzeau, Jérôme-Nicolas Séchard's predecessor and master. The salon, modernized by the late Madame Séchard, was embellished with a hideous wooden wainscoting, painted a barber's blue; the panels were decorated with a paper representing oriental scenes in dark-brown on a white ground; the furniture consisted of six chairs with blue sheep-skin seats and backs made in the shape of lyres. The two arched windows, which looked on Place du Mûrier, were without curtains; the mantelpiece had neither candlesticks nor clock nor mirror. Madame Séchard died in the midst of her schemes of embellishment, and the bear, failing to appreciate the utility of improvements which brought in nothing, had abandoned them.

It was to this room that Jérôme-Nicolas Séchard, *pede titubante,* led his son, and pointed to the table, whereon lay an inventory of the stock in his printing office, prepared under his supervision by the proof-reader.

"Read that, my boy," said Jérôme-Nicolas Séchard, rolling his drunken eyes from the paper to his son and from his son to the paper. "You'll see what a jewel of a printing office I'm giving you."

" 'Three wooden presses supported by iron bars, with the beds of cast-iron—'

"An improvement of mine," interposed old Séchard.

" 'With all their appurtenances, ink-wells, balls and benches, etc., sixteen hundred francs!' Why, father," said David Séchard, letting the inventory fall, "your presses are old rubbish not worth a hundred crowns, good for nothing but to be burned up."

"Old rubbish?" cried old Séchard, "rubbish? Take the inventory and let's go down! You'll see if your wretched blacksmith inventions work like these good old well-tried tools. Then you won't have the heart to insult honest presses that roll as smoothly as post-chaises, and will last all your life without the slightest need of repair. Rubbish! Yes, rubbish in which you'll find salt enough to cook eggs! rubbish your father has used twenty years and that has helped him to make you what you are."

The father shuffled down the rickety, worn-out, shaking staircase without falling through; he opened the door of the passageway that led to the work-room, rushed to the first of his presses, which he had craftily had oiled and cleaned, and pointed to the strong oaken cheeks, which his apprentice had rubbed until they shone.

"Isn't that a love of a press?" he asked.

2

There was a wedding invitation on the press. The old bear lowered the frisket on the tympan, and the tympan on the slab, which he slid under the press; he drew the bar, loosened the cord to draw back the slab, and raised tympan and frisket with the agility of a young bear. The press, thus handled, gave forth a sweet little note such as a bird might have uttered as it flew away after striking against a window.

"Is there an English press capable of doing such work as that?" said the father to his astonished son.

He ran to the second and third presses in succession and went through the same performance upon each of them with equal skill. Upon the last, his hazy eye discovered a spot the apprentice had overlooked; the drunkard, having sworn roundly, took the skirt of his coat to rub it, as a groom polishes the coat of a horse that is for sale.

"With these presses and without a proof-reader, you can earn your nine thousand francs a year, David. As your future partner, I object to your replacing them by those accursed cast-iron presses that wear out the type. You shouted miracles in Paris when you saw the invention of that infernal Englishman, an enemy of France, who has tried to make the fortune of founders. So you wanted to have Stanhopes, did you? a fig for your Stanhopes, which cost twenty-five hundred francs each, almost twice as much as my three jewels together are worth, and break the backs of the letters by their lack of elasticity. I'm not a learned man like

you, but just remember this: the life of the Stanhopes means the death of the type. These three
presses will do you good service, the work will be
done properly, and that's all the good people of
Angoulême want. Whether you print with iron or
wood, with gold or silver, they won't pay a sou
more."

" '*Item*,' David read on, " 'five thousand pounds
of type from the foundry of Monsieur Vaflard—' "

At that name, the pupil of the Didots could not
restrain a smile.

"Oh! laugh, laugh! After twelve years, the
type are still as good as new. That's what I call a
founder! Monsieur Vaflard's an honest man who
supplies durable goods; and to my mind the best
founder is the one you have to call on least often."

" 'Appraised at ten thousand francs,' " continued
David. "Ten thousand francs, father! why that's
at forty sous a pound, and Messieurs Didot only
charge thirty-six sous a pound for their new pica.
Your nail-heads are only worth the value of the
castings, ten sous a pound."

"You give the name of 'nail-heads' to the italics,
running-hand and roundhand of Monsieur Gillé,
formerly printer to the Emperor, type that is worth
six francs a pound, masterpieces of casting purchased five years ago, and some of the pieces with
the white of the casting still on them: see!"

Old Séchard picked up several handfuls of "sorts"
that had never been used and showed them to him.

"I'm no scholar, I don't know how to read or

write, but I know enough to know that the Gillé
written type is the father of your Didots' English
type.   Here's a roundhand," he said, pointing to
a case and taking out an M, "a case of pica roundhand that's not yet out of use."

David saw that it was impossible to argue with
his father.   He must either agree to everything or
nothing; it must be yes or no.   The old bear had
included everything in the inventory, even to the
cords in the drying-room.   The smallest chase, the
shelves, the trays, the stone and the scrubbing
brushes, everything was figured with the scrupulous
exactitude of a miser.   The whole amounted to
thirty thousand francs, including the license as
master printer and the good-will.   David deliber-
ated as to whether it was or was not a practicable
opportunity.   Seeing his son sitting mute over the
figures, old Séchard became uneasy; for he preferred
a violent dispute to silent acquiescence.   In bargains of this sort, discussion indicates a capable
negotiator defending his interests.   *The man who
agrees to everything pays for nothing*, thought old
Séchard.   Watching his son's countenance the
while, he went through the enumeration of the
sorry accessories essential to the working of a provincial printing office; he led him to a polishing
press, a cutting machine for the town work, and
boasted of their long use and their durability.

"Old tools are always the best," he said.   "A
printer ought to be willing to pay more for them
than for new, as gold-beaters do."

Hideous vignettes representing Hymens and Cupids, dead men lifting the stones from their sepulchres, describing a V or an M, enormous borders with masks for play bills, became, by virtue of the vinous eloquence of Jérôme-Nicolas Séchard, objects of immense value. He told his son that the habits of provincials were so deeply rooted that he would try in vain to arouse a taste for anything finer. He, Jérôme-Nicolas Séchard, had tried to sell them better almanacs than the *Double Liégois* printed on sugar paper! but they preferred the genuine *Double Liégois* to the most magnificent almanacs. David would soon realize the value of these old-fashioned things when he found he could sell them for more than the most expensive novelties.

"Ah! my boy, the province is the province, and Paris is Paris. If a man from L'Houmeau comes to order his wedding invitations and you print them for him without a cupid and garlands of roses, he won't believe he's married, and he'll bring them back to you if he sees nothing but an M, such as your Messieurs Didot would give him; they may be the glory of typography, but their inventions won't be adopted in the provinces in less than a hundred years. And there you are."

Generous-minded men are very poor hands at driving a bargain. David was one of those shy, affectionate creatures who shrink from a dispute, and who yield at once when their opponent appeals to their heart. His exalted sentiments and the power the old drunkard had retained over him made

him still more unfit to sustain a discussion concerning money matters with his father, especially when
he credited him with the best intentions; for at
first he attributed the voracity of selfishness to the
old pressman's attachment to his tools. However,
as Jérôme-Nicolas Séchard had purchased the whole
establishment from the widow Rouzeau for ten
thousand francs in *assignats,* and as thirty thousand
francs was a most exorbitant price for them in their
present condition, he cried:

"Father, you are robbing me!"

"I, who gave you your life?—" said the old
drunkard raising his hand toward the drying-room.
"Why, David, what do you value the license at?
Do you know what the legal notices are worth at
ten sous a line,—a privilege that brought in five
hundred francs last month, all by itself? Just open
the books, my boy, and see what the advertisements
and lists of the prefecture produce and the custom
of the mayor's office and the bishopric! You're a
sluggard who doesn't want to make his fortune.
You're haggling over the horse that will take you
to some fine estate like Marsac."

To the inventory were appended articles of partnership between the father and son. The kind
father leased his house to the firm for twelve hundred francs, although he had paid only six thousand for it, and he reserved for himself one of the
two attic rooms. Until David Séchard should pay
the thirty thousand francs, the profits were to be
equally divided; on the day when he paid his

father that sum, he was to become the sole
proprietor of the business. David formed an estimate of the value of the license, the good-will and
the journal, paying no heed to the stock and
machinery; he believed that he could see his way
to make money and he accepted the conditions.
The father, accustomed as he was to the pettifog-
ging shrewdness of the peasantry, and knowing
nothing of the far-reaching projects of Parisian men
of business, was amazed at so prompt a conclusion.
"Can my son have got rich?" he thought, "or is
he now thinking up some way of not paying me?"
With that conjecture in his mind, he questioned
him as to whether he had brought any money home,
so that he might secure it as a payment on account.
The father's inquisitiveness aroused the son's suspicions, and he maintained a close reserve. The
next day, old Séchard bade his apprentice carry his
furniture to his room on the second floor, intending
to send it to his house in the country by wagons
that were returning in that direction empty. He
turned over to his son the three rooms on the first
floor stripped perfectly bare, just as he put him in
possession of the printing office without giving him
a centime to pay the workmen. When David urged
his father, as a partner, to contribute to the fund
that was essential for running the office for their
mutual benefit, the old pressman feigned ignorance.
He was not obliged, he said, to furnish money when
he had furnished the plant; his contribution was all
made. Cornered by his son's logic, he retorted

that, when he bought the plant from the widow Rouzeau, he had made his way without a sou. If he, a poor journeyman, without any sort of knowledge, had succeeded, a pupil of the Didots ought to do even better. Furthermore, David had earned money because of the education his old father had paid for with the sweat of his brow; he might well put it to some use to-day.

"What have you done with your *funds?*" he said, returning to the charge in the hope of gaining some light upon the problem which his son's silence had left unsolved the night before.

"Why, have I not had to live? haven't I bought books?" replied David indignantly.

"Ah! you have bought books? You won't make a good business man. People who buy books are hardly fit to print them," retorted the bear.

David experienced the most horrible of humiliations, that caused by the degradation of one's father: he was forced to submit to the flood of base, cowardly, tearful, commercial reasons with which the old miser supported his refusal. He forced his sorrow back into his heart, realizing that he was alone and unsupported, and finding a vile speculator in his father, whom, through philosophical curiosity, he determined to probe to the bottom. He called his attention to the fact that he had never asked for an account of his mother's fortune. If that fortune was not to enter into the matter of payment for the plant, it should at least be used for the expenses of carrying on the business.

"Your mother's fortune?" said old Séchard; "why her wit and her beauty were her fortune!"

From that reply David gauged his father's character completely, and realized that, in order to obtain an account, he would be compelled to enter upon an expensive, interminable, degrading lawsuit. The noble heart accepted the burden that was cast upon it, for he knew how difficult it would be for him to fulfil his agreements with his father.

"I will work," he said to himself. "After all, if I have bad luck, it's no more than the goodman himself had. Besides, I shall really be working for myself."

"I leave you a great treasure," said the father, disturbed by his son's silence.

David inquired what the treasure might be.

"Marion," was the reply.

Marion was a stout country girl, whose services were indispensable in carrying on the printing office; she soaked the paper and cut it, did the errands and the cooking and washing, unloaded the wagons of paper, collected the money and cleaned the rolls. If Marion had known how to read, old Séchard would have made a compositor of her.

The old man set out on foot for the country. Although highly pleased with his sale, which he disguised under the name of partnership, he was anxious as to his means of obtaining payment. After the agonizing suspense of a sale comes always that of its completion. All the passions are essentially jesuitical. This man, who deemed education useless, forced himself to believe in the influence of education. He based his hopes of realizing his thirty thousand francs on the ideas of honor that education had probably developed in his son. David, being a well brought-up youth, would sweat blood and water to fulfil his undertakings, his knowledge would suggest ways and means, he had shown himself to be actuated by praiseworthy sentiments, and he would pay! Many fathers, who act in this way, believe that they have acted as fathers should and old Séchard had succeeded in so persuading himself by the time he arrived at his vineyard at Marsac, a small village four leagues from Angoulême.

This estate, upon which the last owner had built an attractive little house, had been added to from year to year since 1809, when the old bear purchased it. There he laid aside the cares of the printing-press for those of the wine-press, and he had, as he himself said, been too long among the vines not to know a thing or two about them. During the first year of his retirement, Père Séchard exhibited an anxious face over his vine poles; for he was always in his vineyard, just as he used to be always in his press-room. The thirty thousand francs he almost despaired of receiving intoxicated him more than the September wine; he constantly imagined that he had them between his fingers. The less reason he had to expect the money, the greater his longing to see it safely stowed away in his strong-box. So he often made hurried trips from

Marsac to Angoulême, drawn thither by his anxiety.
He would climb the steps up the cliff on whose summit the town is built, and go at once to the press-
room to see if his son were going out of business.
But the presses were always in their places. The
only apprentice, with his paper cap on his head,
was scraping the dirt off the rolls. The old bear
would hear the squeak of a press upon some invitation, he would recognize his old type, and see his
son and the proof-reader, each in his cage, reading
what the bear took for proofs. Having dined with
David, he would return to Marsac, ruminating over
his fears.

Avarice, like love, has the gift of second sight as
to future contingencies, it scents them and hurries
them on. When he was away from the press-room,
where the sight of his tools fascinated him, taking
him back to the days when he made his fortune,
the vinegrower recalled ominous symptoms of inactivity in his son. The name of *Cointet Frères*
frightened him, he fancied that he saw it overshad-
owing that of *Séchard et Fils*. In short, the old
man scented the wind of misfortune. His presentiment was well-founded: disaster was hovering over
the house of Séchard. But misers have a god.
Through a combination of unforeseen circumstances,
that god was destined to drop the price of the
usurious sale into the old drunkard's purse.

The fall of the Séchard establishment, notwithstanding its elements of prosperity, was due to
the following reason. Indifferent to the religious

reaction which the Restoration produced in the government, and equally indifferent to the cause of liberalism, David maintained a most injudicious neutrality in political and religious matters. It was a time when provincial tradesmen were compelled to profess some opinion in order to have any customers, and one must choose between liberal and royalist tenets. A passion that assailed David's heart, and his absorption in scientific investigations, together with his naturally noble character, kept him from that keen thirst for gain which constitutes the true tradesman, and which would have led him to study the points of difference between the Parisian method of doing business and that in vogue in the provinces. The lines of demarcation that are so sharply marked in the departments, disappear in the constant movement of Paris.

The brothers Cointet adopted monarchical opinions, they fasted ostentatiously, they haunted the cathedral, cultivated the acquaintance of the priests, and reprinted the first religious books of which the supply ran short. Thus the Cointets took the lead in that lucrative branch of the trade, and slanderously accused David Séchard of liberalism and atheism. How, they asked, could anyone employ a man, whose father was a Septembrist, a drunkard, a Bonapartist, an old miser who would die sooner or later and leave heaps of gold? They were poor and burdened with families, while David was a bachelor and would be immensely rich; that was the reason that he took things so easily, etc.

Influenced by these accusations against David, the prefecture and the bishopric finally transferred the privilege of doing such printing as they had to do, to the brothers Cointet. Soon these grasping rivals, emboldened by David's indifference, established a second journal of legal announcements. The old office was thus reduced to the town printing, and the profits of its journal of announcements were cut down one-half. Having realized a considerable sum on their church books and religious publications, the Cointets soon proposed to the Séchards that the latter should sell them their journal, so that the departmental and legal announcements might all appear in the same sheet. David had no sooner transmitted this proposition to his father than the old vinegrower, already alarmed at the progress made by the Cointet establishment, rushed from Marsac to Place du Mûrier with the celerity of the crow that has scented the dead bodies lying on a field of battle.

"Let me handle the Cointets, don't you meddle in this business," he said to his son. The old man soon detected the purpose of the Cointets; he frightened them by his keen insight. His son was on the point of doing a foolish thing which he had come there to prevent, he said.

"What will our custom have to rest upon, if he gives up our journal? The solicitors, the notaries, all the tradesmen of L'Houmeau are liberals; the Cointets have tried to injure the Séchards by accusing them of liberalism, and in that way they have

prepared a plank of salvation for them; the liberal
announcements will still be published by the
Séchards!   Sell the journal?—why we might as
well sell the stock in trade and the license.''

He thereupon asked the Cointets to buy the plant
for sixty thousand francs, in order not to ruin his
son; he loved his son, he would defend his son.
The vinegrower used his son as peasants use their
wives: whether his son was willing or not, he at
last led the Cointets, extorting from them one offer
after another, to give twenty-two thousand francs
for the *Journal de la Charente*.   But David was to
bind himself never to print a journal of any
description, under a penalty of thirty thousand
francs.   This sale was the suicide of the Séchard
printing office; but the old vinegrower was but
little disturbed by that fact.   After the theft comes
always the murder.   The goodman proposed to apply
this sum in part payment for his plant; and, in
order to make sure of it, he would have thrown in
David to boot, especially as that burdensome son
was really entitled to half of the unhoped-for treasure.   In return, the generous father turned over the
printing office to his son, but still insisted upon his
rent of twelve hundred francs.

After the sale of the journal to Cointet, the old
man rarely came to the town, alleging his advanced age as an excuse; but the real reason was
his lack of interest in an establishment that no
longer belonged to him.   He could not, however,
entirely renounce his old affection for his tools.

When his business took him to Angoulême, it would have been very hard to say whether his wooden presses or his son, from whom he went through the form of demanding his rent, were more potent in attracting him to his house. His former proof-reader, who was now employed in that capacity by the Cointets, was able to explain this paternal generosity; he said that the old fox, by allowing the rent to accumulate, had in view the right to intervene, as a privileged creditor, in the settlement of his son's affairs.

David Séchard's indifference was attributable to certain causes which will serve to depict the young man's character. Some days after his installation in his father's printing office, he had fallen in with one of his college friends, then in utterly destitute circumstances. This friend of David Séchard was a young man of about twenty-one, named Lucien Chardon, the son of a former surgeon in the republican army, who was incapacitated for further service by a severe wound. Nature had made the elder Chardon a chemist and chance had established him at Angoulême as a druggist. Death came upon him in the midst of the necessary preparations for exploiting a valuable discovery, to which he had devoted several years of scientific research. He aimed at curing every variety of gout. Gout is the disease of the rich and the rich will pay a high price for health when they are deprived of it. Therefore, the druggist had selected that particular problem for solution among all those that presented themselves to his mind. Placed between science and empiricism, the late Chardon realized that science alone could assure his fortune; he had therefore studied the causes of the disease, and based his remedy upon a special diet which he varied to suit each individual temperament. He died during a visit to Paris, whither he had gone to seek the approbation of the Academy of Sciences, and thus he lost the fruit of his labors. Deeming his fortune assured, the druggist had neglected no means of perfecting the education of his son and of his daughter, so that his family expenses had constantly eaten up the profits of his pharmacy. And so, not only did he leave his children in destitute circumstances, but, unluckily for them, he had brought them up in the hope of a brilliant destiny, which hope died with him. The illustrious Desplein, who attended him in his last illness, watched him die in convulsions of impotent rage. The moving cause of this intense ambition was the ex-surgeon's deep affection for his wife, the last scion of the family of Rubempré, whom he had saved from the scaffold, as by a miracle, in 1793. Without obtaining her consent to the falsehood, he had gained time by saying that she was *enceinte*. Having thus acquired a sort of right to marry her, marry her he did, notwithstanding their common poverty. Her children, like all love children, had no other inheritance than their mother's marvelous beauty, a gift that is so often fatal when accompanied by poverty. Her husband's hopes and toil and despair, which she had so fully shared, had wrought prodigious changes in Madame Chardon's beauty, just as the gradual degradation of want had changed her manners; but her courage and her children's equaled their misfortunes.

The poor widow sold the pharmacy, which was

located on the main street of L'Houmeau, the principal suburb of Angoulême. The sum she received
therefor enabled her to assure herself an income
of three hundred francs, which was quite insufficient
for her own support; but she and her daughter accepted their situation without shame, and devoted
themselves to such work as they could procure.
The mother nursed women in childbed, and her
pleasant manners led to her being preferred to all
others in the wealthy families, where she lived without expense to her children, and earned twenty sous
per day. To spare her son the humiliation of seeing his mother in such a plight, she had taken the
name of Madame Charlotte. Those persons who
desired her services applied to Monsieur Postel,
Monsieur Chardon's successor.

Lucien's sister was employed by a neighbor, a
most respectable woman, much esteemed at
L'Houmeau, one Madame Prieur, a laundress, and
earned about fifteen sous per day. She superin-
tended the other girls, and occupied a sort of superior
position in the establishment, which raised her
slightly above the grisette class. The trifling proceeds of their labor, added to Madame Chardon's
three hundred francs, made a total of about eight
hundred francs a year, with which those three persons had to board and clothe themselves. Even the
strict economy with which the household was conducted could hardly make that sum sufficient, as it
was almost entirely absorbed by Lucien. Madame
Chardon and her daughter Eve believed in Lucien

as Mahomet's wife believed in her husband; their devotion to the interests of his future was absolutely unlimited. The impoverished family lived at L'Houmeau in lodgings let to them for a very moderate sum by Monsieur Chardon's successor, and situated at the end of an inner court, above the laboratory. Lucien occupied a wretched attic room. Being constantly spurred on by a father, who, in his passionate inclination for natural science, had first turned his mind in that direction, Lucien was one of the most brilliant pupils at the College of Angoulême, and was in the third class when David Séchard completed his studies there.

When chance brought these two old schoolmates together, Lucien, weary of drinking from the bitter cup of poverty, was upon the point of adopting one of the extreme courses to which young men of twenty sometimes resort. Forty francs a month, which David generously offered him, together with a proposition to teach him the trade of proof-reader, although a proof-reader was absolutely useless to him, rescued Lucien from despair. The bonds of their college friendship, thus renewed, were soon drawn tighter by the similarity of their destinies and the difference in their characters. Each of them possessed a mind teeming with the material for several fortunes, and that lofty intelligence which places man upon a level with eminence of every sort, and yet they found themselves on the very lowest rung of the social ladder. This injustice on the part of fate was a powerful bond of union.

Furthermore, both had arrived at versifying, but by different roads. Although destined to the loftiest speculations in the natural sciences, Lucien's eyes were turned with ardor toward literary renown; while David, whom his meditative temperament predisposed to poesy, inclined, as a matter of taste, to the exact sciences. This intermingling of characters engendered a sort of mental brotherhood. Lucien soon told David of the lofty views he inherited from his father as to the applications of science to manufacturing, and David called Lucien's attention to the untrodden roads in literature which he proposed to venture upon in order to make a name and a fortune for himself. The friendship of the two young men became in a few days one of those passions which spring into being only on the threshold of manhood.

David was soon presented to Eve and fell in love with her, as melancholy and meditative natures are wont to fall in love. The *Et nunc et semper et in secula seculorum* of the liturgy is the device of the sublime unknown poets whose works consist of magnificent epics born and lost between two hearts! When the lover had fathomed the secret of the hopes that Lucien's mother and sister placed upon that beautiful poetic forehead, when their blind devotion became known to him, he took delight in drawing near his mistress by sharing her sacrifices and her hopes. Thus Lucien was David's brother-elect. Like the ultras who tried to be more royalist than the king himself, David's faith in Lucien's genius surpassed that of his mother and sister, he spoiled him as a mother spoils her child. During one of the conversations, in which, impelled by the lack of money that tied their hands, they considered, like all young men, the different ways of attaining wealth promptly by shaking to no purpose all the trees that have already been stripped of their fruit by earlier comers, Lucien recalled two ideas that his father had suggested to him. Monsieur Chardon had contemplated reducing the price of sugar one-half by the use of a new chemical agent, and of effecting a proportionate reduction in the price of paper, by bringing from America certain inexpensive vegetable substances analogous to those used by the Chinese. David, who knew the importance of this matter, which had already been discussed by the Didots, seized upon the idea, believing that he saw a fortune in it, and he looked upon Lucien as a benefactor to whom he could never hope to pay his debt.

It will readily be understood that the dominant thoughts as well as the private lives of the two friends made them wholly unfitted to manage a printing office. Instead of bringing in fifteen to twenty thousand francs, like the establishment of the brothers Cointet, printers and publishers to the bishopric and proprietors of the *Courrier de la Charente*, now the only journal in the department, the Séchard establishment produced hardly three hundred francs a month, out of which the proof-reader's salary, Marion's wages, taxes and rent had

to be paid; which reduced David's net income to
about a hundred francs a month.   Energetic and in-
dustrious men would have renewed the type, purchased iron presses, and procured books at the
Parisian bookstores which they would have reprinted at a low price; but master and proof-reader,
engrossed by the absorbing labors of the mind, contented themselves with the work their last customers gave them.   The brothers Cointet had come
at last to understand David's character and habits,
and they no longer slandered him; on the other
hand, a wise policy led them to allow his printing
office to live on, and to help to support it in decent
mediocrity, so that it might not fall into the hands
of some dangerous antagonist; they themselves sent
the so-called town work there.   Thus, although he
had no idea of it, David Séchard continued to exist,
commercially speaking, only by virtue of his rivals'
shrewd foresight.   Delighted with what they called
his mania, the Cointets treated him, so far as ap-
pearances went, with the utmost straightforward-
ness and loyalty; but, in reality, they were acting
like the management of the *Messageries Royales*,
when they invent a feigned rivalry in order to
avoid a genuine one.

   The exterior of the Séchard house was in harmony with the shameful avarice that reigned
supreme in the interior, where the old bear had
never repaired anything.   The rain and sun, the
changing seasons, had given the door of the passageway the appearance of an old tree trunk, it was so

furrowed with cracks of all lengths and widths.
The front, wretchedly constructed of stone and
bricks, mingled without any attempt at symmetry,
seemed to bulge out under the weight of a moulder-
ing roof overburdened with the hollow tiles with
which all roofs are covered in the south of France.
The rotting window frames were embellished with
enormous shutters held in place by the thick cross-
bars which the heat of the climate demands. It
would have been difficult to find in all Angoulême
another house as cracked and seamed as this one,
which was held together only by the strength of the
cement. Imagine the press-room, light at both ends,
dark in the middle, the walls covered with hand-
bills; darkened at the lower part by the workmen
rubbing against it for thirty years past, its network
of cords hanging from the ceiling, its piles of paper,
its old presses, its heaps of stones to press the
dampened sheets, its rows of cases, and at the end,
the two cages in which the master and the proof-
reader respectively sat; you will then understand
the existence of the two friends.

In 1821, early in the month of May, David and
Lucien were standing near the window looking on
the courtyard, about two o'clock one afternoon, just
as their four or five workmen left the press-room to
go to dinner. When the master saw his apprentice
close the street door, which had a bell attached, he
led Lucien into the courtyard, as if the smell of the
paper and ink and presses and old wood were unbearable to him. They sat down under an arbor

ANDRÉ DE CHÉNIER

———

"So that is André de Chénier!" cried Lucien more than once. "He drives one to despair," he repeated for the third time, when David, too deeply moved to continue, allowed him to take the book.— "A poet discovered by a poet!" he said, when he saw the signature at the end of the preface.

Xavier Le Sueur

ADRIEN-MOREAU.

from which they could see whatever took place in the press-room. The sunbeams playing among the vine-leaves on the trellis caressed the two poets, enveloping them with their light as with a halo. The contrast between the two characters and the two faces was so strikingly brought out that it would have charmed the brush of a great artist. David had the figure that nature bestows upon beings destined to sustain violent conflicts, open or secret. His broad chest was flanked by sturdy shoulders that harmonized with the amplitude of all his proportions. His full, dark, sunburned face, supported by a thick neck, and surrounded by a dense forest of black hair, resembled at a first glance the faces of the canons of whom Boileau sings; but a second glance disclosed to you, in the furrows of the thick lips, in the dimpled chin, in the profile of a square-cut nose, divided by a strong irregular line, and above all in the eyes, the ever-burning fire of a single passion, the sagacity of the thinker, the ardent melancholy of a mind that could embrace the whole horizon from end to end, penetrating all its windings, and that was readily disenchanted with purely ideal pleasures by subjecting them to the searching light of analysis.

If one could detect in that face the gleams of the genius that will not be restrained, one also saw therein the ashes beside the volcano; hope faded away in a deep-rooted consciousness of the social nullity to which obscure birth and lack of fortune condemn so many superior minds. Beside the poor

printer, who had an intense loathing for his trade,
although it borders so closely on the realm of the
intellect, beside this Silenus who leaned heavily
upon himself and drank long draughts from the cup
of science and poetry, intoxicating himself in order
to forget the woes of provincial life, stood Lucien in
the graceful attitude invented by sculptors for the
Indian Bacchus. His face had the distinguished
outlines of the antique type of beauty; the forehead
and nose were Greek, the skin as velvety and
white as a woman's, the eyes of such a deep blue
that they seemed black, eyes overflowing with love,
the whites as clear and unspotted as a child's.
Those lovely eyes were surmounted by eyebrows
that might have been drawn by a Chinese pencil,
and bordered with long chestnut lashes. Along the
cheeks glistened a silky down, of a color that
harmonized perfectly with the naturally curly,
blond hair. Divine amiability was written upon
his golden-white temples. Incomparable nobility
of character was stamped upon his short, gracefully
curved chin. The smile of a sorrowful angel played
upon his coral lips whose color was heightened by
handsome white teeth. He had the hands of a
patrician, elegant hands, whose slightest sign men
would hasten to obey, such hands as women love to
kiss. Lucien was slender and of medium height.
Upon looking at his feet one would have been inclined to take him for a young woman in disguise,
the more because, like the majority of shrewd, not
to say astute men, his hips were shaped like a

woman's. This indication, rarely misleading, was accurate in Lucien's case, for the bent of his active mind often led him, when he set about analyzing the present condition of society, to act upon the depraved theory peculiar to diplomatists, that success justifies any means, however shameful they may be. One of the misfortunes to which great minds are subjected is the necessity of comprehending everything, vices as well as virtues.

These two young men passed judgment upon society with the greater freedom because of their lowly station therein, for undervalued men take their revenge for the humility of their position by the loftiness of their glance. But, in like manner, their despair was the more bitter because in this way they traveled more rapidly in the direction in which their real destiny impelled them. Lucien had read much and compared much; David had thought much and meditated much. Despite his apparent robust and vigorous health, the printer was a melancholy, sickly genius; he doubted himself; whereas Lucien, being endowed with an enterprising and versatile mind, was audacious to a degree that was not in accord with his effeminate, almost weakly carriage, instinct with the graces of the gentler sex. Lucien had to the highest degree the Gascon character, bold, courageous, adventurous, prone to exaggerate good and to make light of evil, which does not shrink from a sin if there is profit in it, and which laughs at vice if it can use it as a stepping-stone. This ambitious disposition had hitherto been held in check by the seductive illusions of youth, by the ardor that inclined him toward the noble methods that young men who are enamored of renown employ before all others. He was as yet at odds only with his longings and not with the difficulties of life, with his own power and not with the cowardice of men, which sets a fatal example to changeable minds. Thoroughly fascinated by Lucien's brilliant mind, David admired him, while he sought to rectify the errors into which the characteristic French ardor led him. That just man had a retiring disposition not in harmony with his powerful constitution, but he did not lack the persistence of the men of the North. Although he always foresaw all sorts of difficulties, he promised himself that he would overcome them without becoming discouraged; and although he had the firmness of truly apostolic virtue, he tempered it by the charms of inexhaustible indulgence. In this friendship, already of long standing, one of the two loved idolatrously and that one was David. Thus Lucien issued orders like a woman who knows that she is beloved. David obeyed with delight. His friend's physical beauty imported a superiority which he acknowledged, deeming himself stupid and commonplace.

"For the ox, patient agriculture ; for the bird, heedless life," said the printer to himself. "I will be the ox, Lucien shall be the eagle."

For some three years past the friends had thus mingled their destinies, of such brilliant promise for

the future. They read the great works that appeared
upon the literary and scientific horizon after the
peace; the works of Schiller, Gœthe, Lord Byron,
Walter Scott, Jean-Paul, Berzélius, Davy, Cuvier
and Lamartine. They warmed themselves at those
great fires, they tried their own powers in works,
mostly abortive, laid aside and taken up again
with ardor. They worked constantly without ex-
hausting the inexhaustible strength of youth.
Equally poor, but consumed by the love of art
and science, they forgot their present misery, so
engrossed were they in laying the foundations of
their renown.

"Lucien, what do you suppose I have just received
from Paris?" said the printer, taking a little 18mo
volume from his pocket. "Listen!"

David read, as only poets can read, André de
Chénier's idyl, entitled *Néère*, then *Le Jeune Malade*
and then the elegy upon suicide, the first in the
ancient metre, the last two in iambics.

"So that is André de Chénier!" cried Lucien
more than once. "He drives one to despair,"
he repeated for the third time, when David, too
deeply moved to continue, allowed him to take
the book.—"A poet discovered by a poet!" he
said, when he saw the signature at the end of
the preface.

"After producing that book," said David,
"Chénier thought he had done nothing worthy to
be published."

Lucien in his turn read the epic fragment,

L'Aveugle, and several elegies.   When he happened upon the line:

" If they're not happy, is happiness found on earth?"

he kissed the book, and the two friends wept, for
both loved idolatrously.   The vine-leaves took on
a brilliant coloring, the old walls of the house, split
and battered and irregularly traversed by unsightly
cracks, were embellished by fairy fingers with
delicate tracery and carvings, bas-reliefs and count-
less masterpieces of some forgotten school of architecture.   Fancy scattered its flowers and its rubies
on the dark little courtyard.   André de Chénier's
Camille became in David's eyes his adored Eve,
and in Lucien's a great lady to whom he was paying court.   Poetry shook the majestic skirts of its
starry robe over the press-room where the *monkeys*
and *bears* were making wry faces over their work.
The clock struck five, but the two friends were
neither hungry nor thirsty; their life was a golden
dream, they had all the treasures of earth at their
feet.   They saw the corner of the blue horizon
which the finger of Hope points out to those whose
lives are stormy, and to whom her siren's voice
says: "Go, fly, you will escape disaster through
that patch of gold or silver or azure."   At that
moment an apprentice named Cérizet, a Paris gamin
whom David had sent for to come to Angoulême,
opened the small glass door that led from the press-
room into the courtyard, and called the attention of

the two friends to a stranger who came toward them, bowing.

"Monsieur," he said to David, taking from his pocket an enormous roll of paper, "here is a memoir which I desire to have printed; will you kindly estimate the cost?"

"Monsieur, we don't print manuscripts of such length," replied David, without looking at the roll. "See Messieurs Cointet."

"But we have a very pretty type that might be suitable," observed Lucien, taking the manuscript. "We shall have to ask you to be good enough to return to-morrow, and to leave the manuscript with us to estimate the cost of printing."

"Have I not the honor of addressing Monsieur Lucien Chardon?"

"Yes, monsieur," the proof-reader replied.

"I am very happy, monsieur," said the author, "to have met a young poet who has so great a future in store. I am sent by Madame de Bargeton."

When he heard that name, Lucien blushed and stammered a few words expressive of his gratitude for Madame de Bargeton's interest in him. David noticed his friend's blushes and embarrassment, and left him in conversation with the country gentleman, author of a memoir upon the cultivation of silk worms, whose vanity impelled him to have his lucubrations printed in order that they might be read by his colleagues in the Society of Agriculture.

"Well, Lucien," said David, when the gentleman

had taken his leave, "are you in love with Madame de Bargeton?"

"Madly."

"But you are more completely separated by social prejudices than if she were in Pekin and you in Greenland."

"The will of two lovers triumphs over everything," said Lucien, lowering his eyes.

"You will forget us," said the fair Eve's timid lover.

"On the other hand, it may be that I have sacrificed my mistress to you," cried Lucien.

"What do you mean?"

"Despite my love, despite the divers motives that impel me to frequent her house, I have told her that I would never go there again, unless a man whose talents are superior to mine, whose future is certain to be glorious, unless David Séchard, my brother, my friend, were made welcome there. I expect to find an answer at home. But, although all the aristocrats are invited there this evening to hear me read poetry, if the answer is unfavorable, I will never again set foot inside Madame de Bargeton's house."

David wiped his eyes and pressed Lucien's hand fervently. Six o'clock struck.

"Eve will be anxious; adieu," said Lucien abruptly.

He fled, leaving David overwhelmed with the emotion that one never feels so completely as at that age, especially in the situation of these two young

swans whose wings provincial life had not yet
clipped.

"Heart of gold!" cried David, looking after
Lucien as he passed through the workroom.

Lucien went down to L'Houmeau by the beautiful
Promenade de Beaulieu, Rue du Minage, and Porte
Saint-Pierre. His reason for taking the longest road
to his destination was that Madame de Bargeton's
house lay upon that road. He felt so much pleasure
in passing beneath that lady's windows, even without her knowledge, that for two months past he had
not once returned to L'Houmeau by Porte Palet.

When he found himself under the trees of Beaulieu, he reflected upon the distance between Angoulême and L'Houmeau. The customs of the
province had raised barriers much more difficult to
pass than the steps by which Lucien descended.
The ambitious youth, who had made his way into
the Bargeton mansion, exhaling glory, like a flying
bridge between the town and the faubourg, was as
anxious concerning his mistress's decision as a
favorite who dreads disgrace after having attempted
to extend his power. These words may seem obscure to those who have never remarked the peculiar customs in vogue in towns that are divided into
an upper town and a lower town; but it is the more
necessary at this point to set forth a few facts with
relation to Angoulême, because they will be of
assistance in understanding the character of Madame de Bargeton, one of the most important personages of this narrative.

4

*

Angoulême is an ancient town built on the summit
of a rock, shaped like a loaf of sugar, which over-
looks the meadows through which the Charente
flows. This rock is the continuation of a long hill
which falls gradually toward Périgord, and which
it brings to an abrupt termination on the road from
Paris to Bordeaux, forming a sort of promontory
bounded by three picturesque valleys. The importance of this town in the times of the religious wars
is attested by its ramparts, by its gates and by the
remains of a fortress perched on the apex of the
rock. Its situation made it in the old days a
strategic point of equal value to Catholics and Cal-
vinists; but its oldtime strength constitutes its
present weakness; its ramparts and the extremely
steep slope of the rock have prevented it from
spreading out along the Charente and thus have condemned it to the most lamentable inactivity. About
the time when the events recorded in this narrative
took place, the government tried to extend the town
toward Périgord by building the palace of the prefecture, a naval school and military establishments
along the hill, and laying out roads there. But
commerce had taken a start in another direction.
For a long time, the suburb of L'Houmeau had been
growing like a bed of mushrooms at the foot of the

cliff and along the shores of the river which the great highroad from Paris to Bordeaux skirted. Everyone is aware of the celebrity of the paper manufactories of Angoulême, which were established three centuries ago on the Charente and its affluents, where falling water was found. The State had founded its largest foundry for naval guns at Ruelle. Express offices, the post office, inns, wheelwrights, public carriages, all the branches of industry which depend for their maintenance on the road and river, were grouped together at the feet of Angoulême, to avoid the difficulties presented by its approaches. Naturally the tanneries, laundries, all the trades in which water was largely used, remained within call of the Charente; the wine-shops too, the storehouses for all raw materials carried on the river, and lastly, all the warehouses for goods in bond, lay along the river. Thus the suburb of L'Houmeau became a thriving and wealthy town, a second Angoulême viewed with jealous eyes by the Upper Town, where the government buildings, the bishop's palace, the courts of law and the aristocracy still remained. So that L'Houmeau, notwithstanding its activity and its increasing power, was only an annex of Angoulême. Above, the nobility and the constituted authorities; below, commerce and wealth; two social zones that are always at enmity everywhere; and it is difficult to say which of the two hated its rival the more bitterly.

For the past nine years the Restoration had aggravated the condition of affairs, which were

reasonably tranquil under the Empire. The
majority of the houses in Upper Angoulême are
occupied either by noble families or by old bourgeois families who live on their income and form
a sort of aboriginal nation into which strangers are
never admitted. Even after two hundred years of
residence and an alliance with one of the primordial
families, a family from some neighboring province
can only with difficulty make its way into the
charmed circle; in the eyes of the natives it is considered to have come to the province only yesterday.
The prefects, the receivers-general, the successive
administrations of the past forty years, have tried to
civilize these old families, perched on their rock
like suspicious crows; the families have accepted
their parties and their dinners; but, when it came
to admitting them to their houses, they persistently
refused. Scornful, disparaging, jealous, miserly,
these families intermarried, formed themselves into
a compact battalion so that no one could go out or
in. Of the inventions of modern luxury they
knew nothing; in their view, to send a child to
Paris was to seek his ruin. This prudence is
typical of the antiquated morals and customs of
those families, saturated with unintelligent royal-
ism, tainted with religion rather than religious,
who pass their lives as immovable as their town
and its rock. And yet Angoulême enjoys a great
reputation in the neighborhood for the education one
can obtain there. The neighboring towns send
their daughters to the boarding-schools and convents

there.   It is easy to imagine how great an influence
the spirit of caste has upon the feelings that divide
Angoulême and L'Houmeau.   The merchants are
wealthy, the nobles are, generally speaking, poor.
Each takes its revenge upon the other in contempt
that is equal on both sides.   The bourgeoisie of
Angoulême espouse the quarrel.   The tradesman of
the Upper Town says of a tradesman of the suburb,
in an indescribable tone: "That's a man from
L'Houmeau!"

In marking out the position of the nobility in
France and giving it hopes which could not be
realized without a general upheaval, the Restoration
increased the moral distance which was even more
effectual than the physical distance in keeping Angoulême and L'Houmeau asunder.   The social circle
of the nobles, at this time attached to the government, became more exclusive there than in any
other part of France.   The inhabitants of L'Houmeau were veritable pariahs.   Hence the bitter and
deep-seated animosities which gave the Revolution
of 1830 its marvelous unanimity, and destroyed the
elements of a durable social structure in France.
The overbearing pride of the court nobility alienated
the provincial nobility from the throne as much as
the provincial nobility alienated the bourgeoisie
by wounding it in every tender spot.   Therefore
the introduction of a man from L'Houmeau, the son
of a druggist, into Madame de Bargeton's salon
created a small-sized revolution.   Who were responsible for it?   Lamartine and Victor Hugo, Casimir

Delavigne and Canalis, Béranger and Chateaubriand, Villemain and Aignan, Soumet and Tissot,
Etienne and Davrigny, Benjamin Constant and
Lamennais, Cousin and Michaud, in a word, all the
literary celebrities, old and young, liberal and royalist. Madame de Bargeton loved art and letters, an
extravagant taste, a mania deeply deplored in Angoulême, which it is necessary to justify by sketch-
ing the life of this woman, who was born to be
famous, but kept in obscurity by fatal circumstances, and whose influence determined Lucien's
destiny.

Monsieur de Bargeton was the great-grandson of
a former warden of Bordeaux, one Mirault, who was
ennobled under Louis XIII., as a reward for long
service in that office.   Under Louis XIV., his son,
who was known as Mirault de Bargeton, was an
officer in the *gardes de la porte*, and made such a
great marriage, from a pecuniary standpoint, that
his son, under Louis XV. was called Monsieur de
Bargeton simply.   This Monsieur de Bargeton, the
grandson of Monsieur Mirault the warden, was so
bent upon bearing himself as a perfect gentleman
that he ran through all the family property and
checked its rise in fortune.   Two of his brothers,
great-uncles of the present Bargeton, returned to
trade, so that the name of Mirault appeared once
more in the commercial circles of Bordeaux.   As
the estate of Bargeton, situated in Angoumois, having been a dependency of the feudal estate of La
Rochefoucauld, was entailed, as was a house in

Angoulême called the Hôtel de Bargeton, the grandson of Monsieur de Bargeton the Spendthrift inherited those two properties. In 1789, he lost his legal title and retained only the revenues of the estate, which amounted to about ten thousand francs a year. If his grandfather had followed the glorious examples of Bargeton I. and Bargeton II., Bargeton V., who may be called the Silent, would have been Marquis de Bargeton; he would have married into some great family and would have become a duke and peer, like so many others; whereas, he was highly flattered, in 1805, to obtain the hand of Mademoiselle Marie-Louise-Anaïs de Nègrepelisse, the daughter of a gentleman long since forgotten in his little country-seat, although he belonged to the younger branch of one of the oldest families in the south of France. There was a Nègrepelisse among the hostages of Saint Louis; but the head of the elder branch bears the illustrious name of D'Espard, acquired under Henri IV. by a marriage with the heiress of that family.

This gentleman, the younger son of a younger son, lived upon his wife's property, a small estate near Barbezieux, which he cultivated with excellent results, carrying his own wheat to market, burning his wine himself, and snapping his fingers at mockery, so long as he was able to heap up crowns and to add to his domain from time to time. Certain circumstances of rare occurrence in the heart of the provinces had aroused in Madame de Bargeton a taste for music and literature. During the Revolution one Abbé Niollant, Abbé Roze's best pupil, sought shelter in the little castle of Escarbas, bringing thither his stock in trade as a composer. He repaid the old gentleman handsomely for his hospitality by educating his daughter Anaïs, called Naïs for short, who, except for that lucky chance, would have been left to her own devices or, and that would have been even more unfortunate, to those of some evil-minded lady's maid. Not only was the abbé a musician, but he possessed an extensive knowledge of literature, and was familiar with Italian and German. He instructed Mademoiselle de Nègrepelisse in those two languages and in counterpoint; he explained to her the great literary works of France, Italy and Germany, and worked with her upon the compositions of all the great masters of music. Lastly, to combat the slothful tendencies of the profound solitude to which the course of political events condemned them, he taught her Greek and Latin and gave her a smattering of the natural sciences. The presence of a mother did not modify the influence of this masculine education upon a young woman already too prone to assert her independence as a result of her life in the open air.

Abbé Niollant, an enthusiastic, poetic creature, was especially remarkable for the possession of the wit that is the peculiar characteristic of artists, that carries with it many estimable qualities, and rises above bourgeois ideas by the freedom of its judgments and the extent of its perceptions. While, in the world at large, that variety of wit earns forgiveness for its audacity by its originality and depth, it may seem harmful in private life because of the lofty flights it inspires. The abbé did not lack heart, so that his ideas were contagious to a young girl in whom the natural exaltation of youth was strengthened by the solitude of a country life. Abbé Niollant imparted to his pupil his habit of bold scrutiny and his faculty of forming prompt judgments, not reflecting that those qualities, so necessary to a man, become defects of character in a woman destined to fill the humble station of mother of a family. Although the abbé constantly enjoined upon his pupil to be the more amiable and modest, the more extensive her knowledge, Mademoiselle de Nègrepelisse conceived an excellent opinion of herself and a robust contempt for mankind in general. Seeing about her none but inferiors and people eager to obey her, she assumed the haughty manner of great ladies, without their soft and courteous hypocrisy. Flattered in all her vanities by a poor abbé who admired himself in her, as an author admires himself in his work, she was so unfortunate as to have no point of comparison by which to judge herself. The lack of society is one of the greatest drawbacks to life in the country. Having no occasion to make for others the little sacrifices demanded by the toilet and by the laws of courtesy, one loses the habit of putting one's self out for others. Thereupon everything about us depreciates, manners as

well as mind. Being unrestrained by the shackles
of society, the boldness of Madame de Nègrepelisse's
ideas passed into her manners and her expression;
she had that jaunty air which at first glance seems
original, but which is not becoming to women other
than those who lead adventurous lives. Thus her
education, whose asperities would have been worn
smooth in the higher social spheres, was calculated
to make her ridiculous at Angoulême, whenever her
adorers should cease to worship her errors, fascinating only during youth. As for Monsieur de Nègrepelisse, he would have given all his daughter's
books to save a sick ox; for he was so miserly, that
he would never have allowed her one sou over and
above the income to which she was entitled, even
for the purpose of procuring a trifle that was most
essential to her education.

The abbé died in 1802, before his dear child's
marriage, which he would undoubtedly have discouraged. The old gentleman found his hands full
with his daughter when the abbé died. He felt that
he was too weak to sustain the conflict that was
certain to break out between his avarice and the
independent spirit of his child, whose occupation
was gone. Like all young women who have devi-
ated from the traveled road that women are expected to follow, Naïs had made up her mind on the
subject of marriage and cared but little about trying
it. She disliked the thought of submitting her intellect and her person to the uninteresting men,
wholly lacking in personal grandeur, whom it had

been her fortune to meet. She desired to command, and it would be her duty to obey. If she had had to choose between obeying the vulgar caprices of minds that were without indulgence for her tastes, and flying with a lover who caught her fancy, she would not have hesitated an instant.

Monsieur de Nègrepelisse was still enough of a gentleman to dread a *mésalliance*. Like many fathers, he determined to find a husband for his daughter, less for her sake than in the interest of his own tranquillity. He required a nobleman or gentleman of little wit, unlikely to haggle over the guardian's account which he intended to submit to his daughter, sufficiently weak in mind and will to allow Naïs to behave as she chose, sufficiently disinterested to marry her without a marriage-portion. But how to find a son-in-law who would meet the views of both father and daughter? Such a man was the phœnix of sons-in-law. With this twofold object in mind, Monsieur de Nègrepelisse looked over the eligible men in the province, and Monsieur de Bargeton seemed to be the only one who answered all the requirements. Monsieur de Bargeton, then about forty years old and considerably the worse for the dissipated life he had led during his youth, was accused of being extraordinarily feeble-minded; but he retained just enough common sense to manage his property and enough good manners to live in Angoulême society without committing any noticeably awkward or foolish actions. Monsieur de Nègrepelisse set before his

daughter without disguise the negative merit of the
model husband he proposed to her, and impressed
upon her all the advantage she might derive there-
from for her own happiness: she would marry a
coat of arms that was already two hundred years
old; the Bargetons *quarter or three stags' heads*
gules, two and one, alternating with three bulls'
frontals sable, one and two, fesse azure and argent
by six, with six shells or on the azure, three two
and one. Armed with a chaperon, she could
manage his fortune as she chose, sheltered behind
a social position, and with the assistance of the
connections her wit and beauty would procure for
her at Paris. Naïs was fascinated by the prospect
of such liberty of action, Monsieur de Bargeton believed that he was making a brilliant match, considering that his father-in-law would before long
leave him the estate that he was rounding out so
fondly; but at that moment, Monsieur de Nègrepelisse seemed likely to write his son-in-law's
epitaph.

At that time, Madame de Bargeton was thirty-six
years old and her husband fifty-eight. This difference in their ages was the more annoying because
Monsieur de Bargeton seemed to be at least seventy,
while his wife could play the young girl with im-
punity, dress in pink or wear her hair like a child.
Although their fortune did not exceed twelve thousand francs a year, it was classed among the six
most considerable fortunes of the old town, merchants and administrative officers excepted. The

necessity of cultivating their father, whose inheritance Madame de Bargeton was awaiting in order to
go to Paris, and who made her wait so long that his
son-in-law eventually died before him, compelled
Monsieur and Madame de Bargeton to live at Angoulême, where the brilliant qualities of Naïs's
mind and the unpolished jewels hidden in her heart,
bade fair to be wasted without profit, and to change
with time into causes of ridicule.   In truth, our absurdities are caused in great part by noble sentiments, by virtues or mental faculties carried to
extremes.   The pride which is not humbled by contact with the best society becomes stiffness when it
is displayed in connection with trifles, instead of
becoming ennobled in a circle of exalted sentiments.
Exaltation, that virtue within a virtue which gives
birth to saints, which inspires secret devotion and
outspoken poesy, becomes exaggeration when it is
expended upon the trifling concerns of the province.
Far from the centre where great minds shine, where
the air is laden with thoughts, where everything is
constantly changing, knowledge becomes stale, the
taste becomes vitiated like stagnant water.   For
lack of exercise the passions demean themselves by
magnifying small things.   Therein is the explanation of the avarice and gossiping spirit that are the
pests of provincial life.   Ere long the instinctive
imitation of narrow ideas and cringing manners
grows upon persons of the highest distinction.
Thus do men born to be great, sink into insignificance, as well as women who would have been

delightful had they been set right by knowledge of the world and moulded by superior minds.

Madame de Bargeton took up her lyre on the slightest provocation, without distinguishing personal poetic thoughts from poetic thoughts suited for the public eye. For there are misinterpreted sensations that one should keep to one's self. Beyond question a sunset is a grand poem, but does not a woman make herself ridiculous by describing it in high-sounding words before unspiritual people? There are sensuous delights that can only be enjoyed to the full by two congenial souls, poet to poet, heart to heart. She had the fault of using long sentences interlarded with emphatic words, aptly called *tartines* in the vernacular of journalism, which cuts some very indigestible ones every morning for its subscribers, who swallow them uncomplainingly. She was lavish beyond measure of superlatives, and overburdened her conversation with them, making the merest trifles assume gigantic proportions. About this time, she began to *typify, individualize, synthetize, dramatize, superiorize, analyze, poetize, prosaicize, colossify, angelify, neologize* and *tragicize* everything; for we must do violence to the language for a moment in order to convey an idea of the novel freaks that some women indulge in. Her mind took fire, too, as readily as her language. The dithyramb was in her heart and on her lips. Her heart beat fast, she waxed enthusiastic and went into raptures over every occurrence; the devotion of a Gray Sister

and the execution of the Faucher brothers, Monsieur
d'Arlincourt's *Ipsiboé* no less than Lewis's *Ana-
conda,* the escape of La Valette and the heroism of
one of her friends who put robbers to flight by assuming a bass voice. To her everything was sublime, extraordinary, strange, divine, marvelous.
She would become excited or indignant, recoil in
horror, rush forward, fall back, gaze at the sky or
the ground; her eyes would fill with tears. She
wore out her life in constant admiration and consumed her strength in withering disdain. She
formed a mental image of the Pacha of Janina, she
would have liked to contend with him in his harem,
and she discovered something great in being sewn
into a sack and thrown into the water. She envied
Lady Esther Stanhope, the bluestocking of the desert.
She longed to become a sister of Sainte-Camille and
to go and face death from yellow fever at Barcelona,
nursing the sick: that was a great, a noble destiny!
In short, she was athirst for everything that was
not the clear water of her life, hidden beneath its
weeds. She adored Lord Byron, Jean-Jacques
Rousseau and all poetic, dramatic existences. She
had tears to shed for all misfortunes and flourishes
of trumpets for every victory. She sympathized
with Napoléon vanquished, she sympathized with
Mehemet Ali, massacring the tyrants of Egypt. In
a word, she arrayed men of genius in a halo, and
thought that they could live upon incense and light.
To many persons she seemed a madwoman, whose
mania was harmless; but to some perspicacious

observers, these things would surely have seemed
to be the ruins of a magnificent passion that had
crumbled as soon as it was built, the remains of a
celestial Jerusalem, in a word, love without the
lover.   And it was true.

The story of the first eighteen years of Madame
de Bargeton's married life can be written in a very
few words.   She lived for some time upon her own
substance and far-off hopes.   Then, having come to
realize that life in Paris, to which she aspired, was
out of the question on account of the mediocrity of
her fortune, she began to scrutinize the people by
whom she was surrounded and shuddered at her
solitude.   There was no man in her circle who was
capable of inspiring one of those mad passions to
which women abandon themselves, impelled by the
despair consequent upon an objectless, uneventful,
uninteresting life.   She could rely upon nothing,
not even upon chance, for there are some lives into
which chance does not enter.

In the days when the Empire was in its greatest
glory, at the time of Napoléon's march into Spain,
whither he sent the flower of his troops, Madame de
Bargeton's hopes, disappointed hitherto, awoke to
renewed life.   Curiosity naturally led her to study
those heroes who conquered Europe at a word in-
serted in the order of the day, and who re-enacted
the fabulous exploits of the days of chivalry.   The
most parsimonious and the most refractory towns
were compelled to make holiday for the Garde Impériale; the mayors and prefects went out to meet

5

them, with harangues upon their lips, as if to do
honor to royalty. Madame de Bargeton, attending
a *ridotto* given by a certain regiment to the townspeople, lost her heart to a gentleman, a simple sub-
lieutenant, to whom the crafty Napoléon had given
a glimpse of the baton of a marshal of France.
This restrained passion, a grand and noble passion
in striking contrast to the passions that were so
readily formed and abandoned in those days, was
consecrated by death. At Wagram a cannon-ball
shattered, upon the heart of the Marquis de Cante-
Croix, the only portrait that bore witness to Madame de Bargeton's beauty. She long mourned
the noble youth who had become a colonel in two
campaigns, inspired by glory and by love, and who
esteemed a letter from Naïs above all tokens of imperial approbation. Sorrow cast a veil of sadness
over her face. That cloud was not dissipated until
she reached the redoubtable age at which a woman
begins to regret her happy past, although she has
never enjoyed it, at which she sees that her roses
are fading, while the longing for love is rekindled
with the desire to prolong the last smiles of youth.
All her superior qualities wounded her heart at the
moment that the chill of the province attacked it.
Like the ermine, she would have died of grief if
she had chanced to soil herself by contact with men
who think of nothing but playing cards for small
stakes in the evening, after a good dinner. Her
pride preserved her from the melancholy love-affairs
of the province. Between the stupid men who

surrounded her and nothing, a woman of such
superior mind would surely prefer nothing.   Thus
marriage and society were to her a monastery.   She
lived upon poetry, as the Carmelite lives upon religion.   The works of the hitherto unknown illustrious foreigners, which were published from 1815
to 1821, the great treatises of Monsieur de Bonald
and Monsieur de Maistre, those two profound
thinkers, and the less grandiose works of French
literature, which was then putting forth its first
shoots so vigorously, embellished her solitude, but
imparted no elasticity to her mind or her person.
She remained as straight and stiff as a tree that
has been struck by lightning and has not been felled
thereby.   Her dignity overreached itself, her semi-
royalty made her finical and affected.   Like all
those who allow themselves to be adored by courtiers, whoever they may be, she played the queen
with all her faults.

*

Such was Madame de Bargeton's past, a story
without interest, which it was necessary to tell in
order to properly understand her *liaison* with Lucien, whose introduction to her came about in a
peculiar way. During the last winter a person had
arrived in the town who had imparted some animation to the monotonous life Madame de Bargeton
usually led. The post of superintendent of imposts
having fallen vacant, Monsieur de Barante sent
down to fill it a man whose adventurous career
pleaded so strongly in his favor that feminine curiosity served as his passport to the salon of the queen
of the province.

Monsieur du Châtelet, who came into the world
plain Sixte Châtelet, but who had the good sense
to assume a title in 1806, was one of those attractive young men who escaped all the conscriptions
under Napoléon by remaining near the imperial
sun. He had begun his career as secretary to an
imperial princess. Monsieur du Châtelet possessed
all the incapacities demanded by his place. A
shapely, well-favored man, a good dancer, a skilful
billiard-player, proficient in all manly exercises,
a fair amateur actor, a singer of love-songs, quick
to applaud bright remarks, ready for everything,
pliant and envious, he knew everything and nothing. Although he knew nothing of music, he would

(69)

play an accompaniment with more or less success for a woman who obligingly consented to sing a romanza that she had been struggling to learn for a month past. Although he was utterly incapable of a true understanding of poetry, he would boldly ask permission to leave the room for ten minutes to dash off some impromptu verses, a quatrain flat as the palm of your hand, in which ideas were replaced by jingling rhymes. Monsieur du Châtelet was, however, endowed with the talent of filling in a piece of embroidery in which the flowers had been begun by the princess; he held her skeins of silk with exquisite grace while she wound them, telling her idle stories in which the obscenity was hidden beneath a veil with more or less holes in it. Although he was ignorant of the art of painting, he knew how to copy a landscape, draw a profile in crayon, sketch a costume and color it. In short, he had all the petty talents which were such great stepping-stones to fortune at a time when women had more influence than is commonly supposed upon public affairs. He claimed to be very strong in diplomacy, the science of those who have none, and who are deep by their very emptiness; a very convenient science, too, in the sense that it manifests itself simply by undertaking exalted functions; that, having no use for any but discreet men, it permits fools to say nothing, to take refuge in mysterious shakings of the head; and that the man who is most learned in that science is the one who swims along keeping his head above the flood of events, which he thus seems to guide, thereby raising a question of specific gravity. In diplomacy, as in art, you meet a thousand mediocrities for every man of genius.

Despite his ordinary and extraordinary service with her Imperial Highness, the influence of his patroness was not sufficient to secure him a place in the Council of State: not that he would not have made a delightful master of requests, as many others like him have done, but the princess considered him more fitly employed in her service than elsewhere. However, he was made a baron, went to Cassel as envoy extraordinary, and did in truth make a most extraordinary appearance there. In other words, Napoléon made use of him at a critical time as a diplomatic messenger. When the Empire fell, the Baron du Châtelet had been promised the appointment of minister to Jérôme's court of Westphalia. Having missed what he called a family embassy, despair seized upon him; he took a trip to Egypt with General Armand de Montriveau. Separated from his companion by a sequence of strange events, he wandered two years from desert to desert, from tribe to tribe, a prisoner in the hands of the Arabs, who sold him from one to another, unable to derive the slightest benefit from his talents. At last he reached the possessions of the Iman of Mascate while Montriveau was on his way to Tangier; but he had the good fortune to find an English ship at Mascate just about to make sail, and returned to Paris a year before his traveling companion. His recent misfortunes, some

connections of ancient date, and services rendered
to personages then in favor led to his being recommended to the President of the Council, who placed
him with Monsieur de Barante, awaiting the first
vacant post. The part played by Monsieur du
Châtelet in the service of the imperial princess,
his reputation as a man of gallantry, the strange
events of his voyage, his sufferings, all combined
to arouse the interest of the women of Angoulême.
Having made himself familiar with the manners
and customs of the Upper Town, Monsieur le Baron
Sixte du Châtelet conducted himself accordingly.
He played the invalid, the blasé, disgusted man of
the world.

On every occasion, he would take his head in his
hands as if his suffering did not give him a
moment's respite, a little manœuvre which recalled
his travels and made him interesting. He visited
the houses of the higher officials, the general, the
prefect, the receiver-general and the bishop; but
everywhere he exhibited the same polished, cold,
slightly disdainful bearing, like all men who are
not in their proper place and who expect favors
from the powers that be. He left his social talents
to be divined, for it was to their advantage not to
be known; then, after he had made himself popular,
after he had discovered the insignificance of the
men and had knowingly scrutinized the women for
several Sundays at the cathedral, he saw in Madame
de Bargeton the one person with whom he cared to
become intimate. He relied upon music to open to

him the door of that mansion which was pitilessly closed to strangers. He secretly procured a mass by Miroir and practised it on the piano; and, one fine Sunday, when all Angoulême was at mass, he aroused the ecstatic enthusiasm of the ignorant by performing it upon the organ, and rearoused the interest that already attached to his person by causing his name to be freely circulated by the lower clergy. When the service was over, Madame de Bargeton complimented him and expressed her regrets at having had no opportunity to practise music with him; during this premeditated meeting he naturally obtained the passport to her salon, which he would not have obtained if he had asked for it.

The adroit baron called upon the queen of Angoulême and paid her compromising attentions. The old beau—for he was forty-five—discovered in this woman a whole youth to revivify, treasures to bring to light, perhaps a widow, rich in hopes, to marry; in a word, an alliance with the family of Nègrepelisse, which would give him access to the Marquise d'Espard in Paris, whose influence was sufficient to throw open to him a political career. Despite the luxuriant but sombre-hued parasite that disfigured that fine tree, he determined to cling to it, to prune it, to cultivate it, and to obtain delicious fruit from it. Noble Angoulême cried out against the introduction of a *giaour* into the *casbah,* for Madame de Bargeton's salon was the resort of a social circle absolutely without alloy. The bishop alone came there regularly, the prefect was received two or three times a year, the receiver-general never entered the doors; Madame de Bargeton went to his evening parties and his concerts, but never dined with him. Not to receive the receiver-general and to harbor a simple superintendent of imposts—such a reversal of the hierarchical order seemed inconceivable to the slighted functionaries.

Those whose minds are capable of descending to such paltry matters, which, by the way, are to be met with in every social sphere, will understand how imposing the Hôtel de Bargeton was to the bourgeoisie of Angoulême. As for L'Houmeau, the grandeurs of that Louvre on a small scale, the glory of that Angoumois Hôtel de Rambouillet, shone upon the thriving suburb from a distance as great as the sun's. All those who assembled there were the most pitifully deficient creatures in intellectual power, the weakest mortals to be found within a radius of twenty leagues. Political subjects were discussed in verbose, impassioned commonplaces; *La Quotidienne* seemed lukewarm, Louis XVIII. was treated as a Jacobin. As for the women, the greater part of them were foolish and uninteresting, dressed badly and all had some flaw which ruined them; nothing about them was complete, neither their conversation nor their toilets, neither the spirit nor the flesh. Except for his designs upon Madame de Bargeton, Châtelet would not have cared to be admitted. Nevertheless, the manners and the spirit of caste, the gentlemanly bearing, the pride of the nobleman with his little castle and familiarity with the laws of courtesy, covered the void. The nobility of sentiment was much more real there than in the sphere of Parisian grandeur; there were manifestations of an attachment worthy of respect, even if it were to the Bourbons. That society may be compared, if the simile is admissible, to an old-fashioned service of plate, black with age, but heavy. The unchangeableness of its political opinions resembled fidelity. The space between it and the bourgeoisie, the difficulty of gaining admission to it, simulated a sort of superiority and gave it a conventional value. Each of these nobles had his value in the minds of the townspeople, just as shells represent money among the negroes of Bambara.

Several ladies, flattered by Monsieur du Châtelet, and recognizing in him superior qualities which were lacking in the men of their set, allayed the insurrection of wounded self-esteem: one and all hoped to be honored with the succession to the imperial princess. The purists thought that the intruder would be seen at Madame de Bargeton's, but that he would not be received in any other house. Du Châtelet was subjected to divers impertinences, but he maintained his position by cultivating the clergy. Then too he flattered the faults which the queen of Angoulême owed to her country bringing-up, he brought her all the new books, he read the new poems to her as they appeared. They went into raptures together over the works of the younger poets, she in good faith, and he, sadly bored but submitting patiently to the romantic poets, whom, as a man of the imperial school, he hardly understood.

Madame de Bargeton, in her enthusiasm for the renaissance due to the influence of the lily, loved Monsieur de Chateaubriand because he had called Victor Hugo a sublime child. Depressed in spirit because she had no acquaintance with genius except from a distance, she sighed for Paris, where all the great men lived. Thereupon Monsieur du Châtelet believed that he was doing wonders in his own interest by informing her that there was in Angoulême *another sublime child*, a young poet who, unknown to himself, surpassed in brilliancy the rising of the Parisian constellations. A man destined to be great had been born at L'Houmeau! The principal of the college had shown the baron some admirable pieces of verse. Poor and modest, the child was a Chatterton without political cowardice, without the savage hatred of social grandeur that impelled the English poet to write against his benefactors. Among the five or six persons who shared her taste for art and letters, this one because he could scrape a fiddle, that one because he besmeared more or less white paper with sepia, another in the capacity of president of the Society of Agriculture, and another by virtue of a bass voice which enabled him to sing the *Se fiato in corpo avete* after the style of a view-hallo; among those odd figures, Madame de Bargeton had the feeling a half-famished man has before a stage dinner, where all the dishes are of pasteboard.

And so it would be impossible to describe her joy
on hearing this news. She must see this poet, this
angel! she became wildly enthusiastic on the subject, she talked about it for hours at a time. Two
days later, the former diplomatic messenger had
made arrangements through the principal for Lucien's presentation to Madame de Bargeton.

You alone, poor provincial slaves, to whom social
distances are longer to travel than to Parisians, in
whose eyes they grow shorter from day to day, you
who feel so keenly the weight of the bars through
which all the social strata in the world hurl curses
at one another and call one another: *Raca!*—you
alone will understand the upheaval that took place
in the heart and brain of Lucien Chardon, when his
imposing principal informed him that the doors of
the Hôtel de Bargeton were about to be thrown open
to him! renown had forced them to turn upon their
hinges! he would be well received in that mansion,
whose venerable gables attracted his glance when
he walked at Beaulieu with David in the evening,
while they said to each other that their names would
probably never reach ears that were deaf to knowledge when it proceeded from too low a point in the
social scale. Only his sister was admitted to the
secret. Like a good housekeeper, like a divine
seer, Eve took a few louis from the treasury and
went out to purchase some fine shoes for Lucien
from the best shoemaker in Angoulême and a new
suit from the most celebrated tailor. She embellished his best shirt front with a frill which she

laundered and plaited with her own hands. What
joy, when she saw him thus arrayed! how proud
she was of her brother! how many injunctions she
gave him! She detected a thousand little foolish
ways of his. Absorption in his meditations had
given Lucien the habit of putting his elbows on the
table as soon as he sat down; and he would even go
so far as to pull a table toward him to lean upon;
Eve forbade him to indulge in such free-and-easy
perfomances in the aristocratic sanctuary. She
accompanied him as far as Porte Saint-Pierre, and
followed him to a point almost opposite the cathedral, watching him as he walked along Rue de
Beaulieu to the Promenade, where Monsieur du
Châtelet was waiting for him. There the poor girl
remained, deeply moved, as if some great event had
taken place. Lucien at Madame de Bargeton's was
to Eve's mind the dawn of fortune. The saint-like
creature did not know that where ambition begins,
artless, sincere sentiments come to an end.

When they reached Rue de Minage, Lucien was
not awe-struck by the exterior aspect of affairs.
That Louvre, which had assumed such magnified
proportions in his mind, was a house built of a soft
stone peculiar to the province, and gilded by time.
Its appearance, gloomy enough upon the street, was
very simple within; there was the typical provincial courtyard, bare and neat; simple, quasi-monas-
tic architecture, in excellent preservation. Lucien
went up an old staircase with chestnut banisters,
the stairs being of stone only to the first floor.

After passing through a reception-room of mean aspect and a dimly-lighted large salon, he found the sovereign in a small salon with carved wooden wainscoting in the style of the last century, and painted gray. The upper part of the doors was painted in monochrome. The panels were covered with old red damask, badly matched. The stuffing of the old-fashioned chairs was barely hidden beneath covers of alternating red and white squares. The poet discovered Madame de Bargeton sitting on a couch with a little quilted cushion, beside a round table covered with a green cloth and lighted by a candlestick with two wax candles and a shade. The queen did not rise, but turned gracefully on her seat, smiling at the poet, who was deeply moved by that serpentine movement, which seemed to him very distinguished. Lucien's excessive beauty, his timid manners, his voice, everything about him made a deep impression on Madame de Bargeton. The poet was in himself the personification of poetry. The young man glanced timidly at this woman, who seemed to him to harmonize with her reputation; she gave the lie to none of his ideas of what a great lady should be. Madame de Bargeton wore a new style of slashed black velvet cap. That style of headdress conveys a reminiscence of the Middle Ages which imposes on a young man by amplifying the wearer, so to speak; some stray locks of reddish hair escaped from beneath it, shining like gold in the light and with a glint of flame about the edges of the curls. The noble lady had the brilliant complexion with which a woman redeems the alleged drawbacks of that tawny color. Her gray eyes sparkled; they were worthily crowned by the white mass of her prominent, sharply defined forehead, already wrinkled. Below them were pearly circles, and two blue veins on each side of the nose set off the whiteness of that delicate border. The nose presented a Bourbonese curve which added to the animation of her rather long face, forming a salient point at which the royal vivacity of the Condés made itself manifest. Her hair did not entirely conceal her neck. Her dress, carelessly secured, permitted glimpses of a snow-white throat, beneath which the eye could divine a spotless, well proportioned bust. With her tapering, well-kept fingers, albeit a little dry, Madame de Bargeton affably waved the young poet to a chair by her side. Monsieur du Châtelet took an armchair.

Lucien saw that they were alone. Madame de Bargeton's conversation intoxicated the poet from L'Houmeau. The three hours he passed with her were to Lucien one of those dreams one would like to endure for ever. She seemed to him wasted rather than thin, amorous without love, sickly despite her strength; her failings, which her manners exaggerated, pleased him, for young men begin by loving exaggeration, the falsehood of noble hearts. He did not notice the signs of decay or the pimples on her cheeks, to which the *ennui* of her life and some ill-health had given a sort of brick color. His imagination was captured first of all by the eyes of fire, by the graceful curls in which the light was reflected, by the dazzling whiteness of her forehead—luminous points by which he was attracted as a moth is by the candle. And then her heart spoke too eloquently to his to allow him to pass judgment on the woman. The enthusiasm of her exalted mood, the fervor of the somewhat timeworn phrases, which Madame de Bargeton had long been repeating but which seemed new to him, fascinated him the more readily because he desired to find everything as it should be. He had brought no poetry to read to her; but the subject was not mentioned: he had forgotten his verses purposely, in order to have an excuse for coming again; Madame de Bargeton had omitted to speak of them in order to ask him to read to her some other day. Was not this a fair beginning of an understanding between them? Monsieur Sixte du Châtelet was ill pleased with the reception accorded Lucien. He discovered somewhat tardily a rival in the comely youth, whom he escorted on his homeward way as far as the turn in the first flight of steps below Beaulieu, with the design of making him a victim of his diplomacy. Lucien was astonished beyond measure to hear the superintendent of imposts boast of having introduced him, and thereupon assume the right to give him advice.

"God grant you will be better treated than I have been," said Monsieur du Châtelet. "The court is less impertinent than this coterie of noodles. A man receives mortal wounds here, and has to put

6

up with the most maddening contempt. The Revolution of 1789 will begin again if these people don't mend their ways. For my part, my only reason for continuing to go to that house is my liking for Madame de Bargeton, the only passably decent woman in all Angoulême. I have been paying court to her for lack of anything better to do, and I have fallen madly in love with her.'' He went on to say that he should soon possess her, that everything led him to think that she loved him. That haughty queen's submission would be the only vengeance he could wreak upon that idiotic crew of clodhoppers.

Châtelet dilated upon his passion like a man who was quite capable of slaughtering a rival, if he should fall in with one. The old imperial butterfly fell with his whole weight on the poor poet, trying to crush him under his dignity, and to intimidate him. He increased in stature as he described in exaggerated terms the perils of his journey; but, although he may have impressed the imagination of the poet, he did not terrify the lover.

After that evening, in spite of the old dandy, in spite of his threats and his scowling face, like that of a bourgeois bravo, Lucien returned to Madame de Bargeton's, at first with the discretion of a man from L'Houmeau; but he soon became accustomed to what seemed to him at first to be an enormous favor, and he called upon her more and more frequently. The son of a pharmacist was considered by the members of this coterie as being of little consequence. In the beginning, if any gentlemen or ladies who were calling upon Naïs met Lucien there, they treated him with the crushing courtesy which fashionable people adopt with their inferiors. At first Lucien found them very affable; but eventually he fathomed the feeling to which this deceptive esteem was due. Soon he detected patronizing airs which stirred his bile and confirmed him in the detestable republican notions with which many future patricians begin their acquaintance with good society. But how great suffering would he not have endured for Naïs, whom he heard people call by that name, for the elect of that clan, like the Spanish grandees and the *crème de la crème* at Vienna, call one another, men and women alike, by their pet names, the last subtle distinction invented to subdivide the heart of the Angoulême aristocracy.

Naïs was beloved as every young man loves the first woman who flatters him, for Naïs prophesied a great future, unbounded glory, for Lucien. She put forth all her address to install the poet in her salon: not only did she praise him beyond all measure, but she represented him as a youth without resources for whom she wished to find a place; she belittled him in order to keep him; she made him her reader, her secretary; but she loved him more than she thought she could love after the terrible disaster that had befallen her. She was very severe upon herself inwardly, she said to herself that it would be downright madness to fall in love with a young man of twenty, who was already so

far removed from her in social position. Her
familiarity was capriciously contradicted by the
haughty airs inspired by her scruples. She was by
turns arrogant and patronizing, affectionate and
flattering. Intimidated at first by her exalted rank,
Lucien had all the fears, all the hopes and all the
despair that torment a first love and cause it to so
monopolize the heart by alternate blows upon the
chords of suffering and of pleasure. For two months
he saw in her a benefactress who proposed to take
a material interest in him. But confidences began.
Madame de Bargeton called her poet "Dear Lucien;"
then, plain "dear." The poet, emboldened, called
the great lady Naïs. When he first called her by
that name she was angry after the fashion that is
always fascinating to a child; she reproached him
for taking the name by which everybody called her.
The proud and noble Nègrepelisse offered the angelic
creature that one of her names that was still un-
worn; she chose to be Louise to him. Lucien
reached the third heaven of love.

One evening, having entered the room while
Louise was gazing at a portrait, which she hastily
concealed, Lucien insisted upon seeing it. To allay
the despair of the first paroxysm of jealousy, Louise
showed him the portrait of young Cante-Croix, and
told, not without tears, the sad history of her pure
but cruelly disappointed love. Was she trying to
decide to be unfaithful to her dead lover, or had she
conceived the idea of giving Lucien a rival in the
portrait? Lucien was too young to analyze his

mistress; he artlessly manifested his despair, for she opened the campaign, during which women demolish scruples more or less ingeniously fortified. Their discussions concerning duty, propriety and religion are like strong places which they like to see taken by assault. The innocent Lucien did not need such coquetries: he would have fought quite naturally.

"I will not die, I will live for you," he said audaciously one evening, determined to have done with Monsieur de Cante-Croix; and he looked at Louise with an expression indicating a passion that had reached its limit.

Terrified at the progress this new love was making in her own heart and in her poet's, she asked him for the verses he had promised her for the first page of her album, seeking a pretext for a quarrel in his delay in writing them. What were her sensations when she read the two stanzas following, which, of course, seemed to her more beautiful than the choicest productions of the aristocratic poet, Canalis?

> The magic brush, the muses insincere
> Will not for aye adorn the faithful sheet
>   Whereon I write.
> And the shy pencil of my mistress fair
> Will oft to me confide her secret joy
>   Or her dumb grief.
>
> Ah! when from this faded page her fingers stern
> Shall seek accounting of the glorious lot
>   Her future now doth promise,
> Then, may Love grant that of this happy voyage
>   The teeming memento
> May be as sweet to think on as a cloudless sky!

"Was it really I who inspired them?" she said.

This suspicion, suggested by the coquettish instinct of a woman who liked to play with fire, brought a tear to Lucien's eye; she soothed him by kissing him on the forehead for the first time. Lucien was decidedly a great man, whom she proposed to mould; she conceived the project of teaching him Italian and German and perfecting his manners; therein she found pretexts for having him constantly with her, in the face of her wearisome courtiers. What renewed interest it gave to her life! She took up music again for her poet's sake, and threw open to him the doors of the world of music; she played some lovely bits of Beethoven and enchanted him; happy in his delight, she said to him hypocritically, seeing that he was half-fainting with rapture:

"Can you not be content with such happiness as this?"

The poor poet was stupid enough to answer: "Yes."

At last matters reached such a point that Louise had invited Lucien to dine with herself and Monsieur de Bargeton, the preceding week. Despite the precaution of having her husband present, the whole town knew of the fact and considered it so outrageous that everyone asked everyone else if it could be true. It was a shocking rumor. To some people, society seemed on the verge of a revolution. Others cried:

"This is the fruit of liberal doctrines!"

The jealous Du Châtelet discovered that Madame Charlotte, who attended women in childbed, was Madame Chardon, mother of the Chateaubriand of L'Houmeau, he said. This expression was esteemed a *bon mot.* Madame de Chandour was the first to hurry to Madame de Bargeton's.

"Do you know what all Angoulême is talking about, my dear Naïs?" she said; "that wretched little poet's mother is Madame Charlotte, who took care of my sister-in-law when her child was born two months ago."

"My dear," said Madame de Bargeton, assuming a queenly air, "what is there extraordinary in that? isn't she an apothecary's widow? a poor lot for a De Rubempré! Suppose that we hadn't a sou— what should we do for a living, you and I? how would you support your children?"

Madame de Bargeton's sang-froid silenced the lamentations of the nobility. Great minds are always disposed to make a virtue of misfortune. Moreover, there is an invincible attraction in persisting in the doing of a good deed which others blame: innocence has the piquant relish of vice. In the evening, Madame de Bargeton's salon was filled with her friends, who came to remonstrate with her. She gave free rein to her caustic wit; she said that, if gentlemen could not be Molières or Racines or Rousseaus or Voltaires or Massillons or Beaumarchaises or Diderots, we must put up with upholsterers, clockmakers, cutlers, whose children might become great men. She said that genius was always of gentle birth. She reviled the clodhoppers for having so little appreciation of their real interests. In fact, she said many absurd things which would have enlightened less stupid people, but they complimented her on her originality.   Thus she averted the storm by firing heavy guns.

When Lucien, at her summons, entered for the first time the old faded salon where four whist tables were in full blast, she received him affably, and presented him to her guests with the air of a queen who proposes to be obeyed.   She called the superintendent of imposts *Monsieur Châtelet*, and turned him to stone by giving him to understand that she was aware of his illegal assumption of the particle *du*. On that evening Lucien was forcibly thrust into Madame de Bargeton's social circle; but he was accepted there as a poisonous substance which everyone made a mental vow to expel by submitting it to the reactive agency of impertinence. Despite this triumph, Naïs lost her empire: there were dissidents among her subjects, who tempted her to emigrate. By Monsieur Châtelet's advice, Amélie, who was Madame de Chandour, resolved to erect a rival altar by receiving on Wednesdays. Madame de Bargeton opened her salon every evening, and the people who frequented it were such slaves of routine, so thoroughly accustomed to walk upon the same carpets, to play on the same backgammon boards, to see the same people and the same candlesticks, to put on their cloaks and double-soled shoes and hats in the same hall, that they loved the very stairs as dearly as they did the mistress of the house. "They all resigned themselves to put up with the gold-finch* of the sacred grove," said Alexandre de Brébian;—another *bon mot*. The president of the Society of Agriculture finally appeased the sedition by a magisterial observation.

"Before the Revolution," he said, "the greatest noblemen received Duclos, Grimm, Crébillon—all of whom were men of humble station like this little poet from L'Houmeau; but they did not admit tax-collectors, and that's what Châtelet is, after all."

Du Châtelet paid dear for his introduction of Chardon, for everyone turned a cold shoulder on him. When he found that he was attacked, the superintendent of imposts, who, from the moment that Madame de Bargeton called him Châtelet, had sworn that she should be his, at once adopted the views of the mistress of the house; he upheld the young poet and declared himself his friend. This great diplomatist, whose services the Emperor had so ill-advisedly dispensed with, made much of Lucien and told him that he was his friend. To launch the poet in society, he gave a dinner-party at which all the high government officials were present—the prefect, the receiver-general, the colonel of the regiment in garrison, the superintendent of the naval school and the president of the tribunal. The poor poet was flattered so extravagantly that any other than a young man of twenty-two would have strongly suspected some fraud in the praise

* *Chardonneret.*

with which they mocked him. At dessert, Châtelet
asked his rival to recite an ode entitled *Sardanapale
mourant*, the masterpiece of the moment. The
principal of the college, a phlegmatic man, applauded him loudly, saying that Jean-Baptiste
Rousseau had done no better. Baron Sixte Châtelet thought that the little rhymer would burst sooner
or later in the hothouse of praise, or that, in the
intoxication of his anticipated glory, he would permit himself some impertinence which would cause
him to be relegated to his primitive obscurity.
Awaiting the demise of this genius, he seemed to
immolate his pretensions at Madame de Bargeton's
feet; but, with the shrewdness of *roués*, he had decided upon his plan of operations, and followed with
strategic attention the steps of the two lovers,
awaiting an opportunity to exterminate Lucien.

Thereupon there arose in Angoulême and its
neighborhood a dull, rumbling sound that proclaimed
the existence of a great man in Angoumois. Madame de Bargeton was generally applauded for the
attentions she lavished upon this young eagle.
Once her conduct was approved, she was determined
to obtain general sanction. She announced throughout the department with trumpet and drum an evening party with ices, cake and tea, a great innovation
in a town where tea was still sold by the apothe-
caries as a drug useful in cases of indigestion. The
flower of the aristocracy was invited to hear a great
work which Lucien was to read. Louise concealed
from her friend the obstacles she had had to

overcome, but she did say a few words to him on the subject of the conspiracy formed against him by society; for she did not choose to leave him in ignorance of the perils of the career men of genius should follow, a career that bristles with obstacles insurmountable by merely mediocre courage. She used her victory as a means of inculcating a useful lesson. With her white hands she pointed to renown as a treasure to be purchased by constant suffering; she spoke of the tortures of martyrs to be endured at the stake, she buttered for him her finest *tartines* and garnished them with her most pompous expressions. It was a sort of counterfeit of the improvisations that disfigure the novel *Corinne*. Louise deemed herself so great in her eloquence, that she loved the Benjamin who inspired it all the more; she advised him to repudiate his father boldly, by assuming the noble name of Rubempré, heedless of the outcry occasioned by an exchange which the king would legitimize. Being connected with the Marquise d'Espard, a De Blamont-Chauvry, who was high in favor at court, she would undertake to obtain that favor. At those words—the king, the Marquise d'Espard, the court, —Lucien's eyes were dazzled as by a display of fireworks, and the necessity of that rechristening was fully demonstrated.

"Dear boy," said Louise, in a tone of affectionate raillery, "the sooner it is done, the sooner it will be ratified."

She raised one after another the successive strata

of the social structure, and let the poet count the
rungs of the ladder which he could ascend at one
bound by virtue of this judicious decision. In an
instant she made Lucien renounce his plebeian
ideas concerning the chimerical equality of 1793,
she aroused in him the thirst for social distinction
which David's cold reasoning had allayed, she
pointed to the higher levels of society as the only
stage which was suited to his talents. The scornful liberal became a monarchist *in petto*. Lucien
bit at the apple of aristocratic luxury and renown.
He swore to lay a crown at his lady's feet, even
though it were stained with blood; he would win
it at any price, *quibuscumque viis*. To prove his
courage, he described his present misery, which he
had concealed from Louise, taking counsel of that
indefinable modesty characteristic of first loves,
which forbids a young man to display his great
qualities, he takes such keen delight in having his
heart appreciated, even in its disguise. He described the troubles of poverty, endured with pride,
his employment with David and his nights passed in
study. This youthful ardor reminded Madame de
Bargeton of the young colonel of twenty-six, and
her expression softened. When he saw that his
imposing mistress was moved, Lucien seized a hand
that was abandoned to him and kissed it with the
frenzy of a boy, a poet, a lover. Louise went so far
as to allow the apothecary's son to reach her brow
and to press his burning lips upon it.

"Child! child! if anyone should see us, I should

make a very ridiculous appearance," she said,
rousing herself from an ecstatic torpor.

During that evening, Madame de Bargeton's wit
wrought great havoc among what she called Lucien's
prejudices. To hear her, you would have said that
men of genius had neither brothers nor sisters,
fathers nor mothers; the great works they were
destined to build required them to be selfish in appearance, by compelling them to sacrifice everything to their own grandeur. If the family suffered
at first from the pitiless exactions enforced by a
gigantic brain, later it would recover a hundredfold
the value of the sacrifices of every nature demanded
by the first conflicts of a disputed royalty, by sharing the fruits of victory. Genius depended only
upon itself; it was the sole judge of its resources,
for it alone knew the goal to be reached: he ought
therefore to place himself above the laws, being
called upon as he was to revise them; moreover,
the man who fixes his grasp upon his epoch can
take everything, risk everything, for everything is
his. She referred to the early life of Bernard
Palissy, Louis XI., Fox, Napoléon, Christopher
Columbus and Cæsar, of all the illustrious gamblers,
who were at first crushed by debt, or poor, unappreciated, looked upon as madmen, bad fathers, bad
sons, bad brothers, but who subsequently became
the pride of their families, of their countries, of the
world.

These arguments harmonized with Lucien's secret
vices and hastened the corruption of his heart; for,

in the ardor of his desires, he admitted *a priori*
methods. But not to succeed constitutes the crime
of social *lèse-majesté*. Does not one who fails,
destroy all the bourgeois virtues that form the basis
of society, which expels with horror the Mariuses
seated before its ruins? Lucien, who did not
recognize himself between the infamy of the
galleys and the laurel wreaths of genius, hovered
above the Sinai of the prophets without seeing beneath him the Dead Sea, the ghastly shroud of
Gomorrha.

Louise so completely freed her poet's mind and
heart from the swaddling-clothes in which his life
in the provinces had enveloped them, that Lucien
determined to put her to the test, in order to ascertain whether he could conquer that queenly quarry,
without having to undergo the mortification of a refusal. The projected evening party gave him an
opportunity to make the test. Ambition was mingled with his love. He loved and he wished to rise,
a twofold sentiment very natural in young men
who have a heart to satisfy and poverty to struggle
against. By inviting all its children to one great
festival, society awakens their ambitions in the
morning of life. It strips youth of its charms and
vitiates most of its generous sentiments by mingling
worldly scheming with them. Poesy would have
it otherwise; but fact too often gives the lie to the
fiction one would like to believe, to justify us in representing young men as other than they are in the
nineteenth century. Lucien's scheming seemed

to him to have no other object than the promotion of an estimable sentiment, his affection for David.

He wrote a long letter to his Louise, for he found that he was bolder with a pen in his hand than with words in his mouth. In a dozen sheets, three times rewritten, he told of his father's genius, his disappointed hopes, and the horrible poverty that weighed upon him. He described his dear sister as an angel, David as a future Cuvier, who, besides being a great man, was a father, a brother, a friend to him; he should deem himself unworthy of his Louise's love, his first glory, if he did not ask her to do for David what she did for him. He would renounce her forever rather than be false to David Séchard; he desired that David should witness his triumph. He wrote one of those wild letters in which young men threaten pistols in case of a refusal, letters filled with the casuistry of childhood, with the unreasoning logic of noble minds, fascinating verbosity, embellished with those artless declarations that escape from the heart unknown to the writer, and that women like so well. After he had handed the letter to the maid, Lucien went to the office to pass the day correcting proofs, superintending some work that was in progress and arranging a few small matters that needed attention, without saying a word to David. When the heart is still in its infancy, young men sometimes display such sublime reserve. Perhaps, too, Lucien was beginning to dread the axe of Phocion, which David

could handle so well; perhaps he feared a penetrating glance that would reach the very bottom of his
heart.   After reading Chénier, his secret had passed
from his heart to his lips, surprised by a reproach
which he felt like the finger the surgeon lays upon
a wound.

*

Now, imagine, if you can, the thoughts that
thronged Lucien's mind as he went down from Angoulême to L'Houmeau. Was the great lady angry?
would she receive David at her house? would not
he, ambitious wight, be hurled back into his hole at
L'Houmeau? Although, before he kissed Louise on
the forehead, Lucien had been able to measure the
distance that separates a queen from her favorite,
he did not say to himself that David could not cover,
in the twinkling of an eye, the space it had taken
him five months to travel. Not knowing how absolute was the decree of ostracism pronounced
against people of humble extraction, he did not
know that a second experiment of the kind would be
Madame de Bargeton's ruin. Accused and convicted
of having kept low company, Louise would be
obliged to leave the town, while her caste would
shun her as a leper was shunned in the Middle
Ages. The superfine aristocratic clan, and the
clergy too, would defend Naïs against all comers, in
case she should allow herself to commit a sin; but
the crime of consorting with bad company would
never be overlooked; for, if we excuse the sins of
the ruling powers, we condemn them after their
abdication. And would not receiving David be
equivalent to abdication? Even if Lucien did not

7   (97)

grasp that side of the question, his aristocratic instinct gave him a premonition of many other difficulties, which filled him with dismay. Nobility of sentiment does not invariably impart nobility of manners. Although Racine had the air of the noblest of courtiers, Corneille strongly resembled a cattle dealer. Descartes had the appearance of a respectable Dutch tradesman. Visitors at Breda, meeting Montesquieu with his rake over his shoulder and his nightcap on his head, often took him for a common gardener. Social polish, when it is not a gift of noble birth, an accomplishment imbibed with the mother's milk or transmitted in the blood, constitutes an education in itself, which chance should second by some grace of figure, by some distinction of feature, or by an intonation of the voice.

All these great little things were wanting in David, while nature had plentifully endowed his friend with them. Of gentle birth on his mother's side, Lucien had everything even to the curved instep of the Frank, while David Séchard had the flat foot of the Goth and the chest and shoulders of his father the pressman. Lucien realized how the satirical remarks would rain upon David, he could almost see the smile Madame de Bargeton would repress. In fact, without being precisely ashamed of his brother, he promised himself that he would not again listen to his first impulse, but would reflect more fully in the future. Then, after the hour of poetry and devotion, after reading works that showed the two friends the vast field of literature illumined by a new sun, the hour of policy and scheming struck for Lucien. Upon returning to L'Houmeau, he repented of his letter and would have liked to recall it; for he saw as through a vista, the pitiless laws of society. Divining how powerfully acquired fortune would assist ambition, it cost him dear to withdraw his foot from the first rung of the ladder by which he was to mount to the assault upon worldly grandeur. Then. the images of his simple, tranquil life, adorned with the brightest flowers of sentiment; David, a veritable genius, who had so nobly assisted him, who would give his life for him if need were; his mother, so great a lady in her humble station, who believed him to be as good as he was clever; his sister, so charming in her resignation, his pure childhood and his still unsullied conscience; his hopes, from which no blast of the north wind had yet stripped their leaves,—everything bloomed anew in his memory. Thereupon he said to himself that it was far better to pierce the dense battalions of the aristocratic or bourgeois multitude by the vigorous blows of merited triumph than to succeed by the favors of a woman. His genius would shine forth sooner or later, like that of so many men, his predecessors, who had conquered society; and then women would love him! The example of Napoléon, so disastrous to the nineteenth century by reason of the pretensions inspired in so many men of moderate capacities, appeared to Lucien, and he cast his selfish scheming to the winds, rebuking himself for it. So

Lucien was constituted: he veered from bad to good, from good to bad, with equal facility.

Instead of the love that the scholar carries with him into retirement, Lucien had been conscious for a month past of a sort of shame when he saw the shop, with the following sign, in yellow letters on a green background, over the door:

POSTEL, DRUGGIST, SUCCESSOR TO CHARDON.

His father's name, displayed thus in a street through which all the vehicles passed, wounded his eyes. In the evening, when he passed out through the door, embellished with a small grated wicket in wretched taste, on his way to Beaulieu, to walk among the most fashionable young people of the Upper Town, with Madame de Bargeton on his arm, he bitterly deplored the lack of harmony between that abode and his good fortune.

"To love Madame de Bargeton, perhaps to possess her soon, and to live in this rat's nest!" he said to himself as he walked through the passageway into the little courtyard where several bundles of boiled herbs were spread out along the wall, where the apprentice was scouring the retorts from the laboratory, and where Monsieur Postel, in his working apron, retort in hand, was scrutinizing a chemical product and glancing now and again into the shop; if he watched his drug too attentively, he kept his ear on the bell.

The odor of camomile, mint and divers distilled

plants filled the courtyard and the modest apartment reached by one of the steep stairways called millers' stairways, with no other railing than two cords. Above was the only attic chamber, in which Lucien lived.

"Good-day, my boy," said Monsieur Postel, a perfect type of the provincial shopkeeper. "How goes our little health? I've just been making an experiment on treacle, but it would take your father to find what I'm looking for. He was a famous fellow, he was! If I had known his secret remedy for the gout, we would both be riding in our carriages to-day!"

Not a week passed that the druggist, who was as stupid as he was kind, did not stab Lucien to the heart by talking about his father's unfortunate reserve concerning his discovery.

"It's a great misfortune," Lucien replied briefly, beginning to find his father's pupil exceedingly vulgar, after having blessed him many a time: for honest Postel had assisted his master's widow and children more than once.

"Why, what's the matter?" asked Monsieur Postel, laying his test tube on the laboratory table.

"Has any letter come for me?"

"Yes, one that smells like balsam! it's on the counter by my desk."

Madame de Bargeton's letter lying among the bottles of a pharmacy! Lucien darted into the shop.

"Make haste, Lucien! your dinner's been waiting for you an hour, it will be cold," cried a sweet voice through an open window; but Lucien did not hear.

"Your brother's daft, mademoiselle," said Postel with a sniff.

This old bachelor, who much resembled a small cask of eau-de-vie upon which a painter's fancy had drawn a coarse, rubicund face, pitted with the small-pox, assumed as he looked at Eve a ceremonious and at the same time a seductive air, which proved that he was thinking of marrying his predecessor's daughter, but could not put an end to the conflict between love and self-interest in his heart. And he often said to Lucien, with a smile, the words which he now repeated when the young man again passed him:

"Your sister's famously pretty! You're not bad either! Your father did everything well."

Eve was a tall brunette, with black hair and blue eyes. Although she showed symptoms of possessing a virile character, she was sweet, affectionate and devoted. Her innocence, her artlessness, her tranquil resignation to a life of hard work, her virtue, which no slanderous tongue assailed, were well calculated to attract David Séchard. So it was, that, from their first meeting, a quiet, simple passion, of the German sort, had stirred both their hearts, unattended by noisy demonstrations or hasty declarations. Each of them had thought secretly of the other, as if they were kept asunder by some jealous husband, whom that sentiment would have offended. Both hid their feelings from Lucien,

whose prospects they may perhaps have thought
they were likely to injure.   David was afraid of not
pleasing Eve, who, on her side, was influenced by
the timidity natural to poverty.   A real working-
girl would have been bold, but a well-bred girl, who
has fallen upon evil days, adapts herself to her hard
lot.   Modest in appearance, proud in reality, Eve
did not choose to run after the son of a man who
was supposed to be wealthy.   At that moment,
those people who were familiar with the increasing
value of real estate estimated the estate at Marsac
at more than eighty thousand francs, without counting the outlying territory that old Séchard, with his
accumulated savings, always lucky in his crops and
a shrewd hand at selling them, was certain to add
to it as occasion offered.   David was perhaps the
only person who knew nothing of his father's fortune.   To him, Marsac was a hovel purchased in
1810 for fifteen or sixteen thousand francs, to which
he went once a year at harvest time, and where his
father walked him about among the vines, boasting
of crops that the printer never saw and that he
cared very little about.

The love of a student, accustomed to solitude and
inclined to magnify his sentiments while exaggerat-
ing difficulties, required to be encouraged; for, to
David, Eve was more imposing than a great lady
is to a simple clerk.   Awkward and ill at ease in
his idol's presence, in as great haste to depart as to
arrive, the printer restrained his passion instead of
expressing it.   Often, in the evening, he would

invent some pretext for consulting Lucien and would
go down from Place du Mûrier to L'Houmeau, by
way of Porte Palet; but, as he drew near the green
door with the iron grating, he would turn and fly,
fearing that he might be too late, or that he would
seem importunate to Eve, who was doubtless in
bed. Although this great love manifested itself
only in small things, Eve fully understood it; she
was flattered, without pride, to find herself the
object of the profound respect expressed in David's
glances, his words and his manner; but the printer's
greatest charm was his fanatical adoration of Lucien: he had divined the surest way to gratify Eve.
In order to make clear in what respect the silent
pleasures of their love differed from more tumul-
tuous passions, we must compare it to the wild
flowers as opposed to the brilliant products of the
flower-garden. There were glances as soft and
delicate as the blue lotus that floats upon the water,
expressions as fleeting as the faint perfume of the
eglantine, as melancholy and tender as the velvety
moss: flowers of two lovely hearts blooming in rich,
fruitful, unchanging soil. Several times Eve had
caught glimpses of the strength hidden beneath that
weakness; she was so grateful to David for all he
did not dare, that the most trivial incident was
likely to lead to a closer union of their hearts.

Lucien found the door opened by Eve and took
his seat, without speaking, at a small table, consisting of a board placed upon a stool, with no table-
cloth, on which his cover was laid. The poor little

household possessed but three silver covers, and
Eve used them all for her darling brother.

"What's that you are reading?" she said, after
she had placed upon the table a plate that she
took from the fire, and had extinguished the flame
in her movable stove by covering it with the
snuffers.

Lucien did not reply. Eve took a small plate on
which some vine-leaves were tastefully arranged
and put it on the table with a small jug of cream.

"See, Lucien, I have some strawberries for you."

Lucien was paying such close attention to his
reading that he did not hear. Eve thereupon took
a seat beside him, without a murmur; for a
sister's feeling for her brother is such that she
takes a vast amount of pleasure in having him treat
her without ceremony.

"Why, what is the matter with you?" she cried,
as she saw tears glistening in her brother's eyes.

"Nothing, nothing, Eve," he said, taking her by
the waist, drawing her to him and kissing her on
the forehead and the hair and the neck with astonishing effusiveness.

"You are hiding something from me?"

"Well, yes, she loves me!"

"I knew very well that it wasn't I you were
kissing," said the poor sister in a pouting tone,
and blushing.

"We shall all be happy," cried Lucien, gulping
down his soup in great spoonfuls.

"We?" Eve repeated.

Inspired by the same presentiment that had seized upon David, she added:

"You will care less for us!"

"How can you think that, if you know me?"

Eve put out her hand to press his; then she took away the empty plate and the brown earthenware soup tureen, and produced the dish she had prepared. Instead of eating, Lucien reread Madame de Bargeton's letter which the discreet Eve did not ask to see, so much respect had she for her brother: if he chose to tell her about it, she was willing to wait; if he did not choose to, could she demand it? She waited.   The letter was as follows:

" My friend, why should I refuse to your brother in knowledge the support I have given you? In my eyes, all talents have equal rights; but you do not know the prejudices of the persons who belong to my social circle. We cannot make those who compose the aristocracy of ignorance recognize nobility of mind. If I am not sufficiently powerful to force Monsieur David Séchard upon them, I will willingly sacrifice those poor people to you. That will be an old-fashioned hecatomb. But, my dear friend, of course you do not wish to force me to accept the society of a person whose mind or whose manners may not please me. Your flattery has taught me how easily friendship is blinded! Will you take it ill of me, if I place a restriction upon my consent? I wish to see your friend, to make up my mind about him, to ascertain for myself, in the interest of your future, if you are not deceiving yourself. Is this not one of the motherly duties which should be undertaken, my dear poet, by

"LOUISE DE NÉGREPELISSE?"

Lucien did not know how artfully the *yes* is used

in the best society to lead up to a *no*, and the *no* to
lead up to a *yes*.   This letter was in his eyes a
triumph.   David would go to Madame de Bargeton's
and would shine there in all the majesty of genius.
In the intoxication caused by a victory which led
him to believe in the power of his ascendancy over
mankind, he assumed such a proud attitude, such
a world of hope was reflected upon his face in the
radiant expression it wore, that his sister could not
refrain from telling him that he was handsome.

"If that woman has any wit at all, she must love
you dearly!   And how unhappy she will be to-night,
for all the ladies will be making eyes at you.   You
will look very handsome reading your *Saint Jean
dans Pathmos!*   I wish I were a mouse and could
slip into the room!   Come, I have got your clothes
ready in mother's room."

The room in question denoted respectable poverty.
There was a walnut bedstead with white curtains,
and at the foot a narrow strip of green carpet.   A
commode with a wooden top, with a mirror, and
some walnut chairs completed the furniture.   A
clock on the mantelpiece was reminiscent of bygone
affluence.   There were white curtains at the window.   The walls were hung with a gray flowered
paper.   The painted floor was scrubbed by Eve and
fairly shone with cleanliness.   In the centre of the
room was a small table upon which were three cups
and a sugar-bowl of Limoges porcelain on a red
plate with a gilt border.   Eve slept in a closet ad-
joining, which contained a narrow bed, an old couch

and a work-table by the window. The small
dimensions of this seaman's cabin made it necessary that the glazed door should be always left
open, to admit fresh air. Despite the straitened
circumstances which these articles revealed, the
modesty of a studious life breathed there. To those
who knew the mother and her children, the sight
was affecting yet harmonious.

Lucien was tying his cravat when David's step
was heard in the little courtyard, and the printer
appeared at once with the gait and manner of a man
in a hurry.

"Well, David," cried his ambitious friend, "we
triumph! she loves me! you are to go."

"No," said the printer with some embarrassment;
"I have come to thank you for this proof of your
affection, which has caused me to reflect very seriously. My life, Lucien, is marked out for me. I
am David Séchard, the king's printer at Angoulême,
whose name is to be read on all the blank walls, at
the foot of the posters. In the eyes of people of
that caste, I am a mechanic, a tradesman, if you
choose, but a man in business with a shop, on Rue
de Beaulieu, corner of Place du Mûrier. I have
neither the fortune of a Keller, nor the renown of a
Desplein, two varieties of power which the nobility
are still trying to deny, but which—I agree with
them in this—amount to nothing without the tact
and manners of the gentleman. In what way can
I justify this sudden elevation? I should make
myself a laughing-stock to the bourgeois as well as

to the nobles. You are in a different position. A
proof-reader is bound to nothing. You are working
to acquire certain knowledge that is indispensable
to success, you can explain your present occupation
by your future. Besides, you can take up something else to-morrow, study law or diplomacy, or
enter the government employ. In short, you are
neither numbered nor boxed up. Make the most of
your social virginity, walk alone and put your hand
upon the honors that are within your reach! Enjoy
to the full all kinds of pleasure, even those that are
due to vanity. Be happy; I shall rejoice in your
success; you will be a second myself. Yes, my
thoughts will enable me to live your life. Yours be
the fêtes, the excitement of society and the swift
movement of its intrigues. Mine the sober, laborious life of the man of business and the slow occupations of science. You will be our aristocracy,"
he said, glancing at Eve. "If you fall, you will
find my arm ready to support you. If you have
reason to complain of treachery, you can take
refuge in our hearts, there you will find unalterable
love. Patronage, favor, good-will, divided between
two, might become weary, we should mutually injure each other; go forward, you can tow me behind,
if need be. Far from envying you, I devote myself
to you. What you have done for me, running the
risk of losing your benefactress, your mistress perhaps, rather than abandon me or deny me, that
simple, yet grand thing, Lucien, would bind me to
you forever, if we were not already brothers. Have

no remorse or anxiety because you seem to take
the more important part. This division à la Mont-
gomery is to my taste. Indeed, even if you should
cause me some suffering, who knows if I should not
still be your debtor?"

As he spoke, he cast the most timid of glances
toward Eve, whose eyes were filled with tears, for
she had guessed everything.

"At all events," he continued, still addressing
the wondering Lucien, "you have done well, you
have a pretty figure, you wear your clothes gracefully, you look like a gentleman in your blue coat
with yellow buttons, and your plain nankeen trousers; but I should look like a workingman among
all those people; I should be awkward and embarrassed and should either say something foolish or
else say nothing at all; you can satisfy all prejudices on the subject of names by taking your
mother's name and calling yourself Lucien de
Rubempré; but I am and shall always be David
Séchard. Everything would tend to serve you and
to injure me in the social circle you are about to
enter. You are made to succeed there. The women
will adore your angel's face; won't they, Eve?"

Lucien threw his arms about David's neck and
kissed him. This modesty put an end at once to
many doubts, many difficulties. How could he
have failed to feel redoubled affection for a man
whose friendship had led him to make the same reflections that his own ambition had suggested to
him? The path of the ambitious man and lover

was made smooth, the heart of the young man and friend overflowed. It was one of those rare moments when all the fibres are gently drawn tight, when all the chords vibrate and give forth a full volume of sound. But this manifestation of the wisdom of a noble soul aroused in Lucien the tendency that leads a man to refer everything to himself. All of us say, more or less, like Louis XIV. : "I am the State!" The undivided affection of his mother and sister, the devotion of David, the habit of seeing the secret efforts of those three always expended for his benefit, had given him the vices of a spoiled child, and engendered in him the selfishness which devours noble impulses, and which Madame de Bargeton encouraged by inciting him to forget his obligations to his mother and sister and to David. Nothing of the sort had happened yet; but was there not reason to fear that, in drawing the circle of his ambition about him, he would be compelled to think only of himself, in order to maintain himself therein?

This effusion of sentiment having passed, David suggested to Lucien that his poem of *Saint Jean dans Pathmos* was perhaps too biblical to be read before an assemblage to whom the apocalyptic poesy was likely to be unfamiliar. Lucien, who was about to appear before the most censorious audience in the department of the Charente, seemed disturbed. David advised him to take André de Chénier in his pocket and to substitute a certain for an uncertain pleasure. Lucien read perfectly, he must necessarily please his hearers, and his modesty would undoubtedly be of service to him. Like most young people, they attributed their own intelligence and their own virtues to people in society.

If youth which has not yet failed is unindulgent to the mistakes of others, it also attributes to them its magnificent beliefs. Indeed, one must have had a thorough experience of life before realizing that, as Raphaël has well said, to understand is to equal. Generally speaking, the quality of mind that is essential to the true understanding of poetry is rare in France, where wit soon dries up the source of the blessed tears of ecstasy, where no one cares to take the pains to decipher the sublime, or to probe it in order to measure its infinite depth. Lucien was about to undergo his first experience of worldly ignorance and indifference! He went to David's house to get the volume of poems.

When the two lovers were left alone, David was more embarrassed than he had ever been in his life. A prey to innumerable fears, he craved and dreaded words of praise, he longed to escape, for modesty too has its coquetry! The poor fellow dared not say a word which would seem like angling for thanks; every word that came to his lips seemed compromising, and so he held his peace, maintaining the attitude of a convicted criminal. Eve, divining the torments of his modesty, chose to enjoy the silence; but when David began twisting his hat, as if to take his leave, she smiled.

"Monsieur David," said she, "if you do not pass the evening at Madame de Bargeton's, we can pass it together. The weather is fine, would you like to walk along the river? We will talk about Lucien."

David longed to throw himself on his face at the lovely creature's feet. The sound of Eve's voice contained an unhoped-for reward; by the softness of her accent, she had swept away all the difficulties of the situation; her suggestion was more than praise, it was the first favor granted by love.

"Give me a few moments to dress," she said, in response to a gesture from David.

David, who had never, in the whole course of his life, known what a tune was, went out humming, to the amazement of honest Postel, who at once conceived strong suspicions as to the relations between Eve and the printer.

*

The most trivial incidents of that evening had a great effect upon Lucien, whose nature made him prone to listen to first impressions.

Like all inexperienced lovers, he arrived so early that Louise was not yet in the salon. Monsieur de Bargeton was there alone. Lucien had already entered upon his apprenticeship in the petty meannesses by which a married woman's lover purchases his good fortune, and which afford the woman a means of measuring what she can exact; but he had never yet found himself face to face with Monsieur de Bargeton.

That gentleman was one of those shallow-brained creatures who occupy a middle position between the inoffensive nullity which still has a glimmer of understanding, and the haughty stupidity which will neither give nor accept anything. Deeply impressed with his duties toward society and over-anxious to make himself agreeable, he had adopted the stereotyped smile of the ballet-dancer as his only language. Whether he was pleased or displeased, he smiled. He smiled at the receipt of disastrous news as well as when informed of some fortunate occurrence. His smile answered all purposes by virtue of the different expressions he gave it. If direct approbation were absolutely necessary, he reinforced his smile by a condescending laugh,

never uttering a word except in the last extremity.
A tête-à-tête caused him the only embarrassment
that disturbed his vegetative life; he was then
obliged to look for something in the vast void
within.   Generally he avoided the difficulty by re-
curring to the artless customs of his childhood; he
thought aloud, he initiated you into the most trivial
details of his life; he told you of his needs, his
petty sensations, which, to him, resembled ideas.
He never talked about the rain or the fine weather;
he did not resort to the commonplaces of conversation by which fools escape; he addressed his remarks to the most secret concerns of life.

"To oblige Madame de Bargeton, who is very
fond of veal, I ate some this morning," he would
say, "and my stomach is troubling me terribly.
I knew it would, it always does; explain it to me!"

Or else:

"I am going to ring for a glass of *eau sucrée;*
will you have one at the same time?"

Or else:

"To-morrow I am going to ride out and see my
father-in-law."

These brief sentences, which called for no discussion, simply extracted a yes or a no from his inter-
locutor, and then the conversation would fall flat.
Thereupon Monsieur de Bargeton would beg his
visitor's assistance by elevating his asthmatic pug
dog nose toward the west and looking at him with
his great colorless eyes as if to ask: *You were
saying?*   He doted upon the tiresome creatures

who were always eager to talk of themselves; he listened to them with unfeigned, courteous attention which made him so dear to their hearts, that the chattering fools of Angoulême gave him credit for a sly sort of intelligence and claimed that he was misjudged. So, when nobody else would listen to them, these people would come and pour the conclusion of their stories or their arguments into Monsieur de Bargeton's ears, sure of finding his approving smile at their service.

As his wife's salon was always full, he was generally at ease there. He busied himself with the most trivial details; he watched for newcomers, saluted them with a smile and escorted them to his wife; he watched those who left and escorted them to the door, receiving their adieus with his everlasting smile. When the party was an animated one, and he saw that everyone was busily employed for the moment, the fortunate mute would plant himself on his two long legs like a stork, as if he were listening to a political conversation; or he would go and scrutinize the hand of some card-player, understanding nothing of what he saw, for he knew no game; or he would walk about, taking snuff and patting his stomach. Anaïs was the beautiful side of his life; she afforded him infinite pleasure. When she was playing her part as mistress of the house, he would stretch himself out upon a couch and gaze admiringly at her; for she talked for him; again, he took delight in trying to fathom the meaning of her remarks; and, as he frequently did not understand them until long after they were made, he indulged in smiles that went off like buried shells, suddenly exploded. His respect for her amounted to adoration. An adoration of some sort is sufficient to make one's life happy, is it not? Like the clever and generous creature she was, Anaïs did not abuse her opportunities when she discovered that her husband possessed the facile nature of a child, who asks no better fate than to be governed. She had taken care of him as one takes care of a cloak; she kept him clean, brushed him, put him away, used him carefully; and Monsieur de Bargeton, feeling that he was brushed and tended and used with care, contracted a dog-like affection for his wife. It is so easy to bestow happiness that costs nothing! Madame de Bargeton, unaware that her husband cared for anything in the world except good cheer, gave him excellent dinners; she took pity upon him; she never complained; and some people, not understanding that pride kept her silent, attributed invisible virtues to her husband. She had, moreover, subjected him to a sort of military discipline and he obeyed his wife's desires passively in everything. She would say to him: "Call upon Monsieur This or Madame That," and he would go as a soldier goes to take his turn at sentry duty. In her presence he assumed the attitude of a soldier carrying arms, motionless.

At this time there was some talk of electing this dumb man to the office of deputy. Lucien had not

been a favored guest at the house for a sufficiently
long time to have lifted the veil behind which that
enigmatical character kept itself hidden. Monsieur
de Bargeton, buried in his lounging chair, seeming
to see and to understand everything, imparting to
his silence an attribute of dignity, was to him a
prodigiously imposing figure. Instead of taking
him for a granite post, Lucien looked upon him as a
redoubtable sphinx, by virtue of the natural impulse
of imaginative men to magnify everything and to
endow with a soul everything that has shape; and
he deemed it advisable to flatter him.

"I am the first to arrive," he said, saluting him
with a little more respect than was commonly accorded the goodman.

"That is very natural," Monsieur de Bargeton
replied.

Lucien took that remark for the epigrammatic
retort of a jealous husband; he blushed and looked
at himself in the mirror, trying to maintain his
self-possession.

"You live at L'Houmeau," added Monsieur de
Bargeton; "people who live at a distance always
arrive earlier than those who live near."

"Why is that?" said Lucien, assuming a concil-
iatory air.

"I don't know," Monsieur de Bargeton replied,
relapsing into immobility.

"You have not tried to find out," continued Lucien. "A man capable of noticing the fact can discover its cause."

"Ah!" said Monsieur de Bargeton, "final causes! Ha! ha!"

Lucien cudgeled his brains for material with which to rekindle the conversation which expired at that point.

"Madame de Bargeton is dressing, I presume?" he said, shuddering at the absurdity of the question.

"Yes, she is dressing," replied the husband simply.

Lucien looked up at the two exposed rafters, painted gray, with plastered spaces between, but could think of nothing further to say; he noticed, however, with dismay, that the little chandelier with old crystal pendants had been stripped of its gauze covering and supplied with candles. The covers of the furniture had been removed and the red damask displayed its faded flowers. These preparations indicated an extraordinary occasion. The poet was disturbed by doubts as to the propriety of his costume, for he was in boots. He went and gazed in a stupor of apprehension at a Japanese vase that stood upon a garlanded console of the time of Louis XV.; then he feared that he might displease the husband by not paying court to him, and he determined to try and discover whether the goodman had a hobby that he could flatter.

"You rarely leave the town, monsieur?" he said, walking back toward Monsieur de Bargeton.

"Rarely."

Silence again. Monsieur de Bargeton watched,

like a suspicious cat, the slightest movements of
Lucien, who disturbed his repose. Each of them
was afraid of the other.

"Can he have become suspicious of my constant
attentions?" thought Lucien, "for he seems to be
very hostile to me!"

Luckily for Lucien, who was sorely embarrassed
by the uneasy glances with which Monsieur de
Bargeton eyed him as he went back and forth, the
old manservant, who had donned livery for the occasion, announced Du Châtelet. The baron entered
the room with perfect ease of manner, saluted his
friend Bargeton, and bestowed upon Lucien a slight
inclination of the head which was much in vogue
in those days, but which seemed to Lucien brim-
ming over with purse-proud impertinence. Sixte
du Châtelet wore trousers of dazzling whiteness,
with inside straps that kept them in place. He had
dainty shoes and Scotch thread stockings. Over his
white waistcoat floated the black ribbon of his eye-
glass. His black coat was noticeable for its Parisian cut and shape. He was in very truth the
doughty beau that his past life pronounced him to
be; but age had already endowed him with a little
round paunch not easily confined within elegant
limits. His hair and whiskers, which were
whitened by the trials he had undergone on his
travels, were dyed, giving his features a harsh
expression. His complexion, formerly very delicate, had taken on the coppery tinge common to
those who return from the Indies; but his general

bearing, although rendered ridiculous by the pretensions to which he still clung, revealed none the less
the attractive secretary of despatches of an imperial
princess. He took his monocle, gazed at Lucien's
nankeen trousers, his boots, his waistcoat and his
blue coat of Angoulême manufacture—eyed his
rival from head to foot in fact; then coolly replaced
his monocle in his waistcoat pocket, as if he had
said: "I am content."

Overwhelmed by the elegance of the financier,
Lucien thought that he would have his revenge
when he should show his face, illumined by the fire
of poesy, to the assembled guests; but he felt
none the less a sharp pang, which renewed the internal distress that Monsieur de Bargeton's supposed
hostility had already caused him. The baron
seemed to bear down upon Lucien with the full
weight of his fortune in order to humble him the
more. Monsieur de Bargeton, who expected that
he would have no further occasion to speak, was
alarmed by the silence of the two rivals as they
looked each other over; but there was one question
which he held in reserve,—as one keeps a pear for a
possible thirst,—for use when he had exhausted his
resources, and he deemed it necessary to discharge it.

"Well, monsieur, what is there new?" he said
to Châtelet, with a business-like air. "Do you
hear anything?"

"Why, Monsieur Chardon is the novelty," replied the superintendent of imposts maliciously.

"Apply to him.   Have you brought us some pretty little poem," queried the sprightly baron, rearranging the upper curl on one side of his head, which he fancied was out of place.

"I must consult you to find out whether I have succeeded," said Lucien.   "You tried your hand at poetry before I did."

"Bah! a lively vaudeville or two written as a favor, occasional ballads, romanzas that owe their success to the music, my great epistle to a sister of Bonaparte—the ingrate!—give me no claim to the admiration of posterity!"

At that moment Madame de Bargeton made her appearance in all the splendor of a carefully studied toilet.   She wore a Jewish turban embellished with an oriental clasp.   A gauze scarf, beneath which glistened the cameos of a necklace, was gracefully twined about her neck.   Her dress of colored muslin, with short sleeves, allowed her to show several rows of bracelets on her lovely white arms.   This theatrical garb fascinated Lucien. Monsieur du Châtelet gallantly lavished nauseating compliments upon the queen, which made her smile with pleasure, she was so happy to be praised before Lucien.   She exchanged but one glance with her dear poet, and answered the superintendent of imposts with a formal courtesy that mortified him because it expressly excluded him from any claim to intimacy.

Meanwhile, the invited guests were beginning to arrive.   In the first place, came the bishop and his grand-vicar, two dignified and solemn figures, but in striking contrast to each other. Monseigneur was tall and thin; his acolyte was short and stout. Both had bright eyes, but the bishop was pale, while his vicar's face wore the purple flush of most robust health. Both were sparing of their gestures and were rarely moved to animation. Both seemed sagacious; their reserve and their silence awed the beholder, and they were supposed to have great minds.

The two priests were followed by Madame de Chandour and her husband, extraordinary individuals, whom those people who know nothing of the provinces, would be tempted to believe a creation of the fancy. Monsieur de Chandour, whose baptismal name was Stanislas, the husband of Amélie, the woman who posed as Madame de Bargeton's rival, was a *ci-devant* young man, still slender at forty-five, with a face that resembled a sieve. His cravat was always tied in such a way as to present two threatening points, one at the level of the right ear, the other depressed toward the red ribbon attached to his Cross. The skirts of his coat were sharply cut away. His low-cut waistcoat disclosed a wealth of swelling, starched shirt front, secured by pins overburdened with precious stones. In short, all his clothing was characterized by a sort of exaggeration that gave him so marked a resemblance to caricatures, that strangers who met him could not repress a smile.

Stanislas constantly looked himself over from

head to foot, with a sort of smug satisfaction, veri-
fying the number of buttons on his waistcoat, following the wavy lines of his close-fitting trousers,
and caressing his legs with a glance that paused at
the toes of his boots and rested lovingly upon them.
When he ceased to examine himself thus, his eyes
would seek a mirror and he would look to see if his
hair kept its curl; he questioned the ladies with a
jovial eye, putting one of his fingers in his waistcoat
pocket, throwing back his shoulders and posing
three-fourths profile,—chanticleer-like antics that
stood him in good stead in the aristocratic society
of which he was the beau. Most of the time his
conversation consisted of broad remarks such as
were in vogue in the eighteenth century. That
detestable style of conversation procured him some
favor among women, for he made them laugh. Monsieur Châtelet was beginning to cause him some
uneasiness. In fact, the ladies, perplexed by the
disdain of the dandy of the impost office, spurred
on by his affectation in pretending that it was impossible to lift him out of the slough into which he
had fallen, and piqued by his manner, as of a blasé
sultan, the ladies, we say, sought his society more
eagerly than when he first arrived, after Madame
de Bargeton fell in love with the Byron of Angoulême.

Amélie was a woman of small stature, awkwardly
affected, plump and fair, with black hair, carrying
everything to excess, always talking in a loud tone,
strutting about with her head laden with feathers

in summer and with flowers in winter; a fluent talker, but never able to finish her sentence without the accompaniment of the hoarse breathing of unacknowledged asthma.

Monsieur de Saintot, Astolphe by baptism, president of the Society of Agriculture, a tall, heavy man, with a high color, appeared in tow of his wife, in figure resembling a dried fern and familiarly called Lili, an abbreviation of Elisa. This pet name, which implied something infantile in the person on whom it was bestowed, was at odds with the character and manners of Madame de Saintot, a solemn, extremely pious woman, and an ill-natured, fault-finding card-player. Astolphe was supposed to be a scientist of the first order. Although as ignorant as a carp, he had nevertheless written the articles on *Sugar* and *Eau-de-vie* in a dictionary of agriculture, two productions plagiarized outright from newspaper articles and ancient works in which those two products were treated. The whole department believed him to be busily employed on a treatise upon modern methods of cultivation. Although he regularly shut himself up all the morning in his study, he had not written two pages in twelve years. If anyone came to see him, he would be taken by surprise fumbling among his papers, looking for a note he had lost, or cutting his quill; but he employed all the time he remained in his study in profitless pursuits: he would read the newspaper at great length, carve corks with his penknife, draw fanciful designs on his blotter, turn the leaves of a volume of Cicero, to catch on the wing a phrase or a passage, whose meaning might be applied to current events; then, in the evening, he would exert himself to lead the conversation around to some subject which would enable him to say: "There's a passage in Cicero that seems to have been written to fit what is happening nowadays." With that he would repeat the passage, to the vast amazement of his auditors, who would say to one another: "Really, Astolphe is a perfect wellspring of knowledge." The interesting incident would be told all over the town and would confirm the prevalent flattering opinion of Monsieur de Saintot.

After this couple, came Monsieur de Bartas, Adrien by name, the man who sang baritone airs and had enormous pretensions in music. Self-esteem had seated him astride the solfeggio; he had begun by admiring his own singing, from that he had passed to talking about music and had ended by devoting himself exclusively to it. The musical art had become a sort of monomania with him; he never showed any animation except when talking of music, and he suffered agony at an evening party until he was asked to sing. Once he had bellowed one of his airs, life began for him; he posed, he stood on his heels when receiving compliments, he played the modest man; but he went, nevertheless, from group to group culling words of praise; and when everything was said he would return to the piano, and start a discussion about the difficulties of his song, or vaunt the talent of the composer.

Monsieur Alexandre de Brébian, the hero of the crayon, the artist who flooded his friends' rooms with absurd productions and spoiled all the albums in the department, accompanied Monsieur de Bartas. Each of them had the other's wife upon his arm. If the *chronique scandaleuse* were to be believed, the exchange was complete. The two ladies, Lolotte—Madame Charlotte de Brébian—and Fifine —Madame Joséphine de Bartas,—equally absorbed in fichus, lace trimmings and arranging combinations of heterogeneous colors, were consumed by the desire to appear like Parisians, and neglected their households, where everything went wrong. While the two women, squeezed like dolls in dresses cut with great regard to economy of material, presented upon their persons an exhibition of outrageously eccentric coloring, the husbands, in their quality of artists, allowed themselves a truly provincial negligence in the matter of costume, which made them curious spectacles. Their threadbare clothes made them look like the supernumeraries who represent the aristocratic wedding guests at small theatres.

Among the figures that cast anchor in the salon, one of the most original was that of Monsieur le Comte de Senonches, who bore the aristocratic name of Jacques; a great hunter, haughty, reserved, with sunburned face, amiable as a wild boar, suspicious as a Venetian, jealous as a Moor, and on the best of terms with Monsieur du Hautoy, otherwise called Francis, the friend of the family.

Madame de Senonches—Zéphirine—was tall and beautiful, but with some pimples on her face due to an affection of the liver, which gave her the reputation of an exacting wife. Her slender figure, her delicate proportions, justified a languorous manner which savored of affectation, but which indicated the unfailing gratification of the passion and caprices of a dearly loved woman.

Francis was a man of considerable distinction, who had abandoned the consulate at Valentia and his hopes in diplomacy to come to Angoulême and live near Zéphirine, also called Zizine. The former consul looked after the housekeeping, attended to the education of the children, taught them foreign languages and managed the property of Monsieur and Madame de Senonches with whole-souled devotion. Noble Angoulême, official Angoulême, bourgeois Angoulême, had long commented on the perfect unity that prevailed in this household of three persons; but the mystery of conjugal trinity seemed so rare and so attractive that Monsieur du Hautoy would have seemed prodigiously immoral if he had showed any symptoms of marrying. Moreover, people were beginning to suspect the existence of disquieting mysteries in the excessive attachment of Madame de Senonches for a goddaughter, one Mademoiselle de la Haye, who acted as her companion; and notwithstanding some apparent impossibilities connected with dates, a striking resemblance was detected between Françoise de la Haye and Francis du Hautoy. When Jacques was hunting

9

in the neighborhood, everyone would ask him about Francis, and he would describe the trifling indispositions of his self-willed intendant, giving him precedence over his wife. This blindness seemed so strange in a jealous man that his best friends amused themselves by bringing it out, and described it to those who did not know the mystery, in order to entertain them.

Monsieur du Hautoy was a precious dandy, whose solicitude in small matters had developed into finicalness and childishness. He worried about his cough, his sleep, his digestion and his diet. Zéphirine had led her factotum to play the man with delicate health: she wadded his clothes and muffled him up and dosed him; she tempted him with choice dishes like a marchioness's poodle; she ordered or forbade him to eat this or that article of food; she embroidered waistcoats for him and cravat ends and handkerchiefs; she had accustomed him finally to wearing such pretty things, that she metamorphosed him into a sort of Japanese idol. Their understanding was perfect; Zizine looked at Francis on every occasion, and Francis seemed to take his ideas from Zizine's eyes. They blamed and praised together and seemed to consult before uttering the simplest form of greeting.

The wealthiest landowner in the neighborhood, the man who was envied above all others, Monsieur le Marquis de Pimentel, and his wife, who had forty thousand francs a year between them, and who passed their winters in Paris, came from the country in a calèche with their neighbors Monsieur le Baron and Madame la Baronne de Rastignac, accompanied by the baroness's aunt and by their daughters, two charming young ladies, well-bred, poor, but dressed with that simplicity which does so much to set off natural beauty. This party, which certainly composed the élite of the company, were received with a cold silence and respect full of jealousy, especially when everyone noticed the marked distinction with which Madame de Bargeton received them. These two families were of the small number of people who, in the provinces, hold themselves above idle gossip, take part with no clique, live quietly in retirement and maintain an imposing dignity. Monsieur de Pimentel and Monsieur de Rastignac were called by their titles; there was no familiarity between their wives or their daughters and the select society of Angoulême; they were too closely connected with the court nobility to compromise themselves with the absurdities of the province.

The prefect and the general were the last to arrive, accompanied by the country gentleman who had brought his memoir on silkworms to David that afternoon. Doubtless, he was some mayor of a canton whose acquaintance was worth cultivating because of his fine estates; but his manner and his costume betrayed absolute unfamiliarity with society; he was uncomfortable in his clothes, he did not know where to put his hands, he walked around the person with whom he was talking, he rose and

sat down again before replying when he was spoken
to, he seemed ready to do any menial service; he
was by turns obsequious, uneasy, solemn; he made
haste to laugh at a jest, he listened in a servile
fashion, and sometimes he assumed a cunning leer
when he thought that someone was making sport of
him. Several times during the evening, as his
memoir lay heavy on his mind, he tried to talk
about silkworms; but the ill-fated Monsieur de
Séverac fell upon Monsieur de Bartas, who replied
with a few remarks concerning Music, and upon
Monsieur de Saintot, who quoted Cicero to him.
Toward the middle of the evening, the poor mayor
succeeded in coming to an understanding with a
widow and her daughter, Madame and Mademoiselle
du Brossard, who were not the least interesting
figures in the assemblage. A single word will tell
the whole story: they were as poor as they were
noble. Their dress displayed that striving after
elegance which betrays secret poverty. Madame
du Brossard, very unskilfully and on every possible
occasion, vaunted the charms of her tall, stout
daughter, about twenty-seven years of age, who
was supposed to be a fine performer on the piano;
she took care that her daughter should share the
likes and dislikes of all the marriageable men, and
in her desire to see her dear Camille settled in
life, she had, in the course of the same evening,
declared that Camille loved the wandering life of
the garrison, and the tranquil life of landowners
who cultivate their own estates. Both had the

prim, bitter-sweet dignity of persons whom everyone is delighted to pity, in whom people are interested through selfishness, and who have sounded the
empty depths of the consolatory phrases with which
society takes pleasure in greeting the unfortunate.
Monsieur de Séverac was fifty-nine years of age
and a childless widower; therefore the mother and
daughter listened with devout admiration to the
details he gave them of his silkworm nurseries.

"My daughter has always loved animals," said
the mother. "And as the silk the little creatures
make interests us women, I will ask your permission to go to Séverac and show my Camille how it
is gathered. Camille is so intelligent, that she
will grasp at once everything you tell her. Why,
one day she understood the inverse ratio of the
square of distances!"

This phrase brought the conversation between
Monsieur de Séverac and Madame du Brossard to a
glorious termination, after Lucien's reading.

Some habitués of the salon glided freely about
among the guests, and there were two or three
young men of good family, timid and silent, arranged like shrines, happy to have been invited to
this solemn literary function, the boldest of whom
emancipated himself so far as to talk a good deal
with Mademoiselle de la Haye. All the women
seated themselves in a circle, with serious faces,
and the men stood behind them. This assemblage
of strange personages, with eccentric costumes and
made-up faces, became most imposing to Lucien,

whose heart beat fast when he found all eyes fixed upon him. Bold as he was, he found it difficult to undergo that first test, despite the encouragement of his mistress, who bestowed her most ceremonious reverences and her most charming courtesies upon the illustrious luminaries of Angoumois. The distress that he felt was exaggerated by a circumstance readily foreseen, but well calculated to dismay a young man as yet unfamiliar with social tactics.

Lucien, all eyes and all ears, heard himself addressed as Monsieur de Rubempré by Louise, by Monsieur de Bargeton, by the bishop and by some few sycophants of the mistress of the house; and as Monsieur Chardon by the majority of that dreaded audience. Abashed by the questioning glances of the curious, he knew when his plebeian name was coming, from the mere movement of the lips; he divined the anticipatory judgments that were passed upon him with the provincial outspokenness that is often a little too near discourtesy. These constant, unexpected pin-pricks put him on still worse terms with himself. He awaited impatiently the moment for beginning his reading, in order to assume an attitude that would put an end to his internal agony; but Jacques was describing his last hunt to Madame de Pimentel; Adrien was discussing the new musical star, Rossini, with Mademoiselle Laure de Rastignac; Astolphe, who had learned by heart a newspaper description of a new plough, was telling the baron about it. Lucien did not know, poor poet, that not one of those great minds, save Madame de Bargeton's, could understand poetry. All those people, being absolutely without emotions, had hurried to the house entirely astray as to the nature of the spectacle that awaited them. There are words which, like the bugle, the cymbals, the great drum of the puppet-show, always attract the crowd. The words beauty, glory, poetry, have a magic that fascinates the most commonplace minds.

*

When everybody had arrived, when the conversation had ceased, not without numberless warnings given to the interrupters by Monsieur de Bargeton, whom his wife sent about like a church beadle who taps his staff on the flags, Lucien took his place at the round table near Madame de Bargeton, conscious of a terrible sinking of the heart. He announced in a wavering voice that, in order not to disappoint any person's expectations, he proposed to read some recently discovered masterpieces of a great but little known poet. Although André de Chénier's poems were published in 1819, no one at Angoulême had as yet heard of André de Chénier. Everyone chose to discover in this announcement a pretext invented by Madame de Bargeton to spare the poet's self-esteem and put the audience at their ease.

Lucien first read *Le Jeune Malade,* which was received with flattering murmurs; then *L'Aveugle,* a poem which ordinary minds consider too long. While he was reading, Lucien was a prey to such infernal agony as none but eminent artists can realize, or those whom enthusiasm and exalted intelligence place upon the same level. To be translated by the voice, as well as to be understood, poetry demands religious attention. There must be a close alliance between the reader and his auditory, failing which the magnetic communication does not

take place. If such cohesion of minds is lacking,
the poet is like an angel trying to sing a celestial
hymn amid the sneering laughter of the demons of
hell. Now, in the sphere in which their faculties
are developed, men of intellect possess the circum-
spective eyesight of the snail, the scent of the blood-
hound and the ear of the mole; they see, they smell,
they hear everything about them. The musician
and the poet know as quickly whether they are admired or not understood, as a plant withers or
revives in a friendly or hostile atmosphere. The
whispers of the men who had come there only to
please their wives, and who were talking business
with one another, echoed in Lucien's ears, by virtue of this peculiar law of acoustics; just as he saw
the sympathetic gulfs between various yawning
jaws, whose teeth mocked at him. When, like the
dove of the Deluge, he looked about in search of
some favorable corner upon which to let his glance
rest a moment, he met the impatient eyes of people
who were evidently thinking of taking advantage
of this assemblage to question one another as to
some important matters. With the exception of
Laure de Rastignac, two or three young men and
the bishop, everybody in the room was bored.
They who understand poetry try to develop in their
minds what the author has placed in germ in his
lines; but those icy auditors, far from breathing in
the poet's soul, did not even listen to his words.
Lucien was so profoundly disheartened, therefore,
that his shirt was drenched with cold perspiration.

A glance of flame from Louise, toward whom he turned, gave him courage to finish; but his poet's heart was bleeding from a thousand wounds.

"Do you find this very interesting, Fifine?" said the meagre Lili to her neighbor, anticipating perhaps more stage effect.

"Don't ask me for my opinion, my dear; my eyes close as soon as I hear anybody begin to read."

"I hope Naïs won't often give us poetical evenings," said Francis. "When I listen to reading after my dinner, the attention I have to pay to it disturbs my digestion."

"Poor dear," said Zéphirine in a low voice, "drink a glass of *eau sucrée.*"

"It was very well delivered," said Alexandre; "but I prefer whist."

At that remark, which was considered to be clever, because of the English meaning of the word, some enthusiastic card players declared that the reader must need a rest. On that pretext, one or two couples escaped to the boudoir. Lucien, at the earnest request of Louise, the charming Laure de Rastignac and the bishop, re-aroused attention, thanks to the counter-revolutionary energy of the iambics, which several of the guests, carried away by the vigorous warmth of the declamation, applauded without understanding them. People of that sort are worked upon by vociferation, just as ordinary palates are inflamed by strong liquors. While ices were being passed around, Zéphirine sent Francis to look at the volume, and told her neighbor Amélie that the lines Lucien had read were printed.

"Why, that's easily explained," Amélie replied with visible satisfaction, "Monsieur de Rubempré works for a printer. It's as if a pretty woman should make her own dresses," she said, glancing at Lolotte.

"He has printed his poems himself," said the women.

"Why is he called Monsieur de Rubempré then?" demanded Jacques. "When a man of noble blood works with his hands, he ought to change his name."

"He has changed his name, which was plebeian, for that of his mother, who is of noble birth," said Zéphirine.

"As his verses are printed," said Astolphe, "we can read them ourselves."

This stupidity complicated matters until Sixte du Châtelet deigned to explain to this ignorant assemblage that the preliminary announcement was not a mere oratorical precaution, and that the beautiful poems they had heard were from the pen of a royalist brother of the revolutionist Marie-Joseph Chénier. The aristocracy of Angoulême, with the exception of the bishop and Madame de Rastignac and her daughters, who were profoundly impressed by the noble lines, deemed itself imposed upon and took offence at the fraud. A subdued muttering arose; but Lucien did not hear it. Isolated from that hateful assemblage by the intoxication produced by inward melody, he strove to prolong it, and he saw the faces about him as through a cloud. He read the mournful elegy upon suicide, the one in the archaic metre, overflowing with sublime melancholy; then the one in which this line occurs:

"Your lines are sweet, I love to say them o'er."

And he concluded with the smooth-flowing idyl, *Néère.*

Plunged in a delicious reverie, with one hand among her curls, which she had involuntarily uncurled, the other hanging at her side, with distraught eyes, alone in her crowded salon, Madame de Bargeton for the first time in her life, felt that she had been transported to the sphere in which she belonged. Imagine the disagreeable shock she received when Amélie, who had undertaken to voice the general opinion, said to her:

"Naïs, we came here to listen to Monsieur Chardon's poetry, and you give us printed poems. Although they are very pretty, from patriotism these ladies would prefer the wine of the province."

"Don't you think that the French language is ill-suited to poetry?" said Astolphe to the superintendent of imposts. "I find Cicero's poetry a thousand times more poetic."

"The true French poetry is light poetry, the *chanson,*" replied Châtelet.

"The *chanson* proves that our language is very musical," said Adrien.

"I would much like to know the verses that caused

Naïs's fall," said Zéphirine; "but, to judge from the
way she receives Amélie's suggestion, she isn't inclined to give us a specimen."

"She owes it to herself to make him repeat his
own verses," said Francis, "for the fellow's genius
is her justification."

"You have been in the diplomatic service; do
you obtain this treat for us," said Amélie to Monsieur du Châtelet.

"Nothing could be easier," the baron replied.

The ex-secretary of despatches, accustomed to
these little manœuvres, went to the bishop and succeeded in making him prefer the request. Being
urged by Monseigneur, Naïs had no choice but to
ask Lucien to repeat some piece that he knew by
heart. The baron's speedy success in this negotia-
tion earned for him a languorous smile from Amélie.

"Really the baron is very clever," she said to
Lolotte.

Lolotte remembered Amélie's bitter-sweet remark
as to women who made their own dresses.

"Since when have you recognized the barons of
the Empire?" she asked with a smile.

Lucien had essayed to deify his mistress in an
ode which was addressed to her under a title adopted
by all young men on leaving college. That ode,
which he had toiled over so lovingly and embellished with all the love that filled his heart, seemed
to him the only one of his own works worthy to
contend with the poetry of Chénier. He glanced
with a more or less conscious expression at Madame

de Bargeton, as he said: À ELLE! Then he proudly took his place to recite his ambitious essay, for his author's self-esteem was quite at ease behind Madame de Bargeton's skirts. At that moment, Naïs betrayed her secret to the eyes of her own sex. Notwithstanding her habit of dominating these people from the height of her superior intellect, she could not avoid an involuntary tremor for Lucien. Her face was troubled, her glances seemed, in a certain sense, to crave indulgence; finally she was obliged to sit with her eyes fixed on the floor and to conceal her satisfaction as the following strophes fell upon her ear:

TO HER.

Forth from the luminous depths of eternal glory
Where cherubim attentive, on timbrels of gold
In homage bent, repeat to God the prayerful story
    Our sorrowing worlds unfold,

Ofttimes a cherubin whose golden locks appear
Veiling God's glory confusing that illumes her face,
Her argent wings abandons in the heavenly place,
    And seeks our earthly sphere.

God's pitying glance all prompt has she learned to divine:
She lulls the keen pangs of struggling genius distressed;
Like maiden adored, she cheers the days of life's decline
    With flowers in childhood blessed.

Of contrite souls she notes the late repentant cry,
And whispering "Hope" in dreams, relieves the mother's load;
With heart joy-abounding she carefully reckons each sigh
    On want and grief bestowed.

Still with us of those bright angels one remains,
Whom earth all-enamored stays in her march ;
But weeping, and saddened she her gentle gaze strains
    To the paternal arch.

'Tis not the dazzling whiteness that her brow o'ershines,
Has told me all the secret of her noble race,
Nor yet the burning glance, nor pregnant fire, the signs
    Of her celestial grace.

But dazzled, my love that numberless glances assail
Has oft striven with her nature divine to unite
But she has donned the great, the dread archangel's mail
    Impenetrable, bright.

Oh! beware, oh! beware lest he see her aspire,
See the seraph all-glorious mount heavenward again ;
For too soon would he learn the enchanting refrain
    Of the eventide choir.

Then piercing night's veil would you see them appear,
Like gleams of earliest morn, enter the starlit sphere
    In swift flight fraternal ;
And the sailor on watch while awaiting a sign,
Would show the pathway of their feet, a brilliant line
    Like a beacon eternal.

"Do you understand that metaphor?" said Amélie to Monsieur du Châtelet, bestowing a coquettish smile upon him.

"Oh! they are such verses as all of us write more or less when we leave college," replied the baron with a bored expression, to carry out his part of a critic who is surprised at nothing. "Formerly we affected the Ossianic mists. There were Malvinas and Fingals, cloudlike apparitions, warriors who came forth from their tombs with stars above their heads. To-day that poetic frippery is replaced by Jehovah, by the zither, by angels, by seraph's wings, by the whole wardrobe of paradise freshly renovated, with the words 'immense, infinite, solitude, intelligence.' There are lakes and words of God, a sort of Christianized pantheism, enriched with rare rhymes evolved with much toil, *émeraude* and *fraude, aïeul* and *glaïeul,* etc. In short, we have changed our latitude; instead of being in the North, we are in the East; but the shadows are quite as dense there."

"If the ode is obscure," said Zéphirine, "the declaration seems clear enough."

"And the archangel's armor is a decidedly thin muslin dress," said Francis.

Although courtesy demanded that they should pretend to think the ode enchanting on Madame de Bargeton's account, the women, furious because they had no poet at their service to call them angels, rose to their feet as if they were sadly bored, murmuring frigidly: *Very fine! how pretty! lovely!*

"If you love me, you will not compliment the author or his angel either," said Lolotte to her dear Adrien, in a despotic tone which he was bound to obey.

"After all, it's nothing but words," said Zéphirine to Francis, "and love is poetry in action."

"You said then just what I was thinking, Zizine,

10

but I couldn't have expressed it so neatly," rejoined Stanislas, eyeing himself from head to foot with a caressing expression.

"I don't know what I would give," said Amélie to Du Châtelet, "to see Naïs's pride have a fall, for she allows herself to be called an archangel as if she were better than the rest of us, and asks us to meet such *canaille* as the son of an apothecary and a nurse, whose sister is a grisette, and works in a printing office."

"As the father sold biscuits for worms,* he ought to have made his son take them," said Jacques.

"He continues at his father's trade, for what he has just given us seems to me very like a drug," observed Stanislas, assuming one of his most fetching attitudes. "Drug for drug, I prefer something else."

In a moment, everybody was doing his or her best to humiliate Lucien by some aristocratic sarcasm. Lili, the devotee, looked upon it as a charitable action, saying that it was high time to open Naïs's eyes, for she was on the point of making a fool of herself. Francis, the diplomat, undertook to guide this absurd conspiracy, in which all these petty minds were as deeply interested as in the final catastrophe of a melodrama, seeing therein an exciting adventure to be talked about the next day. The ex-consul, who was by no means anxious to fight with a young poet who, before his mistress's eyes, would fly into a rage at an insulting word,

*Vers—The French word for *verse* and *verses* is also the plural form of *ver,* meaning *worm,* hence the French pun is untranslatable.

realized that Lucien must be attacked with a consecrated weapon against which revenge was impossible. He followed the example set by the adroit
Châtelet when he desired to make Lucien recite
some of his own lines. He went and talked with
the bishop, pretending to share the enthusiasm the
ode had awakened in His Grace; then he began to
mystify him by giving him to understand that Lucien's mother was a very superior woman of an
exceedingly modest nature, who supplied her son
with the themes of all his compositions. Lucien's
greatest desire was to see justice done to his mother,
whom he adored. Once this idea was implanted in
the bishop's mind, Francis trusted to the chances
of conversation to bring forth the insulting remark
which he had undertaken to make monseigneur
utter.

When Francis and the bishop returned to the
circle in the centre of which Lucien stood, interest
redoubled among those who were already giving
him hemlock to drink in small doses. The poor
poet, being entirely unfamiliar with the devious
practices of salons, could only look at Madame de
Bargeton and reply awkwardly to the awkward
questions that were put to him. He was ignorant
of the names and rank of most of those present, and
he did not know how to reply to women who said
absurd things to him that made him ashamed.
Moreover, he felt a thousand leagues apart from
those Angoumois divinities, who called him sometimes Monsieur Chardon, sometimes Monsieur de

Rubempré, while they called one another Lolotte, Adrien, Astolphe, Lili, Fifine. His confusion was extreme when, having taken Lili for a man's name, he called the outspoken Monsieur de Senonches Monsieur Lili. The Nimrod retorted with a *Monsieur Lulu?* that made Madame de Bargeton blush to the tips of her ears.

"She must be completely blinded to admit that little fellow here and present him to us!" he said in an undertone.

"Madame la Marquise," said Zéphirine to Madame de Pimentel, in a low voice but loud enough to be overheard, "don't you see a great resemblance between Monsieur Chardon and Monsieur de Cante-Croix?"

"The resemblance is imaginary," Madame de Pimentel replied with a smile.

"Glory has a fascination that one may acknowledge," said Madame de Bargeton to the marchioness. "There are women who fall in love with grandeur as others do with pettiness," she added, glancing at Francis.

Zéphirine did not understand, for in her eyes, her consul was a very great man; but the marchioness went over to Naïs's side, laughing heartily.

"You are very fortunate, monsieur," said Monsieur de Pimentel to Lucien, addressing him as Monsieur de Rubempré, after previously calling him Chardon; "you are never bored, I suppose?"

"Do you work quickly?" Lolotte asked him, in

the tone in which she would have asked a carpenter:
"Does it take you long to make a box?"

Lucien was crushed by that sledge-hammer blow;
but he raised his head as he heard Madame de
Bargeton reply, with a smile:

"My dear, poetry doesn't grow in Monsieur de
Rubempré's head as grass grows in our courtyards."

"Madame," said the bishop to Lolotte, "we cannot have too much respect for the noble minds
which God has illumined with one of His rays.
Yes, poetry is a holy thing. Poetry means suffering. How many silent, wakeful nights were the
price of the strophes you admire! Salute the poet
with affection, for he almost always leads an unhappy life, and God doubtless reserves a place for
him in Heaven, among His prophets. This young
man is a poet," he added, laying his hand on Lucien's head; "do you not see fatality written on
that fine brow?"

Happy at being so nobly defended, Lucien saluted
the bishop with a grateful glance, little thinking
that he was destined to be his executioner.

Madame de Bargeton bestowed on the hostile
circle about her a triumphant glance that buried
itself, like a javelin, in the hearts of her rivals,
whose rage redoubled.

"Ah! monseigneur," said the poet, hoping to
strike those foolish heads with his golden sceptre,
"the ordinary man has neither your intellect nor
your charity. Our sorrows are not known, nor
does anyone know of our toil. The miner has less

difficulty in taking gold from the mine than we have in wresting our images from the entrails of the most ungrateful of tongues. If the aim of poetry be to place ideas at the precise point where all the world may see them and feel them, the poet must constantly run over the scale of human intellects, in order to satisfy them all; he must conceal logic and sentiment, two mighty enemies, beneath the brightest colors; he must enclose a whole world of poetry in a phrase, summarize whole systems of philosophy in a single picture; in a word, his poems are seeds from which flowers should spring and bloom in the hearts of his fellows, seeking the furrows ploughed by individual sentiments. Must one not have felt everything in order to express everything? And to feel keenly is to suffer, is it not? Thus poetry is brought into the world only after painful journeys into the vast regions of thought and of society. Are not those works immortal to which we owe beings whose lives seem more vividly true to us than the lives of those who have really lived; like Richardson's Clarissa, Chénier's Camille, Tibullus's Delia, Ariosto's Angelica, Dante's Francesca, Molière's Alceste, Beaumarchais' Figaro, Walter Scott's Rebecca, Cervantes' Don Quixote?"

"And what will you create for us?" queried Châtelet.

"To announce such creations in advance is to give one's self a certificate of genius. Besides, such sublime productions demand long experience of the world, an exhaustive study of human passions and interests which I have had no opportunity to undertake; but I am beginning!" he added, bitterly, casting a revengeful glance upon the circle. "The brain has a long period of gestation—"

"Your accouchement will be a painful one," interrupted Monsieur du Hautoy.

"Perhaps your excellent mother will assist you," said the bishop.

This shaft so cleverly prepared, this premeditated vengeance, kindled a gleam of joy in every eye. Upon every mouth was a smile of aristocratic satisfaction, augmented by the stupidity of Monsieur de Bargeton, who began to laugh some time after the blow.

"Monseigneur, you are a little too clever for us at this moment, these ladies don't understand you," said Madame de Bargeton, by that single sentence paralyzing the laughter and drawing all eyes to herself. "A poet who draws all his inspiration from the Bible has a veritable mother in the Church. —Monsieur de Rubempré, give us *Saint Jean dans Pathmos*, or *Le Festin de Balthazar*, to show monseigneur that Rome is still the *Magna Parens* of Virgil."

The women smiled at one another when they heard Naïs say the two Latin words.

Early in life the haughtiest courage is not without its moments of depression. The first effect of the blow was to send Lucien straight to the bottom, but he spurned it with his foot and returned to the

surface, registering a vow to override the clique.
Like a bull, irritated by the pricking of a thousand
darts, he stood erect, furious with rage, and obeyed
Louise's command by declaiming *Saint Jean dans
Pathmos*. But most of the card-tables had attracted
their quota of players, who fell back into the rut of
their regular habits, finding a pleasure there that
poetry did not afford them. Moreover, the vengeance of so many wounded self-esteems would not
have been complete without the negative contempt
for native poetry which they displayed by deserting
Lucien and Madame de Bargeton. Everyone seemed
preoccupied; one went to talk about a proposed
departmental road with the prefect, another suggested varying the evening's entertainment with
a little music. The first society of Angoulême, conscious of its own unfitness to pass judgment on the
merits of poetry, was especially curious to learn the
opinion of the Pimentels and Rastignacs concerning
Lucien, and several persons gathered about them.
The great influence which those two families exer-
cised in the department was always recognized on
great occasions; everyone was jealous of them and
fawned upon them, for they all felt that they might
some day need their patronage.

"What do you think of our poet and his poetry?"
said Jacques to the marchioness, on whose estate
he hunted.

"Why, for provincial verses," she said with a
smile, "they're not bad; however, such a comely
poet can do nothing ill."

Everyone thought this an admirable judgment, and they went about repeating it, giving it an ill-natured turn which the marchioness by no means intended. Châtelet was called upon at this juncture to accompany Monsieur de Bartas, who murdered the great aria from *Figaro*. Once the door was opened to music, they must listen to the romanza of the days of chivalry, written under the Empire by Chateaubriand, as rendered by Châtelet. Then came pieces for four hands, executed by young ladies, and called for by Madame du Brossard, who desired to display her dear Camille's talent in the presence of Monsieur de Séverac.

Madame de Bargeton, wounded by the disdainful treatment of her poet, met scorn with scorn by going into her boudoir while the music was in progress. She was followed by the bishop, to whom his grand-vicar had explained the profound irony of his involuntary epigram, and who was desirous to make amends therefor. Mademoiselle de Rastignac, who was fascinated by the poetry, glided into the boudoir, unknown to her mother. As she sat down upon her quilted-cover couch, to which she led Lucien, Louise was able, unseen and unheard, to whisper in his ear:

"Dear angel, they did not understand you! but

"'Your lines are sweet, I love to say them o'er.'"

Lucien, comforted by this flattery, forgot his troubles for a moment.

"Renown is not to be bought cheap," said Madame de Bargeton, taking his hand and pressing it. "Suffer, suffer, my friend; you will be great, your sorrows are the price of your immortality. I would like well to sustain the burden of such a conflict. God preserve you from a colorless life, without battles to fight, a life in which the eagle's wings never have room enough! I envy your suffering, for you are at least alive! You will exert all your strength, you will hope for victory! Your struggle will be a glorious one. When you have reached the sphere where great minds hold sway, remember the poor creatures, disinherited by fate, whose intelligence is made naught by the oppression of a moral nitrogen, and who die, having always known what life was without being able to live it, who have keen eyes and have seen nothing, who have a most delicate sense of smell and have smelt nothing but decaying flowers. Sing then of the plant that is withering away in the heart of a forest, stifled by creepers, by dense, greedy vegetation, having never been caressed by the sun, and that dies without having bloomed. Would not that be a terribly melancholy poem, a most original subject? What a sublime picture would be that of a young girl born beneath Asian skies, or of some maiden of the desert transplanted to some cold western clime, calling to her beloved sun, dying of mysterious grief, overwhelmed alike by cold and by love! It would be the type of many lives."

"You would thus depict the soul that remembers

Heaven," said the bishop; "a poem that must have been written long ago; I have been glad to recognize a portion of it in the Song of Songs."

"Undertake it," said Laure de Rastignac, artlessly expressing her belief in Lucien's genius.

"France lacks a great sacred poem," said the bishop. "Believe me, renown and fortune await the man of talent who will labor for religion."

"He shall undertake it, monseigneur," said Madame de Bargeton with emphasis. "Do you not see the idea of the poem already shining in his eyes like the first gleam of dawn?"

"Naïs is treating us very badly," said Fifine. "What in the world is she doing?"

"Don't you hear her?" replied Stanislas. "She's mounted on her long words, which have no head or tail."

Amélie, Fifine, Adrien and Francis appeared at the door of the boudoir, with Madame de Rastignac, who was looking for her daughter, to take her home.

"Naïs," said the two ladies, delighted to disturb the little party in the boudoir, "it would be very good of you to play us something."

"My dear child," replied Madame de Bargeton, "Monsieur de Rubempré is going to recite his *Saint Jean dans Pathmos*, a magnificent biblical poem."

"Biblical!" echoed Fifine, aghast.

Amélie and Fifine returned to the salon, taking that word with them as food for mockery. Lucien

excused himself from repeating the poem on the
plea of failure of memory. When he reappeared
he no longer aroused the slightest interest. Everyone was talking or playing cards. The poet had
been stripped of all his plumes; the landowners saw
no way in which they could make him useful; the
people with pretensions feared him as a power hostile to their ignorance; the women, who were
jealous of Madame de Bargeton—the Beatrice of this
new Dante, as the grand-vicar expressed it,—cast
coldly disdainful glances upon him.

"And that is society!" said Lucien to himself as
he went down to L'Houmeau by the Beaulieu steps,
for there are moments in life when one likes to take
the longest road, in order to stimulate by the motion
of walking, the movement of the ideas that occupy
one's mind and to which one wishes to give free
rein.

Far from discouraging him, the passion due to
foiled ambition gave Lucien new strength. Like
all those whose instinct leads them to a lofty sphere,
which they reach before they are able to maintain
themselves therein, he resolved to sacrifice everything else in order to retain his foothold in good
society. As he walked along, he extracted one by
one the poisoned shafts that had entered his flesh,
he talked to himself aloud, he reviled the fools with
whom he had to deal; he thought of clever retorts to
the absurd questions they had asked him, and was
in despair to have his wits come to him too late.
When he reached the Bordeaux road which winds

about the foot of the hill and follows the bank of the
Charente, he thought that he saw, by the light of
the moon, Eve and David sitting on a piece of timber
by the river, near a large factory, and he took a
path that led down toward them.

*

While Lucien was hurrying to the torture at Madame de Bargeton's, his sister donned a dress of pink calico with innumerable little stripes, a straw hat and a little silk shawl; a simple costume which would have made one think she was handsomely dressed, as is always the case with those persons whose natural nobility of bearing sets off the poorest accessories. Indeed, when she set aside her working-girl's costume, she awed David prodigiously. Although the printer had determined to talk about himself, he could think of nothing to say when he gave the fair Eve his arm to walk through L'Houmeau. Love delights in this sort of respectful terror, like that which God's glory arouses in the faithful. The two lovers walked silently toward Pont Sainte-Anne on their way to the left bank of the Charente. Eve, who found the silence burdensome, paused in the middle of the bridge to gaze at the river, which, from that point to the point where the powder mill was being built, forms a long sheet, whereon the setting sun threw at that moment a joyous flood of light.

"What a lovely evening!" she said, casting about for a subject of conversation; "the air is balmy and cool at the same time, the flowers smell so sweet and the sky is superb."

"Everything seems to speak to the heart," David replied, trying to work around to his love by analogy. "Those who love derive infinite pleasure from finding in the details of a landscape, in the transparent clearness of the air, in the perfumes that rise from the earth, the poetic feeling that they have in their hearts. Nature speaks for them."

"And she loosens their tongues too," laughed Eve. "You were very silent as we came through L'Houmeau. Do you know, I was really embarrassed!"

"You looked so beautiful that I was spellbound!" replied David artlessly.

"So I am less beautiful now, am I?" she asked.

"No, but I am so happy to be walking alone with you, that—"

He stopped, abashed, and looked at the hills down which the road winds from Saintes.

"If you take any pleasure in this walk, I am delighted, for I feel in duty bound to give you an evening in exchange for the one you sacrificed to me. By refusing to go to Madame de Bargeton's, you were as generous as Lucien was in taking the risk of angering her by his request."

"Not generous, but wise," replied David. "As we are alone here in the open air, with no other witnesses than the reeds and bushes that border the Charente, permit me, dear Eve, to express to you some of the anxious thoughts that Lucien's present course causes me. After what I have just said to him, my fears will seem to you, I hope, a refinement of friendship. You and your mother have done

everything to raise him above his station; but, by
arousing his ambition, have you not imprudently
exposed him to great suffering? How will he sustain himself in the world to which his tastes are
leading him? I know him! it is his nature to like
to reap without labor. Social duties will consume
his time, and time is the only capital of people who
have no fortune but their intellectual powers; he
likes to shine, society will aggravate his longings,
which no amount of money will satisfy; he will
spend money and earn none; in a word, you have
accustomed him to look upon himself as a great
man; but, before acknowledging any sort of superiority, the world demands some striking success.
Now, literary success can be won only in solitude
and by persistent work. What will Madame de
Bargeton give your brother in return for so many
days passed at her feet? Lucien is too proud to
accept help, and we know that he is as yet too poor
to continue to meet her social coterie, which is
doubly ruinous. Sooner or later, that woman will
abandon our dear brother, after she has killed all
taste for work in him, after she has developed in
him the taste for luxury, contempt for our humble
mode of life, love of pleasure, and his inclination to
idleness, the curse of poetic souls. Yes, I tremble
to think that this great lady is amusing herself with
Lucien as a mere plaything: either she loves him
sincerely and will make him forget everything, or
she doesn't love him and will make him unhappy,
for he is daft over her."

11

"You freeze my heart," said Eve, stopping at the lock. "But, as long as my mother has the strength to continue her difficult work, and as long as I live, the proceeds of our toil will be sufficient perhaps to meet Lucien's expenses, and enable him to await the moment when his fortunes will begin to mend. I shall never lose courage, for the idea of working for a person one loves," said Eve, with animation, "takes away all the bitterness and weariness of the work itself. I am happy when I think for whom I am taking so much trouble, if indeed it is trouble. Yes, you need have no fear, we shall earn enough for Lucien to go into the best society. There is where his fortune lies."

"And there lies his ruin too," rejoined David. "Listen, dear Eve. The slow execution of works of genius demands either a considerable fortune ready at hand, or the sublime cynicism of a life of poverty. Believe me! Lucien has such an unbounded horror of the privations of poverty, he has found the aroma of feasts and the vapor of success so pleasant to his senses, his self-esteem has assumed such vast proportions in Madame de Bargeton's boudoir, that he will try everything rather than give it all up; and the proceeds of your toil will never correspond with his needs."

"Ah! you are only a false friend!" cried Eve in desperation. "Otherwise, you would not discourage us so."

"Eve! Eve!" replied David; "I would like to be Lucien's brother. You alone can give me that title, which would make it possible for him to accept everything from me, which would give me the right to devote myself to him with the same devoted love that prompts your sacrifices, but combined with the discernment of one who looks forward to the future. Eve, my dear, loved child, consent to give Lucien a treasury upon which he can draw without shame! Will not a brother's purse be like his own? If you only knew all the reflections that Lucien's new position has suggested to me! If he desires to go to Madame de Bargeton's, the poor boy must not be my proof-reader, he must not live at L'Houmeau, you must not continue to work and your mother must abandon her profession. If you consent to become my wife, everything will be made smooth; Lucien can live on the second floor at my house, while I am building an apartment for him above the lean-to at the end of the courtyard, unless my father will agree to put on a second floor. In that way we could arrange for him an independent life, without care. My desire to support him will give me such courage and energy in money-making as I should never have if I alone were concerned; but it depends upon you to authorize my devotion. Perhaps some day he will go to Paris, the only stage upon which he can show what he really is, and where his talents will be appreciated and rewarded. Life in Paris is very expensive, and three of us will not be too many to support him there. Moreover, do not you, and your mother too, need a support? Dear Eve, marry me for love of Lucien. Later you

will love me perhaps, when you see the efforts I
will make to serve him and to make you happy.
We are both equally modest in our tastes, we need
but little; Lucien's happiness shall be our great
care, and his heart the treasure-chest in which we
will put fortune, sentiments, sensations, everything!"

"The proprieties keep us apart," said Eve, deeply
moved when she saw how his great love humbled
itself. "You are rich and I am poor. One must
love dearly to pass over such a difficulty."

"Then you don't love me enough yet?" cried
David in dismay.

"But perhaps your father would not be willing—"

"Good, good," said David, "if there's only my
father to be consulted, you will be my wife. Eve,
dear Eve, you have, at this moment, made life a
very light burden for me to carry. Alas! my heart
was very heavy with feelings which I could not
express. Just tell me that you love me a little, and
I will find the requisite courage to tell you all the
rest."

"Indeed," said she, "you make me very much
ashamed; but, as we are confiding our sentiments
to each other, I will tell you that I have never in
all my life given a thought to any other man than
you. You have seemed to me one of the men to
whom a woman may well be proud to belong, and I
did not dare to hope for such a great destiny for
myself, a poor working-girl without prospects of
any kind."

"Enough, enough," he said, sitting on the cross-bar of the lock, to which they had returned, for they were walking back and forth over the same ground like fools.

"What is the matter?" she said, expressing for the first time the charming anxiety women feel for the well-being of one who belongs to them.

"Nothing but good," said he. "On looking forward to a long, happy life, the mind is dazzled, as it were, the heart is overwhelmed. Why am I the happier?" he said in a melancholy tone. "But I know why."

Eve glanced at him with a coy, questioning expression which signified her desire for an explanation.

"Dear Eve, I receive more than I give. I shall always love you better than you will love me, because I have more reason to love you: you are an angel and I'm a man."

"I am not so learned," said Eve, with a smile. "I love you dearly—"

"As much as you love Lucien?" he interrupted her.

"Enough to be your wife, to devote myself to you and to try to cause you no sorrow during the life, perhaps a little hard at first, that we shall live together."

"You have seen, dear Eve, haven't you, that I have loved you since the day I first saw you?"

"What woman does not know when she is loved?" she asked.

"Then let me demolish the scruples that my supposed wealth causes you. I am poor, dear Eve. Yes, my father has taken pleasure in ruining me; he has speculated on my work; he has done as many pretended benefactors do to their protégés. If I become rich, it will be through you. This is not mere lover's talk, but the reflection of a man who thinks. I am bound to tell you of my failings, and they are enormous for a man obliged to earn his living. My character, my habits, the occupations I delight in make me unfit for any sort of commerce or speculation, and yet we can become rich only by carrying on some trade. If I am capable of discovering a gold mine, I am singularly incapable of working it. But you who, through love for your brother, have descended to the smallest details, who have the genius of economy, the patient attention of the true business man, you will reap the harvest I have sown. Our situation, for I long ago became one of your family in my own mind, weighs so heavily upon my heart, that I have employed my days and nights seeking opportunities to make money. My knowledge of chemistry and my observation of the necessities of commerce have put me on the track of a valuable discovery. I can tell you nothing about it yet, I foresee too many delays. We shall suffer for some years perhaps; but I shall end by finding industrial processes which others than myself are on the scent of; and which will assure us a large fortune if I reach the goal first. I have said nothing to Lucien, for his impulsive nature would spoil everything; he would convert my hopes into realities, he would live like a grandee and would run in debt perhaps. So do you keep my secret. Your sweet, loving companionship alone can comfort me during this long period of waiting, just as the desire to enrich you and Lucien will give me constancy and persistence—"

"I had guessed also," Eve interrupted, "that you were one of those inventors, like my poor father, who need a wife to take care of them."

"You love me then! Oh! tell me without fear, for I saw in your name a symbol of my love. Eve was the only woman in the world, and what was materially true in Adam's case, is morally true in mine. My God! do you love me?"

"Yes," she said, lengthening that simple syllable by the way in which she pronounced it, as if to depict the extent of her love.

"Well, let us sit down here," he said, leading Eve to a long beam that lay on the ground near the wheels of a paper-mill. "Let me breathe the evening air, listen to the calling of the tree-toads and gaze at the moonbeams shimmering on the water; let me grasp the full meaning of this scene where I seem to see my happiness written upon everything, and which appears to me for the first time in all its splendor, illumined by love, embellished by you. Eve, my dear love, this is the first moment of unalloyed joy I have ever known! I doubt if Lucien is as happy as I am."

As he felt Eve's moist hand trembling in his own, David dropped a tear upon it.

"May I not know the secret?" she said in a coaxing tone.

"You have a sort of right to it, for your father gave much thought to the question, which is becoming a serious one. This is why: the fall of the Empire is going to make the use of cotton rags almost universal, because they are so much cheaper than linen. At this moment, paper is still made from flax and linen rags; but those materials are very expensive, and their high price retards the great forward movement that the French press must necessarily make sooner or later. Now, the production of rags cannot be forced. Rags are the result of the use of cloth, and the population of a country yields only a certain fixed quantity. That quantity can be increased only by an increase in the ratio of births. To produce a perceptible change in its population, a country requires a quarter of a century and revolutionary changes in its customs, in commerce or in agriculture. If, therefore, the requirements of the paper trade exceed the production of rags in France, whether it be twice or three times, it will be necessary, in order to maintain the low price of paper, to use some material other than rags in its manufacture. This reasoning rests upon a fact which is well illustrated in this town. The paper mills of Angoulême, the last to abandon the use of linen rags, see cotton taking its place in the pulp with alarming rapidity."

In reply to a question from the girl, who did not know the meaning of the word *pulp*, David gave her certain information concerning paper-making, which would not be out of place in a work whose material existence is due to the paper as much as to the press; but this long parenthesis between a lover and his mistress will gain in interest no doubt by being somewhat abridged.

Paper, a product no less marvelous than the printing for which it serves as a basis, had long existed in China when it made its way, through the underground passages of commerce, into Asia Minor, where, about the year 750, according to some traditions, they used a paper made of cotton ground and reduced to pulp. The necessity of finding a substitute for parchment, which was very costly, led to the invention, in imitation of the bombycinous paper—such was the name given to the cotton paper of the East—of paper made of rags, some say at Basle in 1170, by Greek refugees; others say at Padua in 1301, by an Italian named Pax. Thus paper approached perfection very slowly and obscurely; but it is certain that, under Charles VI., pulp for playing cards was made at Paris. When the immortal Faust, Coster and Gutenberg had invented THE BOOK, mechanics, unknown to fame like so many great artists of that period, applied paper-making to the necessities of typography. In the fifteenth century, that energetic, guileless epoch, the names of the different sizes of paper, as well as the names given to the type, bore the imprint of the simple manners of the time. Thus the grape, the Jésus, the colombier, the pot, the crown, the shell, the wreath, were so named from the bunch of grapes, the image of Our Lord, the wreath, the crown, the pot, in a word, from the water-mark in the centre of the sheet, just as later, under Napoléon, the water-mark was an eagle; whence the paper called great eagle. In the same way, they called the different type *cicero*—pica—grand canon, or Saint-Augustin—long primer—from the treatises of Cicero, liturgical books and theological works, for which the type were first used. *Italics* were invented by Aldus at Venice; hence the name. Before the invention of machine-made paper, which is made of unlimited length, the sheets of largest size were the *grand jésus* or the *grand colombier;* the latter was seldom used except for atlases or for engravings. As a matter of fact, the dimensions of the paper to be used in printing were governed by the size of the bed of the press. At the time when David was speaking, endless paper was believed in France to be a mere chimera, although Denis Robert of Essonne had invented a machine to manufacture it, about 1799, and Didot-Saint-Leger afterwards tried to perfect it. Vellum, invented by Ambroise Didot, dates only from 1780. This rapid sketch shows conclusively that all the great acquisitions of the mechanical arts and of the intelligence are made very slowly, and by unnoticed development, precisely as nature performs her work. To reach their perfect state, writing,—yes, and language,

perhaps!—had to feel their way just as typography
and paper-making had to do.

"Rag-pickers all over Europe collect rags, old
cloths and purchase the refuse of every sort of tis-
sue," said the printer in conclusion. "This refuse,
carefully sorted out, goes to the warehouses of the
wholesale dealers in rags, who supply the paper-
mills. To give you an idea of the extent of the
business, mademoiselle, in 1814, Cardon the banker,
owner of the mills at Buges and Langlée, where
Léorier de l'Isle tried as long ago as 1776 to solve
the problem that your father worked upon, had a
lawsuit with one Proust concerning an error of two
million pounds of rags in an account involving ten
million pounds, worth four million francs! The
manufacturer washes his rags and boils them down
to a clear pulp, which is strained exactly as a cook
strains her sauce through a sieve, over an iron
framework called a *form*, the interior of which is
filled with a metallic substance with the water-mark
in the centre that gives its name to the paper.
Thus the size of the paper depends upon the size of
the form. When I was with Messieurs Didot, the
question was even then being considered and they
are considering it still, for the process your father
tried to find is one of the most imperative necessities of the time. For this reason. Although the
durability of linen, as compared with that of cotton,
makes the linen less expensive in the long run,
still, as with poor people there is always money to
be paid out, they prefer to pay out less rather than

more, and on the principle of the motto *Væ victis!*
they submit to enormous losses. The bourgeois
class follows the same course as the poor man.
Thus the supply of linen rags is failing. In
England, where cotton has taken the place of linen
with four-fifths of the population, paper is now
made from cotton exclusively. This paper, which,
in the first place, has the drawback of tearing and
cracking, dissolves so quickly in water that a book
made of cotton paper will be reduced to pulp if left
in water a quarter of an hour, whereas an old book
wouldn't be destroyed if it were left for two hours.
When the old book was dried, although it would be
yellow and the type somewhat faded, it would still
be legible and the work would not be ruined. We
are approaching a time when, as fortunes continue
to diminish by the process of equalization, every
one will grow poor; we shall demand cheap cloth and
books, just as there is beginning to be a demand for
small pictures for lack of space to hang large ones.
The shirts and books won't last, that's all. The
solidity of the products of our factories is vanishing
on all sides. Thus the problem to be solved is of
the utmost importance to literature, science and
politics. One day in Paris, in my office, there was
an animated discussion as to the ingredients that
are used in the manufacture of paper in China.
There, thanks to the raw materials, paper-making
has from the very beginning, attained a perfection
that ours lacks. Much was said about Chinese
paper, which is much superior to ours by reason of

its lightness and fineness, for those valuable qualities do not detract from its strength; and, however
thin it may be, it is never transparent. A very
well-informed proof-reader—at Paris you find eminent scholars among readers: Fourier and Pierre
Leroux   are   readers   for   Lachevardière   at   this
moment!—as I was saying, the Comte de Saint-
Simon, temporarily a reader, came to see us in the
midst of the discussion.   He told us that, according
to Kempfer and Du Halde, the *broussonatia* furnished
the Chinese with the raw material for their paper,
which is entirely a vegetable product, like our own,
by the way.   Another reader maintained that
Chinese paper was made principally from an
animal substance, together with silk, which is so
abundant in China.   A wager was made in my
presence.   As Messieurs Didot are printers to the
Institute, the dispute was naturally submitted to
members of that assembly of scholars.   Monsieur
Marcel, formerly manager of the imperial printing-
office, who was agreed upon as referee, sent the two
readers to Monsieur l'Abbé Grozier, librarian at the
Arsenal.   By the decision of Abbé Grozier, both
readers lost their stakes.   Chinese paper is made
neither from silk nor from the *broussonatia ;* its
pulp is made from the pulverized fibres of the bamboo.   Abbé Grozier had a Chinese book, an icono-
graphic as well as technological work, in which
were numerous sketches representing the manufacture of paper in all its stages, and he showed us piles
of bamboo stalks lying in a corner of a paper-factory

drawn with great skill. When Lucien told me
that your father, by a sort of intuition peculiar to
men of talent, had conceived a method of replacing linen rags by an exceedingly common vegetable
substance, taken directly from the ground, as the
Chinese take their fibrous stalks, I went over in my
mind all the experiments tried by my predecessors,
and I began finally to study the question seriously.
The bamboo is a reed: I naturally thought of the
reeds of our own country. The labor amounts to
nothing in China; a day's work is worth three
sous; so the Chinese are able to place their paper,
as soon as it comes from the form, leaf by leaf between tables of heated white porcelain, by means
of which they press it and give it the gloss, the
toughness, the lightness and the satiny softness
which make it the finest paper in the world. Very
good; we must find some machine to do the work
the Chinese do by hand. Machinery is the only
solution of the problem of producing paper at the
low price which the cheapness of labor makes possible in China. If we can succeed in making paper
of similar quality to the Chinese, at a low price, we
shall diminish the weight and thickness of books
by more than one-half. A bound set of Voltaire's
works, which weighs two hundred and fifty pounds,
printed on our glazed paper, will weigh less than
fifty on Chinese paper. And that will certainly be
a triumph. The necessary space for libraries will
become a problem more and more difficult of solution
at a time when the general contraction of men and

things is affecting everything, even their houses. In Paris the great mansions, the great suites, will be demolished sooner or later; soon there will be no great fortunes to harmonize with the mammoth edifices of our fathers. What a disgrace for the times we live in to make books that will not last! Ten years hence Holland paper, that is to say, paper made of linen rags, will have entirely disappeared. Now, your brother has told me your father's idea of using certain fibrous plants in making paper; so you see that, if I succeed, you will be entitled to—"

At that moment Lucien accosted his sister and interrupted David's generous proposition.

"I don't know whether you have enjoyed the evening," he said, "but it's been a cruel one for me."

"My poor Lucien, what has happened to you, then?" said Eve, noticing the excitement depicted on her brother's face.

The angry poet described his suffering, pouring into those loving hearts the flood of thoughts that assailed him. Eve and David listened in silence, distressed at this torrent of grief which revealed as much grandeur as weakness.

"Monsieur de Bargeton," Lucien concluded, "is an old man who will probably be carried off by an attack of indigestion; and then I will have my revenge on that arrogant set: I will marry Madame de Bargeton! I read in her eyes to-night a love as great as my own. Yes, she felt the blows that wounded me; she soothed my suffering; she is as great and noble as she is lovely and charming! No, she will never betray me!"

"Isn't it time we set his mind at rest about the future?" David whispered to Eve.

Eve silently pressed his arm, and David, understanding her thought, hastened to tell Lucien of the plans he had formed. The two lovers were as full of themselves as Lucien was full of himself; so that, in their eagerness to secure his approval of their happiness, they did not notice the gesture of surprise that escaped Madame de Bargeton's lover when he learned of the projected marriage of his sister and David. Lucien was dreaming of arranging some great match for his sister when he should have attained some lofty position, in order to shore up his ambition with the interest of some powerful family, and he was in despair to see in this union an additional obstacle to his success in society.

"If Madame de Bargeton consents to become Madame de Rubempré, she will never be willing to be David Séchard's sister-in-law!"

Such was the exact purport of the thoughts that tortured Lucien's heart.

"Louise is right! people of the future are never understood by their families," he thought bitterly.

If the idea of this union had been presented to him at a time when he had not just killed off Monsieur de Bargeton in his mind's eye, it would probably have called forth expressions of the liveliest satisfaction. Upon reflecting on his present plight and

on the probable destiny of Eve Chardon, a beautiful, penniless girl, he would have looked upon the
proposed marriage as unhoped-for good fortune.
But he was living in one of those golden dreams in
which young men, mounted upon *ifs*, surmount all
obstacles.   He fancied himself dominating society;
it was a severe blow to the poet to fall so quickly
into the sphere of reality.

Eve and David believed that their brother was
silent because such a display of generosity overwhelmed him.   To those two noble hearts, silent
approbation proved true affection.   The painter began to describe with simple, heartfelt eloquence the
happiness that awaited all four of them.   Despite
Eve's exclamations, he furnished his first floor with
the extravagance of a lover; with artless sincerity,
he constructed the second floor for Lucien and the
apartments over the lean-to for Madame Chardon,
toward whom he proposed to display all the affectionate solicitude of a son.   In short, he made the
whole family so happy and his brother so independent that Lucien, seduced by David's voice and
by Eve's caresses, as they walked beneath the
trees along the calm, gleaming Charente, under the
starry vault of heaven, in the balmy night air, forgot the painful crown of thorns that society had
pressed down upon his head.   At last, Monsieur de
Rubempré knew David as he was.   His mobile
nature soon brought him back to the pure, hard-
working, bourgeois life he had hitherto led; he saw
it in the future surrounded with comfort and free

12

from care. The sounds of aristocratic society became fainter and fainter. At last, when he reached the pavements of L'Houmeau, the ambitious youth pressed his brother's hand and assented to the union of the happy lovers.

"But won't your father oppose the marriage?" he asked David.

"You know how much he troubles himself about me! the goodman lives for himself; but I shall go and see him to-morrow at Marsac, to induce him to do such building as we need, if for no other purpose."

David accompanied the brother and sister to Madame Chardon's room, and asked her for Eve's hand with the eagerness of a man to whom the slightest delay would be unbearable. The mother took her daughter's hand and joyfully placed it in David's, whereupon the lover made bold to kiss the forehead of his fair betrothed, who blushed as she smiled upon him.

"Such is the betrothal of poor people," said the mother, raising her eyes as if to implore God's blessing.—"You must have courage, my child," she said to David, "for we are most unfortunate and I fear our ill-fortune may prove to be contagious."

"We are rich and fortunate," said David gravely. "First of all, you must give up your nursing and come and live at Angoulême with your daughter and Lucien."

The three thereupon hastened to tell the wondering mother of their delightful project, plunging into one of the unreserved family talks, in which every seed is joyously garnered, every pleasure enjoyed in anticipation. They were obliged to turn David out; he would have liked that evening to last forever. The clocks were striking one when Lucien walked with his future brother-in-law as far as the Porte Palet. Honest Postel, much concerned about these extraordinary proceedings, was standing behind his blind; he had opened his window, and said to himself, seeing a light in Eve's room:

"What can be going on at the Chardons'?—Ah! my boy," he said as Lucien returned, "what in the world is happening to you all? Do you need my services?"

"No, monsieur," replied the poet, "but, as you are our friend, I can tell you about it; my mother has just given my sister's hand to David Séchard."

Postel's only reply was to close his window abruptly, in despair because he had not himself asked for Mademoiselle Chardon's hand.

*

Instead of returning to Angoulême, David took the Marsac road. He walked all the way to his father's house and reached the home vineyard just as the sun was rising. The lover spied the old bear's head over the top of a hedgerow under an almond-tree.

"Good morning, father," said David.

"Hallo, is it you, my boy! How do you happen to be on the road at this time of day? Come in there," said the vine-grower, pointing to a gap in the hedge where there was a small gate. "My vines have all passed the flowering stage and not a twig frozen! There'll be more than twenty casks to the acre this year; but how it was manured!"

"I have come to talk about some important business, father."

"Well, how are our presses? you ought to have a pile of money as big as yourself."

"I shall make money, father, but just now I am not rich."

"They all blame me here for manuring to death," rejoined the father. "The bourgeois, that is to say, Monsieur le Marquis, Monsieur le Comte, Messieurs This and That, maintain that I injure the quality of the wine. What's the use of education? to befog your mind. Hark ye! those gentry press seven, sometimes eight casks to the acre, and sell at sixty

francs the cask, which makes four hundred francs
an acre at most. I press twenty casks and sell at
thirty francs; total six hundred francs! Who are
the fools? Quality! quality! What do I care for
quality? Let messieurs the marquises keep their
quality for themselves! To my mind, quality is
crowns. You were saying?"

"I am going to be married, father, and I came to
ask you—"

"Ask me? What? nothing at all, my boy.
Marry away, I give my consent; but, as for giving
you anything, I haven't got a sou. Taxes have
ruined me! For two years, I've been paying out
money for manure, taxes and expenses of every
kind; the government takes everything; all the
profits go to the government! For two years the
poor vine-growers haven't made anything. This
year don't look so bad, and yet my wretched casks
are worth eleven francs to begin with! We shall
harvest our grapes for the cooper's benefit. Why
do you get married before the grape-picking?"

"I only came to ask your consent, father."

"Ah! that's another affair. May I ask, without
being too inquisitive, whom you propose to marry?"

"Mademoiselle Eve Chardon."

"What's that? how much is she worth?"

"She's the daughter of the late Monsieur Chardon, the druggist of L'Houmeau."

"You marry a girl from L'Houmeau! you, a bourgeois! you, the king's printer at Angoulême!
That's the result of education! Send your children

to college by all means! Say, my boy, is she
very rich?" said the old vine-grower, drawing near
his son with a wheedling air; "for, if you marry a
girl from L'Houmeau, she ought to have thousands
and hundreds! Good! you'll pay me my rent. Do
you know, my boy, that there's two years and three
months' rent due, which makes twenty-seven hundred francs, and they'd come in handily to pay my
cooper. From any other than my son, I should
have a right to demand interest, for business is
business after all; but I'll give you the interest.
Well, how much has she got?"

"Why, she has just what my mother had."

The old fellow was on the point of saying:
"She's only got ten thousand francs!" but he remembered having refused to render his son any
account, and said:

"She's got nothing!"

"My mother's fortune was her good sense and
her beauty."

"Go to the market with it and you'll see what
they'll lend you on it. Bless my soul, how unlucky
fathers are with their children! David, when I
married I had a paper cap on my head for my fortune, and I had my two arms; I was only a poor
bear; but, with the fine printing office I *gave* you,
with your industry and your learning, you ought to
marry a bourgeoise of the Upper Town, a woman
with thirty or forty thousand francs. Let your
passion go, and I'll find a wife for you myself!
There's a widow of thirty-two within a league, a

miller, with a hundred thousand francs in good land; she's the girl for you. You can add her estate to the Marsac property; they touch! Oh! the fine estate we'd have, and how I would manage it! They say she's going to marry Courtois, her foreman, and you're a better man than he is! I would run the mill while she was showing off her pretty arms in Angoulême.''

''I am bound, father—''

''David, you don't understand anything about business, and I can see that you'll soon be ruined. Yes, if you marry this girl from L'Houmeau, I'll settle my accounts with you, I'll sue you for my rent, for I don't see any prospect of anything. Ah! my poor presses! my presses! it takes money to oil you and keep you in repair and make you go. Nothing but a good wine year would console me for this.''

''It seems to me, father, that I have caused you very little trouble hitherto—''

''And paid very little rent,'' retorted the old vinegrower.

''I came to ask you, in addition to your consent to my marriage, to have the second floor of your house raised for me, and to build an apartment above the lean-to.''

''Not likely; I haven't a sou, as you know very well. Besides, it would be throwing money into the water, for what would I get out of it? Upon my word! you get up early in the morning to come and ask me to do building enough to ruin a king.

Although your name's David, I haven't the treasures
of Solomon. But you're mad! My child was
changed by his nurse. There's a vine that will
bear some grapes!" he said, interrupting himself
to point out a shoot to David. "They are children
that don't disappoint their parent's hopes; you
manure them and they pay you back. I sent you
to the lyceum, I paid enormous sums to make you
a scholar, you studied with the Didots and the result of all that nonsense is to give me a girl from
L'Houmeau for a daughter-in-law, without a sou
of dowry! If you hadn't gone away to study, if
you'd stayed under my eyes, you'd have done as I
wanted you to, and you'd be marrying to-day a
miller with a hundred thousand francs, not counting
the mill. Ah! you had so little wit as to think I'd
reward you for this fine bit of sentiment by building
palaces for you, eh? Why, anyone would think, upon
my word, that the house you live in hadn't sheltered
anyone but pigs for two hundred years, and that
it isn't good enough for your girl from L'Houmeau
to sleep in. Say, is she the Queen of France?"

"Very well, father, then I'll build the second floor
at my own expense; the son will enrich the father.
Although that reverses the natural order of things,
it's sometimes done—"

"How's that, my boy; you have money to build
with and none to pay your rent? You rascal, you're
playing sharp with your father!"

The question thus stated became difficult of solution, for the goodman was enchanted to place his

son in a position which justified him in giving him
nothing, while maintaining a paternal attitude.
Thus David was able to obtain nothing more than
a bare consent to his marriage, and permission to
make at his own expense such additions to his
father's house as he might need. The old bear,
that model for conservative fathers, did his son the
favor not to demand his rent and not to take from
him the savings whose existence he was so impru-
dent as to disclose. David returned home sorely
depressed; he understood that he could not rely
upon any assistance from his father if affairs should
turn out badly.

All Angoulême was talking about the bishop's
remark and Madame de Bargeton's reply. The
slightest incidents were so distorted, exaggerated,
embellished, that the poet became the hero of the
hour.

From the superior sphere in which this tempest
of trifles was rumbling, some drops fell among the
bourgeoisie. When Lucien passed through Beaulieu on his way to Madame de Bargeton's, he observed the envious scrutiny that several young
men bestowed upon him, and caught a sentence
here and there that made him flush with pride.

"There's a lucky fellow," said a solicitor's clerk,
named Petit-Claud, a schoolmate of Lucien, and an
ugly youth, whom the poet treated in a patronizing
way.

"Yes, he's good-looking, he has talent, and

Madame de Bargeton is mad over him," replied
a young man of good family, who was present at
the reading.

He had impatiently awaited the hour when he
knew he should find Louise alone; it was necessary
for him to reconcile this woman, the arbiter of his
destiny, to his sister's marriage. After the experience of the preceding evening, perhaps she would
be more affectionate than usual, and if so, a
moment of happiness might be the result. He was
not mistaken: Madame de Bargeton received him
with an effusion of sentiment that seemed to the
novice in love affairs to denote a most impressive
progress in passion. She abandoned her lovely
golden hair, her hands, her face to the burning
kisses of the poet who had suffered so much the
night before!

"If you had seen your face while you were
reading!" she said, continuing to use the second
person singular, the familiar, caressing form of address which she had adopted the night before when
they sat upon the couch and Louise with her fair
hand wiped away the drops of perspiration that
stood like pearls upon his brow, as if anticipating
the crown she would place upon it. "Your lovely
eyes shot fire! I saw, coming from your mouth,
the chains of gold whereby hearts hang suspended
from a poet's lips. You must read me the whole of
Chénier, he is the poet of lovers. You shall suffer
no more, I will not have it! Yes, dear angel, I will
make an oasis for you, where you shall live your

poet's life, active, inactive, indolent, laborious, pensive by turns; but never forget that your laurels are due to me, that they will be the noble reward of the suffering that will fall to my lot. Poor love, those people will spare me no more than they spared you; they take revenge for all the joys they do not share. Yes, I shall always be looked upon with jealousy; didn't you see it yesterday? Didn't the blood-drinking insects fly quickly enough to drink from the stings they had made? But I was happy! I lived! It was so long since all the chords of my heart had rung full and clear!"

Tears rolled down Louise's cheeks; Lucien seized one hand and kissed it again and again for all response. Thus the poet's vanity was fondled by this woman as it had been by his mother, and sister, and by David. Everyone about him continued to raise higher and higher the imaginary pedestal upon which he placed himself. Upheld in his ambitious hopes by one and all, by his friends and by the vain rage of his enemies, he walked in an atmosphere full of mirages. Youthful imaginations so naturally become accomplices of such flattery and such ideas as these, everybody is so eager to serve a handsome young man, with the future all his own, that more than one stern and bitter lesson is necessary to dispel such illusions.

"Then you will really be my Beatrice, my lovely Louise, but a Beatrice who allows herself to be loved?"

She raised her fine eyes, which she had kept on

the floor, and said, contradicting her words by an angelic smile:

"If you deserve it—later! Aren't you happy? To have a heart all to one's self! to be able to say anything with the certainty of being understood! is not that happiness?"

"Yes," he replied, with the pout of a disappointed lover.

"Child!" she said, laughing at him. "Come, haven't you anything to tell me? You were thinking very deeply as you came in, my Lucien."

Lucien timidly confided to his beloved the story of David's love for his sister, his sister's love for David, and their projected marriage.

"Poor Lucien!" said she; "he is afraid of being beaten and scolded as if he were going to be married himself! Why, where's the harm?" she continued, running her hands through his hair. "What do I care for a family, in which you are an exception? If my father married his housekeeper, would you worry very much about it? Dear child, lovers are a whole family in themselves. Have I any other interest in the world than my Lucien? Be great, succeed in winning renown, that is all that concerns us!"

Lucien was made the happiest man in the world by that selfish reply. While he was listening to the absurd arguments by which Louise proved to him that they were alone in the world, Monsieur de Bargeton entered. Lucien frowned and seemed tongue-tied; Louise made a sign to him and begged

him to stay and dine with them, asking him to read
Chénier to her until the card players and regular
guests arrived.

"You will not only please her," said Monsieur de
Bargeton, "but myself as well. Nothing suits me
better than to listen to reading after my dinner."

Petted by Monsieur de Bargeton, petted by Louise,
waited upon by the servants with the respect they
show for their masters' favored guests, Lucien remained at the Hôtel de Bargeton, identifying himself with all the pleasures of a fortune, the usufruct
of which was turned over to him.   When the salon
was filled with people, he felt so strong in Monsieur
de Bargeton's stupidity and Louise's love, that he
assumed an air of authority which his fair mistress
encouraged.   He tasted the joys of the despotism
won by Naïs, which she loved to have him share
with her.   In short, he attempted throughout that
evening to play the part of the hero of a small town.
Observing Lucien's latest attitude, some persons
concluded that he was, to use an old-time expression,
on the best possible terms with Madame de Bargeton.   Amélie, who came with Monsieur du Châtelet,
asserted the truth of that dire rumor in a corner of
the salon, where the envious and jealous guests had
collected.

"Don't hold Naïs responsible for the vanity of a
paltry youth who is all puffed up with pride to find
himself in a social sphere he never expected to
reach," said Châtelet.   "Don't you see that this
Chardon takes the courteous phrases of a woman of

the world for advances? He hasn't yet learned to distinguish the silence of genuine passion from the patronizing language his beauty, his youth and his talent call forth! Women would be too much to be pitied, if they were guilty of all the desires they arouse in us. He is certainly in love, but as for Naïs—"

"Oh!" rejoined the perfidious Amélie, "Naïs is very happy in his passion. At her age, a young man's love presents so many fascinations! She renews her youth with him, she fancies herself a young girl, and assumes a young girl's manners and scruples, and doesn't think of the absurdity of it. Fancy! a druggist's son putting on the airs of a master in Madame de Bargeton's salon!"

"Love knows naught of those distances," hummed Adrien.

The next day there was not a single house in Angoulême in which people were not discussing the degree of intimacy between Monsieur Chardon, *alias* De Rubempré, and Madame de Bargeton; although guilty of nothing more than a few kisses, society was already accusing them of the most criminal happiness. Madame de Bargeton had to bear the cross of her royalty. Among the eccentricities of society, have you not noticed the caprice of its judgments and the folly of its demands? There are people to whom everything is permitted; they can do the most unreasonable things; from them, everything is as it should be; everyone is eager to justify their acts. But there are others to whom society is

incredibly harsh: they must do everything right,
never make a mistake, never fall short, never do
even a foolish thing; you would say that they were
statues of wonderful beauty, which are taken from
their pedestals as soon as the winter weather has
cracked a finger or a nose; they are not allowed to
be simply human, they are required to be always
divine and perfect. A single glance from Madame
de Bargeton to Lucien was more severely censured
than the whole twelve years' happiness of Zizine
and Francis. A pressure of the hand exchanged by
the two lovers was about to draw down upon them
all the thunders of the Charente.

David had brought back from Paris a little hoard
which he intended for the necessary expenses of his
marriage and for building the second floor of his
father's house. To add to the value of the house
was really equivalent to working in his own interest;
sooner or later, it would revert to him, for his father
was seventy-eight. So he built Lucien's apartment
with a colonnade, in order not to overburden the
old cracked walls of the house. He took great
pleasure in decorating and furnishing attractively
the first floor, where the fair Eve was to pass her
life. Those were days of unalloyed joy and happiness for the two lovers.

Although weary of the pitiful proportions of provincial life, and disgusted with the sordid economy
that magnified a hundred-sou piece into an enormous
sum of money, Lucien bore without a murmur the
necessarily close calculations of poverty and its

deprivations. His gloomy melancholy had given place to a radiant expression of hope. He saw a bright star shining over his head; he dreamed of a glorious future, basing his happiness upon the tomb of Monsieur de Bargeton, who had from time to time sharp attacks of indigestion and the agreeable mania of regarding the failure of his dinner to digest as a disease to be cured by eating a hearty supper.

Toward the beginning of September, Lucien was no longer a proof-reader; he was Monsieur de Rubempré, living in magnificent quarters, compared with the wretched attic in which young Chardon lived at L'Houmeau; he was no longer a man from L'Houmeau, for he lived in Upper Angoulême, and dined about four times a week with Madame de Bargeton. Having won the friendly regard of monseigneur, he was received at the episcopal palace. His occupations entitled him to a place in the most exalted society. In a word, he was likely to take rank some day among the eminent men of France. Certainly, as he cast his eye about a pretty salon, a charming bedroom, and a tastefully decorated study, he could console himself for taking thirty francs a month from the hard-earned wages of his mother and sister; for the day was in sight when the historical romance upon which he had been at work two years, *L'Archer de Charles IX.*, and a volume of poems entitled *Les Marguerites*, would make his name known in the literary world, giving him enough money to discharge his debt to his mother and sister and David. And so, feeling that he had

13

grown in stature, listening to the reverberating echoes of his name in the future, he accepted those sacrifices now with noble self-confidence: he smiled at his past distress, he enjoyed his recent poverty.

Eve and David had put their brother's happiness before their own. The marriage was postponed because the workmen needed further time to finish the furnishing and painting and to hang the papers intended for the first floor, for Lucien's affairs took precedence. No one who knew Lucien would be surprised at their devotion; he was so fascinating! his manners were so coaxing! his impatience and his desires were expressed so charmingly! he had always won his case before he opened his mouth. This fatal privilege ruins more young men than it saves. Accustomed to the attentions that youthful beauty provokes, happy in the selfish patronage society accords a person who takes its fancy, just as it gives alms to the beggar who awakens a sentiment or causes a thrill of emotion, many of these great children simply enjoy this favor instead of trying to exploit it. Deceived as to the meaning and motive power of social relations, they believe that they will always meet deceitful smiles; but there comes a time when society leaves them, like old coquettes and old rags, naked, bald, stripped bare, worthless and penniless, outside the door of a salon or begging alms at a street corner. Eve desired the delay, however, as she wished to make the necessary arrangements for managing her little household economically. What could two lovers refuse a brother who, seeing his sister at work, said with an accent that came from his heart: "I wish I knew how to sew?" And then, too, the grave and observant David was an accessory to this devotion. Nevertheless, since Lucien's triumph at Madame de Bargeton's, he was alarmed by the transformation that was taking place in him; he was afraid that he would soon begin to feel contempt for bourgeois customs. With the purpose of testing his brother, David sometimes forced him to choose between patriarchal family joys and the pleasures of aristocratic society, and when he saw that Lucien sacrificed his vain pleasures to them, he cried: "They will never corrupt him!"

Several times the three friends and Madame Chardon indulged in little pleasure trips of the familiar provincial variety; they would walk through the woods near Angoulême along the bank of the Charente; they would dine on the grass, David's apprentice bringing the provisions to a certain spot at a time agreed upon; then they would return in the evening, a little tired, having spent less than three francs. On great occasions, when they dined at what is called a *restaurât*, a sort of open air restaurant midway between the provincial *bouchon* and the Parisian *guinguette*, they sometimes spent as much as a hundred sous, divided between David and the Chardons. David was infinitely grateful to Lucien for forgetting, during those days in the open air, the satisfaction that he derived from being at Madame de Bargeton's and the

sumptuous dinners of society.   For at this time
every one was anxious to entertain the great man
of Angoulême.

At this juncture, when everything was almost
ready for the young couple to begin housekeeping,
during a call David made at Marsac to obtain his
father's consent to be present at his wedding, hoping that the goodman would be so far fascinated by
his daughter-in-law as to contribute to the enormous
expenditures made necessary by the rearrangement
of the house, one of those events occurred which,
in a small town, entirely change the face of affairs.

Lucien and Louise had in Châtelet a spy in
their innermost circle of friends, who watched, with
the persistence of hatred made up of passion and
avarice combined, for an opportunity to bring discovery.   Sixte desired to force Madame de Bargeton
to declare herself so unequivocally on Lucien's side
that she would be what is called *lost*.   He had
adopted the attitude of a humble confidant of Madame de Bargeton; but, if he admired Lucien on
Rue du Minage, he made short work of him everywhere else.   He had insensibly acquired the right
to call upon Naïs at all times, and she no longer
suspected her old adorer; but he had taken too
much for granted in the case of the lovers, whose
love continued to be strictly platonic, to the great
despair of Louise and of Lucien.   There are, in
fact, passions which start off well or ill, as the
parties to them choose.   Two persons plunge into
the tactical part of sentiment, talk instead of acting,

and fight in the open fields instead of beginning a
siege. In this way, they often surfeit themselves
by wearing out their desires in the void in which
they live. Two lovers at such times give each
other time to reflect, to pass judgment upon each
other. It often happens that passions which have
taken the field with heads erect and colors flying,
hot to overcome all obstacles, return home beaten,
shamefaced, disarmed, besotted with their vain
parade. Such fatalities are sometimes to be explained by the timidity of youth and the temporiz-
ing methods in which women who are just beginning their career take pleasure; for this mutual
deception never happens to coxcombs who know
the trade, or to coquettes who are used to the
manœuvres of passion.

Moreover, provincial life is peculiarly opposed to
contented love and rather favors the intellectual
disputes of passion; so also the obstacles it offers to
the sweet intercourse that binds lovers so closely,
tend to drive ardent hearts to extreme courses.
This life is based upon such minute espionage, upon
such complete knowledge of everything that takes
place in every family, it is so opposed to the intimacy that gives comfort without offending virtue,
the purest relations are so unreasonably calumni-
ated, that many women are smirched, despite their
innocence. Certain ones thereupon revile themselves for not having tasted all the joys of a sin of
which they suffer all the inconveniences. Society,
which blames or criticizes without any serious

scrutiny the visible facts in which long, secret struggles end, is thus primarily accessory to these explosions; but the majority of the people who inveigh against the alleged scandal caused by some women who are wrongfully accused, have never reflected upon the causes which finally lead them to take the course they do. Madame de Bargeton was about to find herself in that anomalous position in which many women have found themselves who have not gone astray until after they were unjustly accused.

At the outset of a passion, the obstacles that arise alarm inexperienced persons; and those encountered by our two lovers strongly resembled the bonds with which the Lilliputians bound Gulliver. There was a multiplicity of nothings which made any sort of movement impossible and nullified the most vehement desires. For instance, Madame de Bargeton must always be visible. If she had closed her door when Lucien was with her, it would have been the end of everything, and she might as well have eloped with him at once. She received him, to be sure, in the boudoir, to which he was so accustomed that he fancied himself master there; but the doors were always conscientiously left open. Everything was as proper as could be. Monsieur de Bargeton walked about the house like a cockchafer, never dreaming that his wife wished to be alone with Lucien. If he had been the only obstacle, Naïs would very soon have found a way to dismiss him or give him something to do; but she was overrun with visitors, and they were the more numerous because of the prevalent curiosity. Provincials are naturally of a teasing disposition, they love to annoy budding passions. The servants went here and there about the house, unsummoned and giving no notice of their approach,—a result of long-continued habit, which a woman who had nothing to conceal had allowed them to adopt. To change the interior economy of her household would have been to confess the love all Angoulême suspected.

Madame de Bargeton could not put her foot out of doors without the whole town knowing where she went. To walk alone with Lucien out of the town would have been a fatal step: it would have been less dangerous to shut herself up with him at home. If Lucien had remained at her house after midnight, when there was no other company, it would have been talked about the next day. Thus, within as well as without, Madame de Bargeton lived always in the public eye. These details will apply to provincial life as a whole; sins are either openly avowed or impossible.

Louise, like all women who act under the impulse of a passion without previous similar experience, realized one by one the difficulties of her position, and she was fairly terrified. Her alarm reacted upon the amorous discussions which occupy the happiest hours, when two lovers are alone. Madame de Bargeton had no estate to which she could take her dear poet, as some women do who, under

one or another skilfully devised pretext, go and
bury themselves in the country. Wearied with
living in public, driven to extremities by this
tyranny whose yoke was harsher than her pleasures
were sweet, she thought of Escarbas and contemplated going thither to see her old father, so disturbed was she by these wretched obstacles.

Châtelet did not believe in so much innocence.
He watched to see when Lucien called at Madame
de Bargeton's and appeared there himself a few
moments later, always accompanied by Monsieur
de Chandour, the most talkative person in the whole
clique, always allowing him to enter first, persisting in the hope that chance would enable them to
surprise the lovers. The part he had undertaken
and the success of his plan were the more difficult, because he must remain neutral, in order to
direct all the actors in the drama he desired to have
played. Thus, in order to allay the suspicions of
Lucien, whom he constantly flattered, and of Madame de Bargeton, who did not lack perspicacity,
he had, to keep himself in countenance, attached
himself to the jealous Amélie. To perfect his sys-
tem of espionage upon Lucien and Louise, he had
succeeded some days before in starting a controversy between himself and Monsieur de Chandour
on the subject of the lovers. Châtelet maintained
that Madame de Bargeton was making sport of Lucien, that she was too well-born, too proud, to stoop
to a druggist's son. This rôle of incredulity suited
the plan he had formed, for he desired to pose as

Madame de Bargeton's defender. Stanislas maintained that Lucien was not a baffled lover. Amélie spurred on the discussion by desiring to ascertain the truth. Each of the two gave his reasons. It often happened, as it will in small towns, that some habitués of the Chandour salon arrived in the midst of a conversation in which Châtelet and Chandour were fortifying their respective opinions with sage observations. It would have been very strange if each of the adversaries had not sought partisans, asking his neighbor: "What do you think about it?" This controversy kept Madame de Bargeton and Lucien constantly in evidence.

At last one day Châtelet remarked that, whenever he and Monsieur de Chandour went to Madame de Bargeton's while Lucien was there, they failed to discover any indication of improper relations: the door of the boudoir was always open, the servants going and coming, there was no air of mystery that pointed to the charming crimes of love, etc. Stanislas, who did not lack a considerable share of stupidity, promised to enter the house the next day on tiptoe, a determination in which he was encouraged by the perfidious Amélie.

The next day proved to be for Lucien one of the days when young men tear their hair and take an oath to themselves that they will no longer ply the absurd trade of sighing swain. He had become accustomed to his position. The poet, who had taken a chair so timidly in the sanctified boudoir of the Queen of Angoulême, was metamorphosed into

an exacting lover.   Six months had sufficed to make
him think himself Louise's equal, and he proposed
now to become her master.   He left his own home,
determined to be very unreasonable, to put his life
at stake, to employ all the resources of impassioned
eloquence, to say that he was losing his mind,
that he was incapable of thinking or of writing a
line.

Certain women have a horror of doing things
deliberately which does honor to their delicacy;
they like to yield to sudden excitement and not with
premeditation.   Generally speaking, no one cares
for a pleasure that is forced upon him.   Madame de
Bargeton noticed upon Lucien's forehead, in his
eyes, in his whole face and in his manner that *air
of excitement* which betrays a resolution already
formed; she determined to defeat it, partly through
a spirit of contradiction, but also through a noble
interpretation of the word love.   Being a woman
made up of exaggerations, she exaggerated the value
of her own person.   In his eyes Madame de Bargeton was a sovereign, a Beatrice, a Laura.   She
took her seat, as in the Middle Ages, beneath the
raised canopy of the literary tournament, and Lucien was sure of winning her after several victories;
he had to efface the memory of the *sublime child*, of
Lamartine, of Walter Scott and of Byron.   The
noble creature deemed her love a generous sentiment; the desires she aroused in Lucien would be
a source of glory to him.   This feminine Don
Quixotism is a sentiment which imparts to love a

consecration of respectability; it utilizes it, magnifies it, honors it.   Persisting in her determination
to play the part of Dulcinea in Lucien's life for
seven or eight years, Madame de Bargeton, like
many provincials, proposed to make him purchase
her person by a sort of serfdom, by a period of
constant devotion which would enable her to judge
him.

When Lucien had opened the battle with one of
those exhibitions of sulkiness at which women laugh
who are themselves heart-free, and which grieve
only those who love, Louise assumed a dignified air
and began one of her long speeches interlarded with
pompous words.

"Is this what you have promised me, Lucien?"
she concluded.   "Do not sow in this delicious present the seeds of remorse which would poison my
life hereafter.   Do not ruin the future! and—I say
it with pride—do not ruin the present!   Have you
not my whole heart?   What more must you have?
Can your love submit to be influenced by the
senses, while a beloved woman's noblest privilege
is to impose silence upon them?   For whom do you
take me, pray? am I no longer your Beatrice?   If I
am nothing more to you than a woman, then I am
less than a woman."

"You would say nothing different to a man you
did not love," cried Lucien frantically.

"If you do not feel all the genuine affection there
is in my ideas, you will never be worthy of me."

"You cast a doubt upon my love in order to evade

a reply," said Lucien, throwing himself at her feet and weeping.

The poor boy wept in all seriousness when he saw that he was to be kept so long at the gates of paradise. They were the tears of the poet who deems himself humbled in his might, the tears of a child in despair at being refused the toy he wants.

"You have never loved me!" he cried.

"You do not believe what you say," she replied, flattered by his violence.

"Then prove to me that you are mine," said Lucien mildly.

At that moment Stanislas arrived, unheard, saw Lucien half prostrate, with tears in his eyes and his head against Louise's knees. Satisfied with that abundantly suspicious tableau, Stanislas abruptly retired upon Châtelet, who was standing at the door of the salon. Madame de Bargeton darted from the boudoir into the salon, but did not catch the two spies, who had hurriedly withdrawn like intruders.

"Who has been here?" she asked her people.

"Messieurs de Chandour and du Châtelet," replied Gentil, her old footman.

She returned to her boudoir, pale and trembling.

"If they saw you thus, I am lost," she said to Lucien.

"So much the better!" cried the poet.

She smiled at this outcry of selfishness overflowing with love.

MME. DE BARGETON'S BOUDOIR

———

"Then prove to me that you are mine," said Lucien, mildly.

At that moment Stanislas arrived, unheard, saw Lucien half prostrate, with tears in his eyes and his head against Louise's knees. Satisfied with that abundantly suspicious tableau, Stanislas abruptly retired upon Châtelet, who was standing at the door of the salon.

*

In the provinces such episodes are magnified by the way in which they are described. In a moment everyone knew that Lucien had been surprised at Naïs's knees. Monsieur de Chandour, delighted with the importance the affair conferred upon him, went first of all to the club to tell of the great event, and then from house to house. Châtelet made haste to announce everywhere that he had seen nothing; but, by thus putting himself outside the fact, he excited Stanislas to talk and to embellish the details; and Stanislas, considering himself exceedingly clever, added something new at every repetition. In the evening, the aristocratic society filled Amélie's salon to overflowing; for, when evening came, the most exaggerated versions of the story were circulating through Angoulême, where every narrator had imitated Stanislas. Men and women alike were impatient to know the truth. The women who veiled their faces, crying scandal loudest of all, were Amélie, Zéphirine, Fifine and Lolotte, all of whom were more or less burdened with illicit joys. The cruel theme was played with variations in every key.

"Well," said one, "you've heard about poor Naïs, I suppose? For my part I don't believe it; she has a whole irreproachable life before her; she's much too proud to be anything more than Monsieur

Chardon's patroness. But, if it is true, I pity her with all my heart."

"She's the more to be pitied because she's making herself so frightfully ridiculous; for she's old enough to be Monsieur Lulu's mother, as Jacques called him. The poetaster is twenty-two at most, and Naïs, between ourselves, will never see forty again."

"To my mind," said Châtelet, "Monsieur de Rubempré's position is in itself a proof of Naïs's innocence. A man doesn't go on his knees to ask for what he's already had."

"That depends!" said Francis, with a waggish air that called forth a disapproving glance from Zéphirine.

"Do, pray, tell us all about it," they said to Stanislas, organizing a secret conclave in a corner of the salon.

Stanislas had ended by composing a little tale full of improprieties, and accompanied it with gestures and poses which threw a prodigiously bad light upon the affair.

"It's incredible!" they said.

"At noon!" said one.

"Naïs is the last one I should have suspected."

"What will she do?"

And then the endless comments and conjectures! —Du Châtelet defended Madame de Bargeton; but he defended her so bunglingly that he fanned the flame of gossip instead of extinguishing it. Lili, in despair at the fall of the loveliest angel in the

Angoumois Olympus, went, bathed in tears, to cry the news at the bishop's palace. When it was certain that the entire town was in a ferment, the delighted Châtelet went to Madame de Bargeton's, where there was, alas! but a single whist table. He diplomatically asked Louise to grant him an interview in her boudoir. They sat down together on the little couch.

"You know, doubtless," said Châtelet in an undertone, "what all Angoulême is talking about?"

"No," said she.

"Well," he rejoined, "I am too good a friend of yours to leave you in ignorance. Indeed, it is my duty to place you in a position to put an end to the calumnies, invented doubtless by Amélie, who has the presumption to consider herself your rival. I came to see you this morning with that monkey, Stanislas, who was a few steps ahead of me; when he got as far as there," he continued, pointing to the door of the boudoir, "he claimed to have *seen* you with Monsieur de Rubempré in a position that made it impossible for him to enter; he fell back upon me all aghast, and dragged me away without giving me time to recover myself; and we were at Beaulieu before he told me the reason of his retreat. If I had understood, I wouldn't have stirred from your house until the affair was cleared up to your advantage; but to return after having once gone, would establish nothing. Now, whether Stanislas saw crooked or whether he is right, *he must be put in the wrong.* Dear Naïs, don't, I pray you, allow a fool to play with your life, your honor, your future; impose silence on him instantly. You know my position here? Although I need everybody's good-will, I am entirely devoted to you. Do what you will with a life that belongs to you. Although you have repelled my advances, my heart will always be yours, and at every opportunity I will prove to you how dearly I love you. Yes, I will watch over you as a faithful servant, without hope of reward, simply for the pleasure it gives me to serve you, even without your knowledge. This morning I said everywhere that I was at the door of the salon and saw nothing. If anybody asks you who informed you of the remarks that are being made about you, use my name. I shall be very proud to be your acknowledged defender; but, between ourselves, Monsieur de Bargeton is the only one who can demand satisfaction of Stanislas. Even if little Rubempré did do some foolish thing, a woman's honor must not be at the mercy of the first rattle-brained boy who throws himself at her feet. That is what I have said."

Naïs thanked Châtelet by an inclination of the head, and sat lost in thought. She was tired, even to disgust, of provincial life. At Châtelet's first word, she had turned her eyes upon Paris. Madame de Bargeton's silence placed her adroit admirer in an embarrassing situation.

"Dispose of me, I repeat," he said.

"Thanks," was her reply.

"What do you mean to do?"

LUCIEN TO PARIS

"*Await results and you will see how dearly I love
you. David, what good would our lofty thoughts
do, if they did not permit us to dispense with the
petty formalities with which the laws entangle sentiments? Despite the distance, will not my heart be
here? shall we not be united in thought? Have
I not a destiny to fulfil? Will the booksellers come
here to look for my* Archer de Charles IX., *and* Les
Marguerites?"

"I shall see."

A long silence.

"Do you really care so much for that little Rubempré?"

She smiled superbly and folded her arms, with
her eyes fixed on the curtains of her boudoir.
Châtelet went away, having failed to decipher the
haughty creature's heart. When Lucien and the
four faithful old men who had come to play their
usual game, unmoved by the doubtful gossip, had
taken their leave, Madame de Bargeton stopped her
husband, who was preparing to go to bed and had
his mouth open to bid his wife good-night.

"Come this way, my dear, I have something to
say to you," she said with a sort of solemnity.

Monsieur de Bargeton followed his wife into the
boudoir.

"Monsieur," she said, "perhaps I have been
wrong to display in my patronizing attentions to
Monsieur de Rubempré a warmth as ill understood
by the idiotic people of this town as by himself.
This morning Lucien threw himself there, at my
feet, and made me a declaration of love. Stanislas
came in just as I was lifting the child from the floor.
Heedless of the obligation that courtesy imposes
upon a gentleman toward a lady under all circumstances, he has declared that he surprised me in an
equivocal situation with that boy, whom I was
then treating as he deserves to be treated. If the
young hothead knew of the calumnious statements
based upon his folly, I know him, he would go at

14

once and insult Stanislas and force him to fight. Such a performance would be equivalent to a public avowal of his love. I have no need to tell you that your wife is pure; but you will agree that it would be dishonorable both to you and myself that Monsieur de Rubempré should be the one to defend her. Go at once to Stanislas and in all seriousness demand satisfaction for the insulting remarks he has made about me; remember that you must not allow the matter to be settled peaceably unless he retracts in presence of a number of well-known witnesses. In this way, you will win the esteem of all honorable people; you will act like a man of spirit and of gallantry, and you will be entitled to my esteem. I will send Gentil at once to Escarbas; my father must be your second; despite his age, I know he is the man to trample on the puppet who blackens the reputation of a Nègrepelisse. You have the choice of weapons, fight with pistols; you are a wonderful shot."

"I will go at once," said Monsieur de Bargeton, taking his hat and cane.

"Good, my dear," said his wife, deeply moved; "that's how I like men to act. You are a gentleman."

She gave him her forehead to kiss, and the proud and happy old man pressed his lips to it. His wife, who had a sort of motherly affection for the great child, could not restrain a tear as she heard the porte cochère close behind him.

"How he loves me!" she said to herself. "The

poor man clings to his life and yet he would lose it for me without a regret."

Monsieur de Bargeton was not at all disturbed at having to stand up in front of another man and look coolly into the barrel of a pistol that was aimed at him; no, he was embarrassed by one thing only, and he shuddered as he betook himself to Monsieur de Chandour's.

"What shall I say?" he thought.   "Naïs ought to have given me an idea."

And he cudgeled his brain to formulate a few phrases that would not sound ridiculous.

But people who live, as Monsieur de Bargeton lived, in silence imposed upon them by their narrow-mindedness and their limited breadth of vision, have at their disposal in the great crises of life a ready-made solemnity of demeanor.   As they speak but little, they naturally make few foolish remarks; and as they reflect abundantly upon what they shall say, their extreme distrust of themselves leads them to study their projected harangues so carefully that they express themselves wonderfully well, by a phenomenon similar to that which loosened the tongue of Balaam's ass.

Thus Monsieur de Bargeton bore himself like a man of superior mould.   He justified the opinions of those who looked upon him as a philosopher of the school of Pythagoras.   He reached Stanislas' house at eleven o'clock at night and found a numerous company assembled there.   He went up to Amélie and saluted her without speaking, and bestowed upon each of the guests an inane smile, which, under the existing circumstances, seemed profoundly ironical. His advent was followed by a painful silence, as in nature when a storm is approaching. Châtelet, who had returned, glanced significantly from Monsieur de Bargeton to Stanislas, whom the offended husband saluted courteously.

Châtelet grasped the meaning of a call made at an hour when the old man was always in bed; Naïs was evidently working that feeble arm: and, as his relations to Amélie gave him the right to intervene in the affairs of the household, he rose, took Monsieur de Bargeton aside and said to him:

"You want to speak to Stanislas?"

"Yes," said the goodman, delighted to find an intermediary who would perhaps do the talking for him.

"Very well, go to Amélie's bedroom," said the superintendent of imposts, well pleased at the prospect of a duel which might make Madame de Bargeton a widow, while making it impossible for her to marry Lucien, the cause of the duel.

"Stanislas," said Châtelet to Monsieur de Chandour, "Bargeton has come, without doubt, to demand satisfaction for what you have been saying about Naïs. Come to your wife's room and act, both of you, like gentlemen. Don't make any noise over it, be exceedingly polite, in short, be as cool and dignified as a Briton."

A moment later Stanislas and Châtelet had joined Bargeton.

"Monsieur," said the outraged husband, "you claim to have found Madame de Bargeton in an equivocal situation with Monsieur de Rubempré?"

"With Monsieur Chardon," rejoined Stanislas ironically, for he fancied that Bargeton was not a strong man.

"Very good," returned the husband. "If you don't contradict your statements in presence of those who are your guests at this moment, I beg you to select a second. My father-in-law, Monsieur de Nègrepelisse, will call upon you at four in the morning. Let us both make all necessary arrangements, for the affair can be settled in no other way than that I have indicated. I select pistols, as I am the insulted party."

On his way to the house, Monsieur de Bargeton had ruminated over this speech, the longest he had ever made in his life; he delivered it without passion and with the simplest manner imaginable. Stanislas turned pale and said to himself:

"What did I see, after all?"

But between the shame of retracting his statements before the whole town, in presence of this dumb creature who seemed unable to take a joke, and the fear, the ghastly fear that grasped his neck in its burning hands, he chose the more distant danger.

"Very well. Until to-morrow," he said to Monsieur de Bargeton, believing that the matter could be arranged.

The three men returned to the salon and everyone

scrutinized their faces: Châtelet was smiling,
Monsieur de Bargeton was exactly the same as if
he were in his own house; but Stanislas was as
pale as death. At sight of him some of the ladies
divined the object of the conference. The words:
"They are going to fight!" passed from ear to ear.
Half of the party believed that Stanislas was in the
wrong, for his pallor and his expression accused
him of falsehood; the other half admired Monsieur
de Bargeton's bearing. Châtelet assumed a grave,
mysterious air. Monsieur de Bargeton remained a
few moments, examining the faces of those about
him, and then withdrew.

"Have you pistols?" whispered Châtelet to
Stanislas, who shuddered from head to foot.

Amélie understood the meaning of it all and
showed symptoms of fainting; the ladies were all
anxious to assist in carrying her to her bedroom.
There was a tremendous uproar there, everybody
talking at once. The men remained in the salon
and declared with one voice that Monsieur de
Bargeton was within his rights.

"Did you suppose the goodman was capable of
acting thus?" said Monsieur de Saintot.

"Why," said the pitiless Jacques, "in his
younger days he was most expert with firearms.
My father has often told me of Bargeton's exploits."

"Bah! you place them twenty paces apart and
they'll both miss if you give them horse pistols,"
said Francis to Châtelet.

When everybody else had gone, Châtelet encouraged Stanislas and his wife, assuring them that all would be well, and that, in a duel between a man of sixty and a man of thirty-six, the advantage was all with the latter.

The next morning, when Lucien and David, who had returned from Marsac without his father, were breakfasting together, Madame Chardon rushed into the room, terrified beyond measure.

"Well, well, Lucien, have you heard the news everyone is talking about, even in the market place? Monsieur de Bargeton almost killed Monsieur de Chandour at five o'clock this morning in a meadow belonging to Monsieur Tulloye, a name that they make puns upon. It seems that Monsieur de Chandour said yesterday that he surprised you with Madame de Bargeton."

"It's false! Madame de Bargeton is innocent," cried Lucien.

"A man from the country, whom I heard describing the details of the affair, saw it all from his wagon. Monsieur de Nègrepelisse arrived at three o'clock in the morning to assist Monsieur de Bargeton. He told Monsieur de Chandour that, if anything happened to his son-in-law, he would take it on himself to avenge him. An officer of the cavalry regiment lent his pistols and Monsieur de Nègrepelisse tried them several times. Monsieur du Châtelet objected to their trying the pistols, but the officer they took for a referee said that unless they wanted to act like children they must use weapons

that were in proper condition.   The seconds placed
the duelists twenty-five paces apart.   Monsieur de
Bargeton, who acted just as if he were out for a walk,
fired first and hit Monsieur de Chandour in the
neck; he fell and couldn't return the fire.   The surgeon from the hospital said just now that Monsieur
de Chandour's neck will be crooked for the rest
of his life.   I hurried home to tell you the result
of the duel, to prevent your going to Madame de
Bargeton's or showing yourself in Angoulême,
for some of Monsieur de Chandour's friends may
insult you."

At that moment Gentil, Monsieur de Bargeton's
footman, entered the room, escorted by the apprentice from the printing office and handed Lucien
this letter from Louise:

"Doubtless you have learned, my friend, the result of the
duel between Chandour and my husband. We shall be at
home to no one to-day. Be prudent, do not show yourself; I
ask it in the name of your affection for me. Do you not
think that the best way to pass this sad day is to come and
listen to your Beatrice, whose life is completely changed by
this occurrence, and who has a thousand things to say to
you?"

"Luckily," said David, "my wedding is appointed
for the day after to-morrow; you will have an excuse for going to Madame de Bargeton's less frequently."

"Dear David," Lucien answered, "she asks me to
come and see her to-day; I think I must do as she

asks; she knows better than we how I ought to act
under such circumstances."

"Is everything ready here?" asked Madame
Chardon.

"Come and see," cried David, delighted to ex-
hibit the apartments on the first floor in their transformed condition, everything being fresh and new.

They exhaled the sweetness that reigns in young
households where orange flowers and the bridal veil
still crown the home life, where the springtime of
love is reflected in everything, where everything is
white and clean and blooming.

"Eve will be like a princess," said the mother;
"but you have spent too much money, you have
been foolish!"

David smiled without replying, for Madame
Chardon had placed her finger upon a raw secret
wound which caused the poor lover cruel suffering:
his ideas had been so exceeded in carrying them out
that it was impossible for him to build over the
lean-to. His mother-in-law would not for a long
time to come have the apartment that he intended
her to have. Generous minds feel the keenest
sorrow in breaking promises of that sort, which are,
in a certain sense, the little vanities of affection.
David carefully concealed his embarrassment, in
order to avoid giving pain to Lucien, who might
well have felt crushed by the burden of the sacrifices
made for him.

"Eve and her friends have worked hard too," said
Madame Chardon. "The trousseau, the house

linen, everything is ready. The girls are so fond of her that they have covered her mattresses with white fustian edged with pink, without her knowledge. It's very pretty! it makes one long to be married."

The mother and daughter had expended all their savings in furnishing David's house with the things of which young men never think. Knowing how luxuriously he was doing his part, for they had heard of a dinner service ordered at Limoges, they had tried to make the things they contributed harmonize with those purchased by David. This little struggle between love and generosity was destined to cause pecuniary troubles for the young husband and wife from the very beginning, amid all the outward indications of bourgeois comfort which would be esteemed luxury in an old-fashioned town such as Angoulême then was.

As soon as Lucien saw his mother and David go into the bedroom, whose blue and white hangings and pretty furniture were so familiar to him, he made his escape and hurried to Madame de Bargeton's. He found Naïs breakfasting with her husband, who was eating heartily, entirely unmoved by what had taken place, his appetite having been sharpened by his early walk. The old country gentleman, Monsieur de Nègrepelisse, an imposing relic of the old French nobility, was with his daughter. When Gentil announced Monsieur de Rubempré, the white-haired old man bestowed upon him the searching glance of a father eager to pass judgment upon the man his daughter has distinguished. Lucien's extraordinary beauty impressed him so deeply that he could not repress an expression of approval; but he seemed to look upon his daughter's *liaison* as an ephemeral affair, a mere whim rather than a lasting passion. The breakfast came to an end. Louise rose, leaving her father and Monsieur de Bargeton in the dining-room and motioning to Lucien to follow her.

"My dear," she said in a tone that was at once sad and joyful, "I am going to Paris and my father is to take Bargeton to Escarbas, where he will stay during my absence. Madame d'Espard, a Blamont-Chauvry, with whom we are connected through the D'Espards, the elder branch of the Nègrepelisses, enjoys great influence just at this time, through her own charms as well as through her connections. If she deigns to acknowledge us, I propose to cultivate her acquaintance assiduously; by her influence she can obtain a place for Bargeton. My solicitations may lead the court to express a desire that he be chosen deputy from the Charente, which will assist his chances of election here. His having a seat in the Chamber may later be of assistance to my plans in Paris. You are the one, my darling child, who have led me to make this change in my life. This morning's duel compels me to close my house for some time, for there are people who will take sides with the Chandours against us. In our present position, especially in a small town, absence is always necessary to give hard feeling time to be softened. But, either I shall succeed and shall never see Angoulême again, or I shall fail; and in that event, I shall await at Paris the time when I can pass all my summers at Escarbas and my winters at Paris. That is the only life for a woman *comme il faut,* and I have delayed too long about taking it up. The day will suffice for all our preparations; I shall start to-morrow night, and you will go with me, won't you? You must go on ahead. Between Mansle and Ruffec I will take you into my carriage, and we shall soon be in Paris. There, my dear, is the stage for people of superior minds. One is never at ease except with one's equals; anywhere else one suffers. Moreover, Paris, the capital of the intellectual world, is the field wherein you can achieve success; hasten to pass the space that separates you from it. Do not let your ideas rust in the provinces, but put yourself promptly in communication with the great men who will represent the nineteenth century. Draw near to the court and the seat of power. Neither distinctions nor dignities will seek out the talent that is running to seed in a small town. Name me any notable works that were ever executed in the provinces! On the other hand, see the sublime, poverty-stricken Jean-Jacques irresistibly attracted by that moral sun which creates renown, warming men's minds by the constant friction of rivalries! Should you not hasten to take your place among the constellations that every generation produces? You would not believe how useful it is to youthful talent to be exhibited for the first time in the best society. I will persuade Madame d'Espard to receive you; no one finds it easy to gain admission to her salon, where you will find all the great personages, ministers, ambassadors, the orators of the Chamber, the most influential peers, and numbers of wealthy or famous men and women. One must be quite devoid of tact to be unable to arouse their interest, when one is handsome, young, and running over with genius. Great talents are not narrow-minded, they will lend you their support. When you are known to occupy a lofty position, your works will acquire enormous value. The great problem for artists to solve is how to place themselves where they can be seen. Thus you will find there innumerable opportunities to make your fortune, some sinecure, or a pension on the privy purse. The Bourbons are so devoted to letters and the arts! be at once a religious poet and a royalist poet. Not only will that be worthily done, but you will make your fortune. Does the opposition, does liberalism, give places and rewards and make the fortune of authors? So take the pleasant road, and come where all men of genius go. You have my secret, preserve the most absolute silence and make your arrangements to accompany me.—Don't you want to?'' she added, amazed at her lover's silent attitude.

Lucien, dazed by the rapid glance he cast upon Paris as he listened to these seductive words, felt as if he had hitherto used only half of his brain; it

seemed to him as if the other half were just beginning to bestir itself, so rapidly did his ideas expand;
he looked upon himself, in Angoulême, as a frog
under his stone in the heart of a swamp. Paris and
its splendors, Paris, which looms in all provincial
imaginations as a sort of Eldorado, appeared to him
then in her golden robe, her head adorned with cir-
clets of royal gems, her arms open to talent. Illustrious men would come forth to give him a fraternal
greeting. There, everything smiled on genius.
There were no jealous country squires to utter cutting remarks to humiliate the writer, no stupid
indifference to poetry. Thence the works of poets
shed their refulgent light; there they were paid and
made known to the world. After reading the first
few pages of his *Archer de Charles IX.*, the booksellers would open their cash-boxes and say: "How
much do you want?" He understood, too, that, after
a journey in which they would be married by circumstances, Madame de Bargeton would be his absolutely, that they would live together.

To the question: "Don't you want to?" he
replied with a tear, seized Louise around the waist,
pressed her to his heart and reddened her neck by
the ardent pressure of his kisses. But suddenly he
paused, as if something had just come to his mind,
and cried:

"Great God! my sister is to be married on the
day after to-morrow."

That cry was the last sigh of the noble, pure-
hearted child. The powerful bonds that attach

young hearts to their families, to their early friends, to all the primitive sentiments, were about to receive a terrible blow.

"Well," cried the haughty Nègrepelisse, "what has your sister's marriage in common with the progress of our love? Are you so bent upon being the good fairy of that bourgeois and working-girl's wedding, that you cannot sacrifice its noble delights? A sacrifice indeed!" she added, with bitter contempt. "I sent my husband out this morning to fight a duel on your account! Go, monsieur, leave me! I have deceived myself."

She fell fainting on her couch. Lucien followed her thither, imploring her forgiveness, cursing his family, David and his sister alike.

"I had such faith in you!" she said. "Monsieur de Cante-Croix had a mother whom he idolized, but, for the sake of obtaining a letter from me in which I should say to him: *I am satisfied!* he died on the battlefield. And you, forsooth! cannot give up a wedding-breakfast for the sake of taking a journey with me!"

Lucien swore that he would kill himself, and his despair was so sincere, so profound, that Louise forgave him, but made him feel that he would have to atone for his sin.

"Go," she said at last, "be discreet, and to-morrow night at midnight, wait for me a hundred yards beyond Mansle."

Lucien felt the earth grow small beneath his feet; he returned to David's house, attended by Hope as

Orestes was by his Furies, for he foresaw a thousand obstacles, all of which were included in that terrible question: "What about money?" David's perspicacity terrified him so that he shut himself up in his pretty study to recover from the bewilderment caused by his new position. He must leave that apartment, furnished at so great a cost, and render useless so many sacrifices. It occurred to Lucien that his mother might live there, and thus David could dispense with the costly structure he had planned to build at the end of the courtyard. His departure would be an advantage to his family; he found a thousand peremptory reasons for going away, for there is nothing so jesuitical as a desire. He hastened at once to his sister at L'Houmeau, to tell her of his new prospects and come to an understanding with her. As he passed Postel's shop, he thought that, if there were no other way, he would borrow from his father's successor the sum necessary for a year's stay in Paris.

"If I live with Louise, a crown a day will be a fortune to me, and that makes only a thousand francs a year," he said to himself. "And in six months I shall be rich!"

Eve and her mother listened to Lucien's confidences under a promise of absolute secrecy. Both wept as they heard what the ambitious youth had to tell them; and when he sought to learn the cause of their grief, they informed him that all they possessed had been absorbed by the table and household linen, by Eve's trousseau and by a multitude of purchases of which David had not thought, and which they were happy to have made, for the printer had settled ten thousand francs on Eve. Thereupon, Lucien told them of his idea of a loan, and Madame Chardon undertook to ask Postel for a thousand francs for one year.

"But Lucien," said Eve, with a feeling of oppression at her heart, "you won't be at my wedding? Oh! come back; I will wait a few days! Surely she will let you come back after a fortnight, when you have escorted her to Paris! She certainly can spare us a week, when we have brought you up for her! Our marriage will turn out badly if you are not there.—But will a thousand francs be enough?" she said, suddenly interrupting herself. "Although your coat becomes you divinely, you have only one! You have only two fine shirts, the other six are coarse linen. You have only three lawn cravats, the other three are common jaconet; and then your handkerchiefs are not fine enough. Will you find a sister in Paris to wash and iron your linen for you the very day you need it? you must have more of it. You have only one pair of nankeen trousers made this year; last year's are too short for you; so you will have to buy clothes in Paris, and Paris prices are different from Angoulême prices. You have only two white waistcoats fit to wear, I have mended the others already. I advise you to borrow two thousand francs."

David, entering the room at that moment, seemed to have overheard the last sentence, for

15

he looked earnestly at the brother and sister without speaking.

"Don't conceal anything from me," he said at last.

"He is going away with her," cried Eve.

"Postel agrees to let you have the thousand francs," said Madame Chardon, returning to the room without seeing David, "but for six months only, and he wants your note of hand endorsed by your brother-in-law, for he says you don't offer any security."

As she spoke, she turned and saw her future son-in-law, and the four stood looking at one another in absolute silence. The Chardon family knew how they had abused David's generosity. They were all ashamed. A tear stood in the printer's eye.

"Then you won't be at my wedding?" he said; "you won't stay with us? And to think that I have spent all I had! Ah! Lucien, I have brought Eve her poor little bridal jewels; I didn't know," he added, wiping his eyes and taking several cases from his pocket, "that I should have to regret having brought them."

He placed the morocco-covered boxes on the table, in front of his mother-in-law.

"Why do you think so much of me?" said Eve, with an angelic smile that contradicted the implied reproach.

"Dear mamma," said the printer, "go and tell Monsieur Postel that I consent to endorse the note,

for I see from your face, Lucien, that you are fully
decided to go."

Lucien bowed gently and sadly, saying a moment
later:

"Don't think ill of me, my beloved angels."

He drew Eve and David to him and embraced
them, adding:

"Await results and you will see how dearly I love
you. David, what good would our lofty thoughts
do, if they did not permit us to dispense with the
petty formalities with which the laws entangle sentiments? Despite the distance, will not my heart
be here? shall we not be united in thought? Have
I not a destiny to fulfil? Will the booksellers come
here to look for my *Archer de Charles IX.*, and *Les
Marguerites?* Must I not do at some time, sooner
or later, what I am doing to-day? shall I ever find
circumstances more favorable? Is it not worth a
whole fortune to me simply to make my *début* in
Paris in the Marquise d'Espard's salon?"

"He is right," said Eve. "Didn't you say yourself that he ought soon to go to Paris?"

David took Eve's hand, led her into the narrow
closet in which she had slept for seven years, and
whispered in her ear:

"Did you say that he needs two thousand francs,
my love? Postel lends him only one thousand."

Eve looked at her future husband with a heart-
rending expression that betrayed all her suffering.

"Listen, my adored Eve; we are going to begin
life badly. Yes, my expenses have absorbed all I

possessed. I have but two thousand francs left, and half of that is indispensable to keep the printing-office at work. To give your brother a thousand francs is to give him the bread out of our mouths, to endanger our happiness. If I were alone, I know what I would do; but there are two of us. Decide."

Eve threw herself wildly into her lover's arms, kissed him fondly, and whispered to him, her eyes wet with tears:

"Do as you would do if you were alone; I will work to earn the money."

Despite the most ardent kiss that lovers ever exchanged, David left Eve sorely depressed, and returned to Lucien.

"Don't be distressed," he said, "you shall have your two thousand francs."

"Go and see Postel," said Madame Chardon, "for you both have to sign the note."

When the two friends returned, they surprised Eve and her mother on their knees, praying. Although they knew how many hopes his future return from Paris was likely to fulfil, they felt at that moment all that they lost in bidding him farewell; for they considered that possible happiness to come was not worth the price of a separation which would break up their family life and cast them upon a sea of anxiety concerning Lucien's destiny.

"If you ever forget this scene," said David in Lucien's ear, "you will be the lowest of men."

Doubtless the printer deemed those solemn words

necessary; Madame de Bargeton's influence alarmed
him no less than Lucien's deplorably fickle nature,
which was as likely to lead him into evil courses
as into honorable ones. Eve soon had Lucien's
clothes ready for him. This literary Fernando
Cortez took but few things with him. He wore
his best redingote, his best waistcoat and one of his
two fine shirts. All his linen, his famous dress
coat, his other clothes and his manuscripts made
such a small bundle, that, to conceal it from Madame de Bargeton, David proposed to send it by the
diligence to his correspondent, a dealer in paper, to
whom he would write to hold it subject to Lucien's
orders.

Despite Madame de Bargeton's precautions to conceal her departure, Châtelet learned of it and determined to ascertain whether she made the journey
alone or in Lucien's company; he sent his valet to
Ruffec, with instructions to examine all the carriages
that changed horses at the posting-station.

"If she takes her poet with her," he thought,
"she is mine."

Lucien started the next morning at daybreak,
accompanied by David, who had hired a horse and
cabriolet, saying that he was going to see his father
on business; a little falsehood which, under existing
circumstances, was not improbable. The two
friends drove to Marsac, where they passed part of
the day with the old bear; then, in the evening,
they drove a little beyond Mansle, to wait for Madame de Bargeton, who arrived toward morning.

As he caught sight of the old sexagenarian calèche that he had so often seen in the carriage-house, Lucien experienced one of the keenest thrills of emotion of his whole life; he threw himself into David's arms.

"God grant this may prove to be for your good!" said David.

The printer re-entered his wretched cabriolet and drove away with an oppressed heart, for he had gloomy forebodings of the destiny that awaited Lucien in Paris.

PART SECOND

A PROVINCIAL GREAT MAN AT PARIS

*

Neither Lucien nor Madame de Bargeton, Gentil, nor Albertine, the maid, ever spoke of the events of that journey; but it may well be believed that the constant presence of servants made it very irksome to a lover who was anticipating all the pleasures of an elopement. Lucien, who then traveled by post for the first time in his life, was dismayed to find that almost the whole sum he had expected to live upon for a year was scattered along the road from Angoulême to Paris. Like most men who combine the charms of boyhood with the energy of talent, he made the mistake of expressing his ingenuous amazement at the sight of things that were new and strange to him. A man should study a woman carefully before allowing her to see his emotions and his thoughts in their crude state. A mistress as loving as she is noble smiles at such childish ways and understands them; but let her be ever so little vain, and she never forgives her lover for being childish, vain or trivial. Many women carry their adoration to such a point that they always expect to find a god in their idol; while those who love a man for himself, before loving him for themselves, adore his pettinesses as well as his great qualities. Lucien had not yet discovered that in Madame de Bargeton's case, love was grafted upon pride. He made the mistake of not seeking an explanation of certain smiles that escaped Louise during the journey, when, instead of restraining himself, he indulged in the pretty antics of a young rat just out of his hole.

The travelers alighted at the *Hôtel du Gaillard-Bois*, Rue de l'Echelle, before daybreak. They were so fatigued that Louise desired beyond everything to go to bed, and she did so, having told Lucien to request a room above the apartments that she engaged. Lucien slept until four in the afternoon. Madame de Bargeton sent to waken him for dinner; he dressed himself hurriedly when he learned the time, and found Louise in one of those vile chambers which are the disgrace of Paris, where, despite all its pretensions to splendor, there does not as yet exist a single hotel where a wealthy traveler can find the comforts of home.

His eyes were dimmed by the haze left by a sudden awakening, and he did not recognize his Louise in that cold, sunless room, with faded curtains, a wretched, uncarpeted floor and ugly, worn furniture, very old or bought at second-hand. It is a fact that there are some people who have not the same aspect or the same attractiveness when they are separated from the figures, the objects, the localities which have served them as a frame. Living faces have a sort of atmosphere that is suited to them, just as the *chiaro-oscuro* of Flemish paintings is necessary to the vitality of the figures which the painter's genius has placed therein. Almost all provincials come within this category. Then, too, Madame de Bargeton seemed more reserved, more thoughtful, than she should have been at the moment when a life of unfettered happiness was dawning. But Lucien could not complain. They were waited upon by Gentil and Albertine. The dinner lacked the abundance and essential excellence which are the distinguishing characteristics of provincial dinners. The dishes, brought from a neighboring restaurant, were insufficient in quantity, carefully subdivided, and our lovers dined on short commons. Paris does not shine in those little matters to which people of moderate fortune are condemned. Lucien waited until the end of the dinner to question Louise, whose changed bearing was inexplicable to him. He was not mistaken. A serious event—for reflections are events in one's moral life—had occurred while he was sleeping.

About two in the afternoon, Sixte du Châtelet appeared at the hotel, sent a servant to waken Albertine, told her that he wished to speak with her mistress, and returned after allowing Madame de Bargeton barely sufficient time to make her toilet. Anaïs, whose curiosity was aroused by Monsieur du Châtelet's unexpected appearance on the scene—for she thought she had covered her tracks perfectly—received him about three o'clock.

"I followed you, taking the risk of a reprimand from headquarters," he said, as he bowed to her, "for I foresaw what would happen. But, even if I lose my place, you shall not be lost!"

"What do you mean?" cried Madame de Bargeton.

"I see that you love Lucien," he continued, with an air of tender resignation, "for one must love a man very dearly to throw reflection to the winds, to forget all the proprieties, which nobody is more familiar with than you! Do you imagine, pray, my dear, adored Naïs, that you will be received at Madame d'Espard's, or in any salon in Paris, when it is known that you have practically eloped from Angoulême with a young man, and especially after Monsieur de Bargeton's duel with Monsieur de Chandour? Your husband's stay at Escarbas looks like a separation. In such cases, men of the world begin by fighting for their wives' honor, and then leave them free. Love Monsieur de Rubempré, patronize him, do whatever you please in everything, but do not remain together! If anyone here should know that you had made the journey in the same carriage, you would be excommunicated by the social set you are desirous to enter. And again, Naïs, do not make such sacrifices as this for a young man whom you have as yet compared to nobody, who has been subjected to no test, and may forget you for some Parisian woman, deeming her more necessary than you to his ambitious projects. I have no wish to injure the man you love, but you will permit me to place your interests before his,

and to say to you: 'Study him! Realize the full
meaning of what you are doing.' If you find the
doors closed, if ladies refuse to receive you, at least
do not regret your sacrifice, being certain that he
for whom you make it, will always be worthy of it
and will understand it. Madame d'Espard is the
more rigid and exacting in such matters because she
is herself living apart from her husband, for some
reason which society has never been able to discover; but the Navarreins, the Blamont-Chauvrys,
the Lenoncourts, all her relatives, have taken her
up, the most straitlaced women go to her house and
receive her at their houses with great respect, so
that the Marquis d'Espard is in the wrong. The
very first time that you call upon her, you will
realize the correctness of what I say. I, knowing
Paris as I do, can predict just what will happen as
you enter the marchioness' salon, you will be in
despair lest she should learn that you are at the
Hôtel du Gaillard-Bois with an apothecary's son,
though he does call himself Monsieur de Rubempré.
You will have rivals here much more astute and sly
than Amélie, and they will not fail to ascertain who
you are, where you are, whence you come and what
you are doing. You relied upon your incognito, I
see; but you are one of those persons for whom
there is no such thing as an incognito. Won't you
fall in with Angoulême everywhere? there are the
deputies from the Charente who have come up for
the opening of the session; there is the general in
Paris on leave; but it will be enough that a single

person from Angoulême should see you, to check your career with extraordinary promptitude; you would be nothing more than Lucien's mistress.   If you need me for any purpose, I am at the receiver-general's, Rue du Faubourg-Saint-Honoré, within two steps of Madame d'Espard.   I know the Maréchale de Carigliano, Madame de Sérizy and the President of the Council well enough to present you to them; but you will see so many people at Madame d'Espard's that you won't need me.   Far from desiring to go to this or that salon, your presence will be desired in all the salons.''

Madame de Bargeton allowed Châtelet to speak without interruption: she was impressed by the justness of his observations.   The Queen of Angoulême had, in fact, relied upon her incognito.

''You are right, my dear friend,'' she said, ''but what am I to do?''

''Let me find you a suitable furnished apartment,'' said Châtelet; ''in that way, you will live less expensively than at a hotel, and you will be at home; if you take my advice, you will sleep there to-night.''

''But how did you know my address?'' she said.

''Your carriage was easy to recognize, and, besides that, I followed you.   At Sèvres, the postilion who drove you gave my postilion your address. Will you permit me to be your quartermaster?   I will write you a line soon to let you know where I have found quarters for you.''

''Very well, do so,'' she said.

Those words seemed unimportant, but they were really of the utmost importance. The Baron du Châtelet had spoken the language of society to a society woman. He had appeared before her in all the elegance of Parisian costume; a pretty cabriolet, well-appointed, had brought him to the hotel. By chance, Madame de Bargeton walked to the window to reflect upon her position, and saw the old beau drive away. A few moments later, Lucien, awakened from a sound sleep, having dressed in great haste, appeared before her in his last year's nankeen trousers, with his shabby little redingote. He was handsome, but ridiculously dressed. Put a water-carrier's costume on the Apollo Belvedere or the Antinous; would you then recognize the divine creature of the Greek or Roman chisel? The eyes make comparisons before the heart has rectified their rapid, instinctive judgment. The contrast between Lucien and Châtelet was too sudden not to make an impression upon Louise.

When the dinner was at an end, about six o'clock, Madame de Bargeton motioned to Lucien to come and sit beside her on a wretched couch covered with a red chintz with yellow flowers.

"My Lucien," she began, "don't you think that, if we have done a foolish thing that will ruin us both alike, we ought to do our best to undo it? We must neither remain together in Paris, my dear child, nor allow it to be suspected that we came hither in company. Your future depends in a great measure upon my position, and I must be careful not to compromise it in any way. So I am going, this evening, into lodgings a few steps away; but you will remain in this hotel and we can see each other every day without giving anyone an opportunity to criticize us."

Louise explained the laws of society to Lucien, who listened with wide open eyes. Although he did not realize that they who regret their follies regret their love, he did realize that he was no longer the Lucien of Angoulême. Louise spoke only of herself, her interests, her reputation and society; and, to excuse her egotism, she tried to make him believe that his own interests were at stake. He had no rights over Louise, who had so suddenly become Madame de Bargeton again, and—worse still! —he had no power over her. So he could not keep the great tears from gathering in his eyes.

"If I am your glory, you are much more than that to me, you are my only hope and my whole future. I understood that, if you shared my successes, you were to share my failure too, and now we are to separate so soon!"

"You criticize my conduct," said she; "you don't love me."

Lucien looked at her with such a piteous expression that she could not forbear saying to him:

"Dear boy, I will stay here if you wish; we shall ruin ourselves and be left without support. But, when we are equally wretched and both frowned upon by society; when failure, for we must consider every possibility, has driven us back to

Escarbas, remember, my love, that I prophesied that result, and that I proposed to you at the beginning to win success according to the laws of society by bowing to those laws."

"Louise," he replied, kissing her, "I am terrified to find you so prudent. Remember that I am a child, that I yielded absolutely to your dear will. I intended to triumph over men and things by sheer force of will; but I can succeed more quickly with your aid than alone, I shall be very happy to owe all my fortune to you. Forgive me! I have placed myself too entirely in your hands, not to fear everything. To me, separation is the herald of desertion; and desertion is death."

"But, my dear child, society asks very little of you," she replied. "It is simply a question of sleeping here, for you can stay with me all day, and no one will have a word to say."

A caress or two restored Lucien's tranquillity. An hour later, Gentil brought a note from Châtelet informing Madame de Bargeton that he had found an apartment on Rue Neuve-de-Luxembourg. She ascertained the location of that street, which was not very far from Rue de l'Echelle, and remarked to Lucien:

"We are neighbors."

Two hours later, Louise entered a carriage sent by Châtelet to take her to her new quarters. The apartment, one of those which upholsterers furnish and let to rich deputies or great personages, who have come to Paris for a short time, was sumptuous

16

but inconvenient. Lucien returned about eleven
o'clock to his little *Hôtel du Gaillard-Bois*, having as
yet seen nothing of Paris but that part of Rue
Saint-Honoré that lies between Rue Neuve-de-Luxembourg and Rue de l'Echelle. He went to bed in
his wretched little room, which he could not refrain
from contrasting with Louise's magnificent suite.
Just as he left Madame de Bargeton's, Baron du
Châtelet arrived there, returning from the Ministry
of Foreign Affairs in all the splendor of a ball costume. He came to advise Madame de Bargeton of
the agreements he had made in her behalf. Louise
was disturbed, her luxurious surroundings terrified
her. Provincial manners had reacted upon her at
last; she had become very fastidious in her accounts;
she was so careful that she was likely to be considered miserly in Paris. She had brought with
her an order on the receiver-general for twenty
thousand francs, intending that sum to cover her
surplus expenses for four years; she already feared
that she would not have enough and would run in
debt. Châtelet informed her that the apartment
would cost her only six hundred francs a month.

"A mere trifle," he said, noticing Naïs's start.
"You have a carriage at your service for five hundred francs a month, making fifty louis in all. You
will have nothing to think of except your dress. A
lady who intends to go into the best society cannot
do otherwise. If you want to make Monsieur de
Bargeton a receiver-general or obtain a place for
him in the king's household, you must not live in

poor style. Here people give only to the rich. It's very lucky," he added, "that you have Gentil with you and Albertine to dress you, for servants are a ruinous expense in Paris. You will seldom take your meals at home, with the start in society you will have."

Madame de Bargeton and the baron talked about Paris. Châtelet told her the news of the day, the thousand and one trifles which one must know under penalty of not being considered a Parisian. He advised Naïs as to the shops she should patronize: he mentioned Herbault for caps, Juliette for hats and bonnets; he gave her the address of the only dressmaker who could fill Victorine's shoes; in a word, he impressed upon her the necessity of *disangoulêming* herself. Then he launched the last shaft of wit that he had had the good fortune to conceive.

"To-morrow," he said, carelessly, "I shall probably have a box at some theatre or other; I will come and take you and Monsieur de Rubempré, for you will permit me to do the honors of Paris to both of you."

"He has more generosity in his nature than I supposed," said Madame de Bargeton to herself, when he invited Lucien.

In the month of June, ministers do not know what to do with their boxes at the theatres; the ministerial deputies and their constituents are gathering their grapes or looking after their crops, and their most persistent acquaintances are in the country or traveling; and so, at that season, the best boxes in the Parisian theatres are filled with guests of curious appearance, whom the regular habitués never see again and who produce upon the audience an impression of worn-out tapestry. It had occurred to Châtelet that, owing to that circumstance, he might, without spending much money, afford Naïs the entertainments that are most attractive to provincials.

The next morning, the first time that he called, Lucien did not find Louise. She had gone out to make some indispensable purchases. She had gone out to take counsel with the grave and illustrious authorities on the subject of feminine garb whom Châtelet had recommended to her, for she had written to the Marquise d'Espard, to inform her of her arrival in Paris. Although Madame de Bargeton had that confidence in herself that a long-continued habit of domination imparts, she had a curious fear of seeming provincial. She had sufficient tact to realize how much the future relations of women to one another depend upon first impressions; and, although she knew that she was capable of attaining the level of superior women like Madame d'Espard, she felt that she needed kindly support on her first appearance, and above all things, she desired to neglect no element of success. Thus she was infinitely grateful to Châtelet for having pointed out to her the way to place herself in harmony with the best Parisian society.

By a strange chance, the marchioness was in a

position in which she was enchanted to render a
service to one of her husband's family.   Without
apparent cause, the Marquis d'Espard had withdrawn from the world; he paid no attention to matters of business, to political affairs, to his family or
to his wife.   Having thus become her own mistress,
the marchioness felt the necessity of being smiled
upon by society; she was therefore glad to replace
the marquis at this juncture by becoming the
patroness of his family.   She proposed to make a
great parade of her patronage in order to make her
husband's fault the more notorious.   In the course
of the same day she wrote to *Madame de Bargeton,
née Nègrepelisse,* one of those charming notes which
are so prettily worded that one needs time to discover their lack of depth:

"She was overjoyed that circumstances had
brought within speaking distance a person of whom
she had often heard, and whom she was anxious to
know, for Parisian friendships were not so enduring
that she did not long to have one more friend to
love on earth; and if that longing were not to be
gratified, it would simply be one illusion more to
be buried with the others.   She wished to place
herself entirely at her cousin's disposal, and she
would go to see her at once were it not for a slight
indisposition which kept her at home; but she considered herself indebted to her for having thought
of her."

During his first aimless walk along the boulevards
and the Rue de la Paix, Lucien, like all newcomers,

paid much more heed to things than to persons.   At
Paris, the massiveness of everything first claims
the attention; the magnificence of the shops, the
height of the buildings, the swarm of carriages, the
constant contrast between extreme luxury and extreme destitution impress one first of all.   Amazed
at the throng, which was an entirely unfamiliar
sight to him, this man of vivid imagination felt
something like a tremendous belittling of himself.
Those persons who enjoy any sort of consideration
in the provinces, and who meet at every step there
a proof of their eminence, are not accustomed to
this sudden, total loss of their importance.   To be
somebody in one's province and nobody in Paris
are two states which require some transitionary
stages; and those who pass too abruptly from one
to the other, fall into a dazed, inanimate condition.
For a young poet, who found an echo of all his feelings, a confidante for all his thoughts, a heart to
share his lightest sensations, Paris was certain to
be a horrible desert.

Lucien had not gone to get his fine blue coat, so
that he was embarrassed by the shabbiness, not to
say the dilapidation of his costume, as he betook
himself to Madame de Bargeton's when she was
likely to have returned; he found there the Baron
du Châtelet, who took them both to dine at the
Rocher de Cancale.   Lucien, bewildered by the rapid
movement of the Parisian vortex, could say nothing
to Louise, for they were all together in the carriage;
but he pressed her hand and she replied amicably

to all the thoughts that he expressed in that way. After dinner, Châtelet took his two guests to the Vaudeville. Lucien had a secret feeling of disgust at Châtelet's appearance in Paris and cursed the chance that brought him there. The superintendent of imposts attributed his trip to the capital to his ambition; he hoped to be appointed general secretary of a department, and to enter the Council of State as a Master of Requests; he had just demanded a fulfilment of the promises that had been made him, for such a man as he could not remain superintendent of imposts; he preferred to hold no office, to become a deputy, to re-enter the diplomatic service. He added to his own stature; Lucien recognized vaguely in this old beau, the superiority of the man of the world who is thoroughly at home in Parisian life; he was especially ashamed of owing his pleasures to him. Where the poet was ill at ease and embarrassed, the former secretary of despatches was like a fish in water. Châtelet smiled at the hesitation, the amazement, the questions, the petty errors of etiquette which lack of familiarity with society led his rival to commit, as the old sea-dog laughs at the novices who have not their sea-legs on.

The pleasure that Lucien experienced in attending the play in Paris for the first time atoned for the dissatisfaction due to his confusion. The evening was a noteworthy one because of his secret repudiation of a vast number of his ideas concerning provincial life. His mental horizon expanded,

society assumed different proportions. The proximity of several pretty Parisian women, fashionably
and coquettishly dressed, called his attention to
the antiquated appearance of Madame de Bargeton's
costume, although it was 'reasonably ambitious;
neither the·materials nor the colors nor the cut were
in the prevailing fashion. The style of wearing
the hair, which was considered so bewitching at
Angoulême, seemed to him in frightfully bad taste,
compared with the dainty contrivances by which
the other ladies about him commended themselves
to public notice.

"Will she always be like that?" he said to himself, unaware that the day had been employed in
arranging a transformation.

In the provinces, there is no opportunity to select
or compare; constant familiarity with the same
faces gives them a conventional sort of beauty. A
woman who is considered pretty in the provinces
does not attract the slightest attention when transported to Paris, for she is beautiful only by virtue of
the proverb: *In the kingdom of the blind, the one-
eyed are kings.* Lucien's eyes made the comparison
that Madame de Bargeton had made the night before between him and Châtelet. On her part, Madame de Bargeton indulged in some strange reflections concerning her lover. Despite his extraordinary beauty, the poor poet had no style. His
redingote, the sleeves of which were too short, his
shocking provincial gloves, his scanty waistcoat,
made him prodigiously absurd beside the young

men in the balcony; Madame de Bargeton thought
him a pitiful object. Châtelet, unpretentiously
interested in her welfare, and watching over her
with an attentiveness that betrayed a profound passion; Châtelet, refined and as thoroughly at ease as
an actor returning to the boards of his theatre,
regained in two days all the ground he had lost in
six months. Although it is not commonly admitted
that the sentiments change suddenly, it is certain
that lovers often part much more quickly than they
came together. On the part of both Madame de
Bargeton and Lucien, a season of disenchantment
was approaching of which Paris was the cause.
Life assumed larger proportions there in the eyes
of the poet, as society took on a new face in Louise's
eyes. In either case, only an accident was needed
to cut the bonds that united them. The blow, terrible to Lucien, was not long in coming. Madame
de Bargeton set down the poet at his hotel and
returned to her own quarters, accompanied by
Châtelet, an arrangement exceedingly distasteful
to the poor lover.

"What will they say about me?" he thought as
he went up to his gloomy bedroom.

"That poor boy is terribly tiresome," said Châtelet with a smile, when the carriage door was closed.

"That is true of all those who have a world of
thoughts in the heart and the brain. Men who have
so many things to express in great works which
they have long meditated over, profess a certain contempt for conversation, in which the mind lowers

itself by making itself common," said the haughty
Nègrepelisse, who still had the courage to defend
Lucien, less on Lucien's account than her own.

"I willingly grant you that," said the baron,
"but we are living with persons, not with books.
I see, dear Naïs, that there is nothing between you
as yet, and I am overjoyed. If you decide to import
into your life an interest that you have lacked
hitherto, do not, I implore you, let it be for this pretended man of genius. Suppose you should be mistaken! suppose that, a few days hence, upon
comparing him with men of genuine talent, with
the really noteworthy men you are going to meet,
you should see, my dear, lovely siren, that you
have taken upon your dazzlingly beautiful back and
carried into port, not a man armed with a tuneful
lyre, but a little monkey, unmannerly, of no depth, a
conceited fool, who may have wit at L'Houmeau,
but who becomes in Paris an exceedingly ordinary
young man! Why, volumes of verses are published
here every week, the poorest of which is worth
more than the whole of Monsieur Chardon's poetry.
For mercy's sake, wait and compare! To-morrow,
Friday, there is a performance at the Opéra," he
said, as the carriage entered Rue Neuve-de-Luxembourg; "Madame d'Espard has the box of the first
gentlemen of the chamber at her disposal, and will
take you, I doubt not. In order to see you in all
your glory, I will go and sit in Madame de Sérizy's
box.   They are to give *Les Danaïdes.*"

"Adieu," said she.

*

The next day, Madame de Bargeton tried to arrange a suitable morning costume in which to call
upon her cousin, Madame d'Espard.   It was slightly
cold and she could find nothing better among her
old-fashioned Angoulême properties than a certain
green velvet dress, rather richly trimmed.   Lucien,
too, deemed it essential to go and get his famous
blue coat, for he had conceived a horror of his
shabby redingote, and he determined to appear on
all occasions as well dressed as possible, thinking
that he might meet the Marquise d'Espard, or go to
her house unexpectedly.   He took a cab in order to
bring his bundle home at once.   In two hours' time,
he spent three or four francs, which caused him to
think seriously of the financial side of life in Paris.
After he had reached the superlative degree in the
matter of toilet, he went to Rue Neuve-de-Luxembourg, and there, on the doorstep, he met Gentil accompanied by an outrider magnificently beplumed.

"I was on my way to you, monsieur; madame
sends you this little note," said Gentil, who did
not know the gradations of respect in vogue in
Paris, accustomed as he was to the simple provincial manners.

The footman took the poet for a servant.   Lucien
unfolded the note, from which he learned that Madame de Bargeton was to pass the day with Madame

la Marquise d'Espard and to go to the Opéra in the evening; but she bade Lucien be there, for her cousin allowed her to offer the young poet a place in her box, being delighted to afford him that pleasure.

"She loves me then! my fears are unfounded," said Lucien to himself; "she will present me to her cousin this evening."

He leaped for joy and determined to pass pleasantly the hours that separated him from the happy evening. He hurried away to the Tuileries, thinking that he would walk there until it was time for him to go and dine at Véry's. Behold Lucien caracoling and prancing, elated with happiness, debouching upon the Terrasse des Feuillants, and walking across it, eying the promenaders, the pretty women with their swains, the dandies, two by two, arm in arm, saluting one another with a glance as they passed. What a contrast between that terrace and Beaulieu! The birds upon that magnificent perch were very different from those at Angoulême! It was like comparing the splendor of coloring that characterizes the ornithological species of the Indies or America with the dull colors of European birds.

Lucien passed two cruel hours at the Tuileries; he indulged in some serious reflections and judged himself. In the first place, he did not see a frock-coat upon one of the fashionable dandies. If he did occasionally spy a man in a frockcoat, it was some old man to whom the laws of fashion did not apply, some poor devil of an annuitant from the Marais, or a clerk from some office. After he had discovered that there was a difference between the correct garb for the evening, the poet of keen emotions and penetrating glance discovered the ugliness of his costume, the anomalies that made his frockcoat ridiculous, its antiquated cut, its faded blue color, its shockingly disgraceful collar, and its skirts, which had been worn too long and lapped over each other in front; the buttons were rusty and the seams marked with deadly white lines. His waistcoat was too short, also, and so grotesquely provincial that, in order to hide it, he abruptly buttoned his coat. Lastly, he saw no nankeen trousers except upon the common people. The fashionable folk wore lovely fancy stuffs, or else the always correct white! Moreover, all the trousers were worn with straps, whereas his hardly reached the heels of his boots, for which the frayed edges of the stuff manifested a violent antipathy. He had a white cravat, the ends of which were embroidered by his sister, who had lost no time, after seeing that Monsieur du Hautoy and Monsieur de Chandour wore ties of that description, in making some of them for her brother. Not only did no one save serious-minded persons, old financiers and stern-faced magistrates, wear white cravats in the morning, but Lucien saw through the iron fence on the sidewalk on Rue de Rivoli, a grocer's boy with a basket on his head and two floating cravat ends embroidered by some charming grisette. That sight stabbed Lucien to the heart, that still ill-defined organ in which our sensitiveness takes refuge and upon which men have laid their hands, in moments of excessive joy as well as of excessive sorrow, since sentiments have existed in the world.

Do not tax this narrative with puerility. Of course, to the wealthy who have never known suffering of this sort, there is something paltry and incredible about it; but the agony of the unhappy is no less deserving of attention than the crises that revolutionize the lives of the powerful and privileged ones of earth. Indeed, do we not find as much grief in the one case as in the other? Suffering magnifies everything. Change the conditions, if you please; in place of a costume of more or less magnificence, take a ribbon, a mark of favor, a title. Have not those apparently trivial things been the torment of many a brilliant existence? Moreover, the question of costume is one of vast moment to those who wish to appear to have what they have not; for that is often the best means of procuring it later. Lucien felt a cold perspiration break out upon him when he thought that he had proposed to appear in the evening, in that costume, before the Marquise d'Espard, the kinswoman of one of the first gentlemen of the chamber to the king, before a woman whose salon was frequented by the most eminent men in all walks of life, by the choicest minds of the age.

"I look like an apothecary's son, a genuine counter-jumper!" he said to himself, raging inwardly as he watched the graceful, dandified,

fashionable young men of Faubourg Saint-Germain,
all of whom had a manner peculiar to themselves,
which made them all resemble one another in their
slender figures, their noble bearing and their general
expression; and all differ from one another in the
frames that each had selected in which to display
his charms. All of them made the most of their
good points by a sort of stage setting which young
men in Paris understand as well as women. Lucien
inherited from his mother the same invaluable
physical qualities whose privileges were flaunted
before his eyes by these dandies; but the gold was
in the quartz and still unworked. His hair was
badly cut. Instead of keeping his head erect by a
flexible whalebone, he felt all drawn together in his
uncomfortable shirt collar; and his cravat offered
no resistance to his tendency to hang his humiliated
head. What woman could have imagined the pretty
feet that were hidden in the shapeless boots he had
brought from Angoulême? What young man would
have envied his graceful figure disguised in the blue
bag he had hitherto believed to be a coat? He saw
fascinating buttons upon shirts that fairly gleamed
with whiteness; his own was rusty! All the fashionable dandies were elegantly gloved, and he wore
regular gendarme's gloves! One toyed with a
beautifully mounted cane. Another wore dainty
little gold buttons in his wristbands. One of them,
as he talked with a lady, swung a pretty hunting
crop, and his baggy trousers slightly spotted with
mud, his glistening spurs and his closely buttoned

riding coat, showed that he was about to mount one
of the two horses held by a tiger no larger than
one's fist.   Another took from his pocket a flat
watch of the size of a hundred-sou piece, and
looked at the time, like a man who was before or
behind the hour fixed for an appointment.   As he
noticed these pretty trifles, whose existence he had
not suspected, Lucien began to conceive some idea
of the multitude of necessary superfluities, and he
shuddered as he thought that it must require an
enormous capital to ply the trade of a fashionable
bachelor!   The more he admired these young men
with their joyous, off-hand manners, the more conscious he became of his own strange manner, the
manner of a man who has no idea whither the road
leads that he is following, who does not know the
Palais-Royal when he is touching it, and who asks
the whereabouts of the Louvre from a passer-by, to
receive the answer: "You are there now."   Lucien felt that an abyss lay between him and those
others; he asked himself by what means he could
cross it, for he was determined to make himself like
those slender and refined Parisian youths.   All the
young patricians were constantly bowing to divinely
dressed and divinely beautiful women, for a single
kiss from whom Lucien would gladly have been cut
in pieces, like the Comtesse de Kœnigsmark's page.
In the recesses of his memory, Louise appeared like
an old woman, in comparison with those queens of
beauty.   He met several of those women whose
names will appear in the history of the nineteenth

century, and whose wit and beauty and love will be
no less famous than those of the queens of the past.
He passed one sublime creature, Mademoiselle des
Touches, so well known under the name of Camille
Maupin, an eminent writer, as remarkable for her
beauty as for her superior mind, whose name was
repeated in undertones by all the promenaders,
both young men and women.

"Ah!" said he to himself, "there is poesy."

What was Madame de Bargeton beside that angel,
radiant with youth and hope and future renown,
whose smile was so sweet, and whose black eye was
as vast as the vault of heaven, as ardent as the
sun? She was laughing and talking with Madame
de Firmiani, one of the most delightful women in
Paris. A voice cried to him: "Intellect is the
lever with which the world is moved." But another
voice answered that the fulcrum of the lever of intellect is money. He did not choose to remain amid
his ruins and on the stage of his discomfiture, so he
betook himself to the Palais-Royal, having first
asked where it was, for he did not as yet know the
topography of his own quarter. He went to Véry's,
and ordered, as an initiation into the pleasures of
Paris, a dinner that somewhat allayed his chagrin.
A bottle of Bordeaux, Ostend oysters, a fish, a
partridge, an ice and some fruit were the ne plus
ultra of his desires. He relished his little dissipation, thinking how he would demonstrate his wit in
the evening in the Marquise d'Espard's presence,
and atone for the shabbiness of his anomalous garb

17

by the manifestation of his intellectual powers. He was awakened from his dreams by the footing of his account, which despoiled him of the fifty francs with which he expected to do a great deal in Paris. That one dinner cost as much as he spent in a whole month at Angoulême. So he respectfully closed the door of that palace, thinking that he would never again put his foot therein.

"Eve was right," he said to himself as he walked homeward through the stone gallery, in order to replenish his purse; "Paris prices differ from prices at L'Houmeau."

On his way he gazed admiringly into the tailors' shops, and, as he remembered the costumes he had seen in the morning, he cried:

"No, I will not appear before Madame d'Espard in such a rig as this!"

He ran like a deer to the *Gaillard-Bois*, went up to his room, took a hundred crowns and hurried back to the Palais-Royal to refit from head to foot. He had noticed the shops of bootmakers, haberdashers, vestmakers and hairdressers at the Palais-Royal, and his future elegance was scattered through ten establishments. The first tailor he visited made him try on as many coats as he would consent to try on, and persuaded him that they were all in the latest style. Lucien, when he took his leave, possessed a green coat, white trousers and a fancy waistcoat, all for the sum of two hundred francs. He soon found a very neat pair of boots that fitted him perfectly. Finally, after he had purchased

everything he required, he sent for the hairdresser
to come to his room, where each dealer brought the
goods he had bought. At seven in the evening, he
called a cab and was driven to the Opéra, curled
like an image of Saint-Jean in a procession, well
waistcoated, well cravated, but a little uncomfortable in the sort of mould in which he was incased
for the first time in his life. Following Madame de
Bargeton's directions, he asked for the box assigned
to the first gentleman-in-waiting. Seeing a man
whose borrowed elegance gave him the air of the
best man at a wedding, the ticket-taker requested
him to show his ticket.

"I have none."

"Then you cannot go in," was the sharp reply.

"But I am invited by Madame d'Espard," he
said.

"We are not supposed to know that," said the
attendant, exchanging an imperceptible smile with
his associates.

At that moment a coupé drove under the peristyle.
An outrider, whom Lucien did not recognize, let
down the step and two ladies in full dress alighted.
Lucien, who did not wish to receive from the ticket-
taker an impertinent request to stand aside, made
room for the two ladies.

"But this lady is the Marquise d'Espard, whom
you claim to know, monsieur," said the ticket-taker
ironically to Lucien.

Lucien was the more abashed because Madame
de Bargeton did not seem to recognize him in his

new plumage; but, when he walked toward her, she smiled at him and said:

"This is extraordinary; come!"

The attendants had become serious once more. Lucien followed Madame de Bargeton, who, as they ascended the spacious staircase of the Opéra, presented her Rubempré to her cousin. The box of the first gentleman-in-waiting is in one of the flattened corners at the rear of the hall; there one can be seen from and can see all parts of the great auditorium. Lucien took a chair behind Madame de Bargeton, well pleased to sit in the shadow.

"Monsieur de Rubempré," said the marchioness, in a flattering tone, "this is your first visit to the Opéra; you must see all there is to be seen, so take this chair at the front of the box; we will excuse you."

Lucien obeyed; the first act of the opera was just coming to an end.

"You have employed your time to good advantage," said Louise in his ear, amazed at the change in Lucien's appearance.

Louise remained the same. The proximity of a woman of fashion, the Marquise d'Espard, the Madame de Bargeton of Paris, was so disadvantageous to her; the brilliant Parisian brought into such bold relief the imperfections of the woman from the provinces, that Lucien, doubly enlightened by the gorgeous company assembled in that superb hall, and by his eminent hostess, at last saw Anaïs de Nègrepelisse as she really was, as the people of

Paris saw her: tall, thin, pimply, faded, more than
red-haired, angular, stiff, formal, conceited, provincial in her speech, and above all things, badly
dressed! In Paris a dress may be old and still its
folds will attest its owner's taste; you can understand it and divine what it once was; but an old
provincial dress is an inexplicable mystery, it is
laughable. The dress and its wearer were alike devoid of charm and freshness, the velvet was mottled
like the complexion. Lucien, ashamed of having
loved such a cuttle-bone, determined that he would
take advantage of Louise's first spasm of virtue to
leave her. His excellent eyesight enabled him to
see all the opera-glasses brought to bear upon the
aristocratic box, *par excellence.* The most fashionable women were certainly scrutinizing Madame de
Bargeton, for they all smiled as they talked to one
another.

If Madame d'Espard gathered, from the gestures
and smiles of those of her own sex, the source of
their amusement, she was entirely indifferent to
it. In the first place, everyone was sure to recognize in her companion the poor kinswoman from the
provinces, with whom every Parisian family is
likely to be afflicted. Then, too, her cousin had
mentioned the subject of her toilet, expressing some
apprehension in that direction; she reassured her,
for she saw that when Anaïs was once properly
dressed, she would soon acquire Parisian manners.
If Madame de Bargeton lacked practice, she had the
inborn *hauteur* of a woman of noble birth, and the

indefinable something that may be called *race*. On the following Monday, therefore, she would have her revenge. Moreover, when it was once known that her guest was her cousin, the marchioness knew that the public would suspend its raillery and await an opportunity to examine her more closely before passing judgment upon her.

Lucien did not foresee the change that would be wrought in Louise by a scarf wound about her neck, a pretty dress, a fashionable arrangement of her hair and Madame d'Espard's advice. Even as they ascended the stairs, the marchioness told her cousin not to carry her handkerchief unfolded in her hand. Good or bad taste depends upon innumerable little trifles of this sort, which a bright woman grasps at once and which some women will never understand. Madame de Bargeton, whose will was of the best, was more clever than she required to be to discover wherein she went astray. Madame d'Espard, sure that her pupil would do her credit, did not shirk the task of moulding her. In fact, an agreement had been entered into by the two women, and cemented by their mutual interests. Madame de Bargeton had suddenly become a devoted worshiper of the idol of the day, whose manners, wit and surroundings had fascinated, dazzled, enchanted her. She had recognized in Madame d'Espard the occult power of the ambitious great lady, and had said to herself that she would strive to become the satellite of that planet: she had therefore frankly expressed her admiration. The marchioness was touched by her undisguised conquest, and had at once taken a deep interest in her cousin, finding her to be poor and unfriended; she had shrewdly laid her plans to found a school of her own by having a pupil, and she asked nothing better than to acquire in Madame de Bargeton a sort of lady-in-waiting, a slave who would sing her praises, a treasure rarer among Parisian women than an honest critic in the literary world. But the general curiosity became too perceptible for the newcomer not to notice it, and Madame d'Espard determined courteously to mislead her as to the cause of the excitement.

"If they come and call on us," she said, "perhaps we shall find out to what we owe the honor of such earnest attention on the part of all these ladies."

"I strongly suspect my old velvet dress and my Angoumois figure of amusing the Parisians," said Madame de Bargeton, laughing.

"No, it's not you; there's something I can't understand," she added, turning to the poet, whom she then looked at for the first time and seemed to think strangely attired.

"There's Monsieur du Châtelet," said Lucien at that moment, raising his finger to point to Madame de Sérizy's box, where the old beau, thoroughly renovated, had just made his appearance.

At that gesture, Madame de Bargeton bit her lips with annoyance, for the marchioness could not restrain a glance and a smile of amazement, which said so contemptuously: "Where does this young man come from?'' that Louise felt deeply humiliated in her love, the most painful sensation a French woman can experience, and one that she never forgives her lover for causing. In that society, where trifles are magnified into great things, a gesture, a word, may ruin the chances of a beginner. The principal advantage of the fine manners and the tone of good society is to present a harmonious whole, in which everything is so perfectly blended that nothing offends. The very persons who, whether it be through ignorance or because their thoughts are engrossed by something else and fail to observe the laws of this science, will all agree that a single discordant note is, as it is in music, a complete nullification of the art itself, for all its conditions must be fulfilled to the least detail, under pain of ceasing to exist at all.

"Who is that gentleman?" asked the marchioness, indicating Châtelet. "Do you know Madame de Sérizy?"

"Ah! so that is the famous Madame de Sérizy, who has had so many adventures and still is received everywhere!"

"An unheard-of thing, my dear," the marchioness replied, "a thing capable of explanation, but unexplained! The most redoubtable men are her friends, and why? No one dares probe the mystery. Is yonder gentleman the lion of Angoulême?"

"Why, Monsieur le Baron du Châtelet," said Anaïs, through vanity bestowing upon her adorer in Paris the title she denied him in the country, "is a man who has been much talked of. He is Monsieur de Montriveau's traveling companion."

"Ah!" exclaimed the marchioness, "I never hear that name without thinking of the poor Duchesse de Langeais, who has disappeared like a shooting star.—There," she continued, pointing to another box, "are Monsieur de Rastignac and Madame de Nucingen, the wife of a contractor, banker, agent, broker on a large scale, a man who forces himself into Parisian society by virtue of his wealth, and is said to be by no means scrupulous as to methods of increasing it; he takes unheard-of pains to make people believe in his fidelity to the Bourbons; he has already tried to be introduced to my house. By taking Madame de Langeais's box, his wife thought she would inherit her charms, her wit and her success! The old fable of the jackdaw in peacock's feathers!"

"How do Monsieur and Madame de Rastignac, whom we know to have less than three thousand francs a year, manage to support their son in Paris?" said Lucien to Madame de Bargeton, amazed at the style and luxury displayed in the young man's dress.

"It is easy to see that you come from Angoulême," said the marchioness satirically, without taking her opera-glass from her eyes.

Lucien did not understand; he was entirely engrossed in looking at the boxes, divining the criticisms that were being made upon Madame de Bargeton, and the curiosity of which he was himself the object. For her part, Louise was deeply mortified by the marchioness's lack of appreciation of Lucien's beauty.

"Then he can't be as handsome as I thought!" she said to herself.

From that point, it was but a step to thinking that he was less clever. The curtain fell. Châtelet, who had come to pay his respects to the Duchesse de Carigliano, whose box was quite near Madame d'Espard's, bowed to Madame de Bargeton, who replied with a slight inclination of the head. A woman of the world sees everything, and the marchioness noticed Châtelet's superior bearing. At that juncture, four persons entered the marchioness's box, one after another—four Parisian celebrities.

The first was Monsieur de Marsay, a man famous for the passions he aroused, and especially remarkable for his girlish beauty, soft and effeminate, but redeemed by a fixed, calm glance, as fierce and uncompromising as a tiger's; he was loved and feared. Lucien, too, was handsome; but his glance was so gentle, his blue eye so clear, that he did not seem capable of the strength and power which attract women. Moreover, nothing had as yet shown the poet's temper, while De Marsay had a flow of wit, a certainty of pleasing, a costume adapted to his character, which crushed all his rivals. Imagine how Lucien, grim, solemn, stiff and new as his clothes, would appear beside him! De Marsay had earned the right to say impertinent things by the wit he imparted to them and by the charming manners with which he accompanied them. The marchioness's reception made clear at once to Madame de Bargeton the power of the man.

The second was one of the two Vandenesses, he who had caused the Lady Dudley scandal, a sweet-tempered, clever, modest young man, whose success was due to qualities diametrically opposed to those upon which De Marsay plumed himself, and whom the marchioness's cousin, Madame de Mortsauf, had warmly recommended to her.

The third was General de Montriveau, author of the ruin of the Duchesse de Langeais.

The fourth was Monsieur de Canalis, one of the most illustrious poets of that epoch, a young man still at the dawn of his renown, who, prouder of being a gentleman than of his talent, posed as Madame d'Espard's devoted slave, in order to conceal his passion for the Duchesse de Chaulieu. Despite his charming manners, somewhat marred by affectation, his friends already suspected the soaring ambition that led him at a later period into the tempests of political life. His almost girlish beauty and his flattering ways hardly disguised his profound selfishness and the constant scheming of an existence which was at this time an unsolved problem; but his choice of Madame de Chaulieu, a woman past forty, secured for him the favor of the court, the approbation of Faubourg Saint-Germain, and the insults of the liberals, who called him a poet of the sacristy.

When she saw those four noteworthy faces, Madame de Bargeton understood the slight attention the marchioness had paid to Lucien. And when the conversation began, when each of those keen, subtle minds made itself manifest by remarks that contained more sense and more depth than all that Anaïs heard in a month in Angoulême; when the great poet especially uttered vibrating words that reflected the positive character of the time, but gilded with poesy, she realized the truth of what Châtelet had said to her the day before: Lucien was nothing at all. One and all glanced at the unhappy stranger with such cruel indifference, his position was so exactly that of a foreigner unacquainted with the language, that the marchioness took pity on him.

"Permit me, monsieur," she said to Canalis, "to present Monsieur de Rubempré. You occupy too lofty a position in the literary world not to welcome a beginner. Monsieur de Rubempré is just from Angoulême, and he will need your patronage, I doubt not, with those whose business it is to bring genius to light. He has as yet no enemies to make his fortune by attacking him. Would it not be an undertaking so original as to be worth trying, to obtain for him through friendship, what you owe to hatred?"

The four young men looked at Lucien while the marchioness was speaking. Although he was within two feet of the newcomer, De Marsay took his monocle to look at him; his eyes went from Lucien

to Madame de Bargeton and from Madame de Bargeton to Lucien, coupling them together with a sneering glance that mortified them both cruelly; he
looked them over as if they were two strange animals, and he smiled. His smile was a dagger-
thrust to the provincial great man. Félix de
Vandenesse assumed a charitable expression. Montriveau bestowed a glance upon Lucien that probed
him to the marrow.

"Madame," said Canalis, bowing, "I will obey
you, notwithstanding the personal interest that in-
clines us not to assist our rivals; but you have
accustomed us to miracles."

"Very well; give me the pleasure of your company at dinner with Monsieur de Rubempré on
Monday; you can then talk over literary matters
more comfortably than here; I will try to collect
some of the tyrants of literature and the celebrities
who take it under their wing; the author of *Ourika*
and some well-inclined young poets.

"Madame la Marquise," said De Marsay, "if you
take monsieur under your protection for his wit, I
will take him under mine for his beauty; I will
give him some good advice which will make him
the luckiest dandy in Paris. After that he can be
a poet if he chooses."

Madame de Bargeton thanked the marchioness by
a glance overflowing with gratitude.

"I didn't know that you were jealous of bright
men," said Montriveau to De Marsay. "Happiness
kills poets."

"Is that why monsieur is anxious to marry?"
said the dandy, addressing Canalis, in order to see
if Madame d'Espard would be hit by the question.

Canalis shrugged his shoulders, and Madame
d'Espard, who was Madame de Chaulieu's niece,
began to laugh.

Lucien, who felt in his new clothes like an Egyp-
tian mummy in its sheath, was ashamed to make
no reply.   At last he said to the marchioness in his
soft voice:

"Your kindness, madame, dooms me to have
nothing but success."

At that moment Châtelet, seizing the opportunity
by the hair to secure Montriveau, one of the kings
of Paris, as his sponsor with the marchioness, entered the box.   He bowed to Madame de Bargeton
and begged Madame d'Espard to forgive the liberty
he took in invading her box; it was so long since
he had seen his traveling companion!   It was the
first time he and Montriveau had met since they
parted in the desert.

"To part in the desert and meet at the Opéra!"
said Lucien.

"It's a genuine stage meeting," said Canalis.

Montriveau presented the Baron du Châtelet to
the marchioness, and the marchioness accorded the·
ex-secretary of despatches to her Imperial Highness
the more flattering welcome, because she had seen
that he was well received in three boxes, because
Madame de Sérizy admitted none but available
men, and lastly because he was Montriveau's

traveling companion.   This last title to her regard
was so powerful that Madame de Bargeton could see
in the tone, the expressions and the manners of the
four men that they recognized Châtelet as one of
themselves without hesitation.   The sultan-like
manner adopted by Châtelet in the provinces was
at once explained to Naïs.   Lastly Châtelet recognized Lucien and gave him one of those cool, abrupt
nods by which one man casts discredit upon another,
indicating to his fellows the infinitely humble position that that other occupies in society.   He accompanied his salutation with a sardonic smile, which
seemed to say: "How does he happen to be here?"
Châtelet's manner was fully understood; for De
Marsay leaned over to Montriveau and whispered
in his ear, loud enough for the baron to hear:

"Ask him who this extraordinary young man is,
who looks like a manikin at a tailor's door."

Châtelet spoke for a moment aside with his old
friend, as if they were renewing their acquaintance,
and doubtless he cut his rival in small pieces.   Surprised by the ready wit, by the acuteness with which
these men shaped their replies, Lucien was bewildered by what is called the *trait*, the *mot*, and especially by the freedom of their conversation and
their ease of manner.   The luxury that had dismayed him in the morning as applied to things, he
found now displayed in ideas.   He asked himself by
what mysterious means these people always found
brilliant thoughts ready to their tongues, repartees
which he could not have invented except after long

meditation. And then these five men of the world were entirely at ease, not only in their speech, but in their clothes; they wore nothing new and nothing old. Nothing about them glistened with newness, but everything attracted the eye. Their splendor of to-day was that of yesterday and would be that of to-morrow. Lucien realized that he acted like a man who was dressed for the first time in his life.

"My dear fellow," said De Marsay to Félix de Vandenesse, "that young Rastignac is soaring like a kite! there he is with the Marquise de Listomère, he is making progress; he's looking at us! Doubtless he knows monsieur?" added the dandy, addressing Lucien but not looking at him.

"It is strange," said Madame de Bargeton, "if the name of the great man of whom we are so proud has not reached his ears; his sister recently heard Monsieur de Rubempré read some very beautiful verses."

Félix de Vandenesse and De Marsay took leave of the marchioness and went to the box of Madame de Listomère, Vandenesse's sister. The second act began and Madame d'Espard, her cousin and Lucien were left alone. Some went to explain Madame de Bargeton to the ladies who were puzzled by her presence, others told of the poet's arrival and laughed at his costume. Canalis returned to Madame de Chaulieu's box and remained there. Lucien was glad of the diversion afforded by the renewal of the performance. Madame de Bargeton's apprehensions relative to him were augmented by the attention her cousin had paid to the Baron du Châtelet, which was very different from her patronizing courtesy to Lucien. During the second act, Madame de Listomère's box continued full of people and its occupants seemed excited by a conversation of which Madame de Bargeton and Lucien were the theme. Young Rastignac was evidently the entertainer of the party; he set the key for that Parisian laughter, which, seeking every day a new feeding-ground, hastens to exhaust the latest subject by converting it into something old and worn out in a single moment. Madame d'Espard, knowing that a person who is wounded by a calumny is never left long in ignorance of it, uneasily awaited the end of the act.

When the sentiments have begun to scrutinize themselves as in the case of Lucien and Madame de Bargeton, strange things come to pass in a short time: moral revolutions are governed by the law of swift results. Louise had always present in her memory the wise and politic words concerning Lucien that Châtelet had said to her in returning from the Vaudeville. Every sentence was a prophecy, and Lucien seemed to have undertaken to bring them all to pass.

Losing his illusions concerning Madame de Bargeton as she lost hers concerning him, the poor fellow, whose destiny was not unlike Jean-Jacques Rousseau's, imitated him to the extent of being fascinated by Madame d'Espard, and he fell in love with her at once. Young people and men who remember

18

their youthful emotions, will understand how natural
and likely to be aroused that passion was. The
pretty little manners, the refined speech, the melodious voice, the willowy, nobly-born woman, so
highly placed, so envied, a queen, appeared to the
poet as Madame de Bargeton appeared to him at
Angoulême. The mobility of his character impelled
him strongly to desire such eminent patronage; the
surest way was to possess the woman, then he
would have everything! He had succeeded at Angoulême, why should he not succeed in Paris? Involuntarily, and despite the fascinations of the
Opéra which were entirely novel to him, his eyes,
attracted by the magnificent Célimène, constantly
returned to her; and the more he looked at her, the
more he longed to look at her! Madame de Bargeton surprised one of his speaking glances; she
watched him and saw that he was more engrossed
by the marchioness than by the performance. She
would have resigned herself gracefully to be neglected for the fifty daughters of Danaus; but when
a more ambitious, more ardent, more significant
glance than the others told her what was taking
place in Lucien's heart, she became jealous, less for
the future than for the past.

"He never looked at me that way," she thought.
"*Mon Dieu*, Châtelet was right!"

She realized thereupon the error of her love.
When a woman reaches the point of repenting of
her weakness, she passes a sponge over her life, as
it were, to wipe it all out. Although every one of

Lucien's glances angered her, she remained out-
wardly calm.   De Marsay returned between the
acts with Monsieur de Listomère.   The middle-aged
man and the young fop lost no time in informing
the haughty marchioness that the wedding guest in
his Sunday clothes whom she had had the ill-fortune
to admit to her box was no more Monsieur de Rubempré than a Jew has a baptismal name.   Lucien
was the son of an apothecary named Chardon.
Monsieur de Rastignac, who was thoroughly posted
upon Angoulême affairs, had already amused two
boxes at the expense of the species of mummy
whom the marchioness called her cousin, and of
that lady's wise precaution in having an apothecary
always in attendance, for the evident purpose of
keeping up her artificial life with drugs.   In a word,
De Marsay repeated a few of the innumerable jests
which amuse Parisians for a moment and are forgotten as soon as made, but behind which was Châtelet, the artisan of this particular example of
Punic faith.

"My dear," said Madame d'Espard behind her
fan to Madame de Bargeton, "I pray you, tell me if
your protégé is really named De Rubempré?"

"He has taken his mother's name," said the embarrassed Anaïs.

"But what is his father's name?"

"Chardon."

"And what does this Chardon do?"

"He was a druggist."

"I was very sure, my dear friend, that all Paris

would not make sport of a woman whom I take up.
I don't care about receiving visits here from jocose
young men, delighted to find me with an apothecary's son; if you wish to gratify me, you will go
out with me, and at once."

Madame d'Espard assumed a decidedly impertinent expression, Lucien being entirely unable to
guess in what way he had occasioned the alteration
in her features. He thought that his waistcoat
must be in bad taste, which was true; that the cut
of his coat exaggerated the prevailing fashion,
which was also true. He realized, with secret bitterness of heart, that he must procure his clothes
from a fashionable tailor, and he determined that
he would go the next day to the most famous of
them all, so that he might be able on the following
Monday to hold his own with the men he was to
meet at Madame d'Espard's. Although he was lost
in his reflections, he was interested in the third act,
and his eyes did not leave the stage. While he
watched the pompous progress of that unique spectacle, he abandoned himself to his dream concerning Madame d'Espard. He was in despair at her
sudden coldness, which thwarted sadly the intellectual ardor with which he attacked this new passion,
heedless of the enormous difficulties which he per-
ceived in his path and which he vowed that he
would overcome. He roused himself from his profound meditation to look again at his new idol; but,
when he turned his head, he found that he was
alone; he had heard a slight noise, it was the door

closing behind Madame d'Espard and her cousin.
Lucien was surprised to the last degree by this sudden desertion, but he did not think about it long,
just because he found it inexplicable.

When the two women had entered their carriage
and were rolling through Rue de Richelieu toward
Faubourg Saint-Honoré, the marchioness said, dis-
guising her wrath:

"My dear child, what are you thinking about?
pray wait till an apothecary's son is really famous
before taking an interest in him. The Duchesse
de Chaulieu doesn't acknowledge Canalis yet, and
he is famous and a gentleman. This fellow is
neither your son nor your lover, is he?" said the
haughty woman, darting a keen, piercing glance at
her cousin.

"How lucky for me that I always kept the little
fool at a distance and never granted him anything,"
thought Madame de Bargeton.

"Very well," continued the marchioness, taking
the expression in her cousin's eyes for a reply,
"drop him, I implore you. What presumption to
assume an illustrious name!—why, that's the kind
of audacity that society punishes. I admit that it's
his mother's name; but consider, my dear, that the
king alone has the right, by royal decree, to confer
the name of Rubempré on the son of a daughter of
that family; if she has married beneath her, it
would be a very great favor, and, to obtain it, one
must have immense wealth or very exalted patronage, or must have rendered some service to the

government. That costume of a dressed-up shopkeeper proves that the boy is neither rich nor of
gentle birth; he has a beautiful face, but he seems
to me a great booby; he doesn't know how to act
or speak; in short, he has no *breeding*. How do you
happen to have him under your wing?"

Madame de Bargeton, who denied Lucien as Lucien had denied her in his mind, shuddered to think
that her cousin might learn the truth touching her
journey.

"I am in despair at having compromised you,
my dear cousin."

"I am not to be compromised," said Madame
d'Espard with a smile. "I am thinking only of
you."

"But you invited him to dine with you Monday."

"I shall be ill," replied the marchioness, hastily;
"you must write and tell him of it and I will give
my people orders to keep him out whichever name
he gives."

*

It occurred to Lucien to walk in the foyer between the acts, as he saw that everybody seemed to do it. In the first place, none of the men who had come to Madame d'Espard's box bowed to him or seemed to pay any attention to him, a fact which seemed most extraordinary to the provincial poet. In the second place, Châtelet, to whom he attempted to cling, watched him out of the corner of his eye and constantly avoided him. Having become further convinced, after watching the men who were strolling about the foyer, that his costume was absurd, Lucien returned to his place in the corner of the box and, during the remainder of the performance, his mind was engrossed in turn by the magnificent spectacle of the ballet in the fifth act, famous for its representation of *Hell;* by the auditorium, where his eyes wandered from box to box, and by his own reflections, which were most profound in the presence of Parisian society.

"This is my kingdom," he said; "this is the world I must conquer!"

He returned home on foot, musing on all that had been said by the people who came to pay court to Madame d'Espard; their manner, their gestures, their way of entering and leaving the box, everything came back to his memory with astonishing accuracy. The next day, toward noon, he made it his business to call upon Staub, the most celebrated tailor of the time. By dint of entreaties and by the persuasive power of cash, he obtained a promise that his clothes should be ready for the famous Monday. Staub went so far as to promise him a beautiful redingote, a waistcoat and a pair of trousers for the decisive day. Lucien ordered shirts and handkerchiefs, in short, a complete little trousseau at a haberdasher's, and was measured for boots and shoes by a famous bootmaker. He purchased a pretty cane at Verdier's, gloves and shirt buttons at Madame Irlande's; in a word, he tried to place himself on the level of the dandies. When he had satisfied all his fancies, he went to Rue Neuve-de-Luxembourg and found that Louise had gone out.

"She dines with Madame la Marquise d'Espard and will not return till late," said Albertine.

Lucien dined for forty sous at a restaurant in the Palais Royal and went to bed early. On Sunday he called upon Louise about eleven o'clock; she had not risen. He returned at two o'clock.

"Madame does not receive yet," said Albertine, "but she gave me a little note for you."

"She doesn't receive yet?" Lucien repeated. "But I am not—"

"I don't know," said Albertine with an impertinent toss of her head.

Lucien, less surprised at Albertine's reply than to receive a letter from Madame de Bargeton, took the note and read these crushing words:

" Madame d'Espard is not well, she will not be able to receive you on Monday; I am not well myself, and yet I am going to dress and go and sit with her. I am in despair at this difficulty; but I am comforted when I think of your talents; you will make your way without charlatanism."

"No signature!" said Lucien to himself, finding himself in the Tuileries without any consciousness of having walked thither.

The gift of second sight that talented men possess, made him suspect the catastrophe foreshadowed by this cold note. Lost in his thoughts, he walked straight ahead, staring at the monuments on Place Louis XV. It was a beautiful day. Handsome carriages rolled by him in endless succession on their way to the broad Avenue des Champs-Elysées. He followed the throng of promenaders and saw the three or four thousand carriages that always drive back and forth on a pleasant Sunday and make of it an improvised Longchamp. Dazzled by the magnificence of the horses, the toilets and the liveries, he went on and on until he reached the Arc de Triomphe, recently begun. What were his thoughts when, as he turned back, he saw Madame de Bargeton and Madame d'Espard driving toward him in an admirably appointed calèche, behind which appeared the waving plumes of the footman, whose gold-embroidered green coat first drew his attention to them. The long line of carriages stopped in consequence of a block, and Lucien saw Louise in her transformed state; she was hardly recognizable: the colors of her costume were chosen to suit her complexion;

her dress was lovely; her hair was beautifully
arranged and became her wonderfully, and her
hat, which was in exquisite taste, was noticeable
even beside Madame d'Espard's, who ruled the
fashion.   There is an indescribable way of wearing
a hat: put it a little too far back and you have a
brazen look; put it too far forward and you have a
cunning look; on one side, your appearance becomes
rakish; but *comme il faut* women wear their hats
as they please and always look well.   Madame de
Bargeton had instantly solved that curious problem.
A pretty girdle encircled her slender waist.   She
had copied her cousin's manners and gestures; sitting in the same attitude, she was playing with a
dainty smelling-bottle, attached to one of the fingers
of her right hand by a gold chain, and in that way
exhibited her shapely, well-gloved hand without
apparently intending to show it.   In short, she had
made herself like Madame d'Espard without simply
aping her; she was the worthy cousin of the marchioness, who seemed to be proud of her pupil.
The men and women who were walking on the foot-
way stared at the superb carriage with the arms of
the D'Espards and the Blamont-Chauvrys, the two
escutcheons being placed back to back.

Lucien was amazed at the great number of persons who bowed to the cousins; he was not aware
that all Paris, which consists of about twenty
salons, already knew all about the relationship
between Madame de Bargeton and Madame d'Espard.
Young men on horseback, among whom Lucien

recognized De Marsay and Rastignac, rode beside
the calèche, to escort the cousins to the Bois. It
was easy for Lucien to see, by the actions of the
two fops, that they were complimenting Madame
de Bargeton on her metamorphosis. Madame
d'Espard was glowing with grace and health; her
indisposition therefore was simply a pretext for not
receiving Lucien, as she did not fix another day for
the dinner. The poet, in a frenzy, approached the
carriage, walking very slowly, and, when he was
within the two ladies' range of vision, bowed to
them: Madame de Bargeton pretended not to see
him, the marchioness stared at him through her
glass and did not acknowledge his salutation. The
reprobation of the Parisian aristocracy was not like
that of the sovereigns of Angoulême: by putting
themselves out to wound Lucien, the provincial
clodhoppers acknowledged his power and admitted
that he was a man; whereas, to Madame d'Espard,
he simply did not exist. It was not a decree, it
was a denial of justice. A deathly chill seized the
poor poet when De Marsay put his glass to his eye
and stared at him; the Parisian let his glass drop
in such a peculiar way that it seemed to Lucien
like the knife of the guillotine. The calèche passed
on. Impotent rage, a mad thirst for vengeance,
seized upon the disdained youth; if he had had his
hands upon Madame de Bargeton, he would have
strangled her; he imagined himself Fouquier-Tin-
ville in order to have the pleasure of sending Madame d'Espard to the scaffold; he would have liked

to subject De Marsay to one of the refined torments
invented by savages. He saw Canalis pass on
horseback, elegantly attired as befitted the most
flattering of poets, and saluting the prettiest women.

"My God! I must have money at any cost!"
cried Lucien; "Money is the only power at whose
feet these people kneel."—"No!" cried his conscience, "but glory, and glory means work! Work!
that is David's watchword."—"My God! why am
I here? But I will triumph! I will drive along
this avenue with a carriage and footmen! I will
have Marquises d'Espard!"

With these frantic words on his lips, he dined at
Hurbain's for forty sous. The next morning at nine
o'clock, he called upon Louise to reproach her
for her barbarity; not only was Madame de Bargeton not at home to him, but the concierge would not
even admit him; he remained in the street, watching until noon. At noon, Châtelet came out, saw
the poet out of the corner of his eye and tried to
avoid him. Lucien, cut to the quick, pursued his
rival; Châtelet, finding that he was hard pressed,
turned and bowed, with the evident intention of
making sail again at once after this act of courtesy.

"In pity's name, monsieur," said Lucien, "give
me one second of your time; I have a few words to
say to you. You have manifested some friendliness
to me, and I invoke your friendship to confer upon
me the most trivial of favors. You have just left
Madame de Bargeton; tell me why I am in disgrace
with her and Madame d'Espard."

"Monsieur Chardon," replied Châtelet with feigned kindliness, "do you know why those ladies left you at the Opéra?"

"No," said the poor poet.

"Well, you have been badly served from the beginning by Monsieur de Rastignac. That young dandy, when he was questioned about you, answered baldly that your name was Chardon and not De Rubempré; that your mother was a monthly nurse; that your father in his lifetime was an apothecary at L'Houmeau, a suburb of Angoulême; that your sister was a charming girl who laundered shirts beautifully, and that she was going to marry a printer named Séchard. That is society! Put yourself forward and it picks you to pieces. Monsieur de Marsay came and laughed about you with Madame d'Espard, and the two ladies took flight at once, thinking that they would be compromised by remaining with you. Don't try to call upon either of them. Madame de Bargeton would not be received by her cousin if she continued to see you. You have genius, try to take your revenge. Society looks down on you, look down on society. Take refuge in an attic, produce a few masterpieces there, seize upon power of some sort and you will see society at your feet; then you will repay the wounds it has inflicted on you in the same place where they were so inflicted. The more friendship Madame de Bargeton has shown you heretofore, the more she will hold aloof from you now. That's the way with a woman's sentiments. But at this moment, it's not a question of winning back Anaïs's friendship, but of not making an enemy of her, and I will tell you how to avoid it. She has written to you; send back all her letters and she will appreciate such a chivalrous proceeding; and later, if you need her assistance, she won't be hostile to you. As for myself, I have such an exalted opinion of your future, that I have taken your part everywhere, and from this time on, if I can do anything for you here, you will find me always ready to do you a service.''

Lucien was so dejected, so pale, so crushed, that he did not return the parting salutation bestowed upon him by the old beau, rejuvenated by the atmosphere of Paris. He returned to his hotel, where he found Staub in person, who had come less for the purpose of trying on his clothes, which however he did try on, than to find out from the landlady of the *Gaillard-Bois*, the financial standing of his unknown customer. Lucien had arrived in Paris by post, Madame de Bargeton had brought him home from the Vaudeville in her carriage the preceding Thursday. This information was satisfactory. Staub called Lucien "Monsieur le Comte," and called his attention to the skill with which he had set off his shapely figure.

"A young man dressed like that, can walk in the Tuileries gardens," he said, "and marry a rich Englishwoman in a fortnight."

The German tailor's pleasantry and the perfect fit of his clothes, the fineness of the materials, the grace which he discovered in his own person as he looked himself over in the mirror, all these trifles tended to make Lucien less melancholy. He said to himself, vaguely, that Paris was the capital city of chance, and for a moment he believed in chance. Had he not a volume of poems and a magnificent romance, the *Archer de Charles IX.*, in manuscript? He had great hopes of his destiny. Staub promised the redingote and all the other garments for the next day. The next day the bootmaker, the haberdasher and the tailor appeared, all armed with their bills. Lucien, not knowing how else to get rid of them, and being still under the spell of provincial customs, paid them; but after he had paid them, he had but three hundred and sixty francs left of the two thousand francs he had brought from Angoulême; and he had been in Paris a week! However, he dressed and went to take a turn on the Terrasse des Feuillants. There he had his first taste of revenge. He was so well dressed, so graceful, so handsome, that several women looked at him, and two or three were sufficiently impressed by his beauty to turn around. Lucien studied the gait and the bearing of the young men, and took his lesson in refined manners, thinking all the time of his three hundred and sixty francs. In the evening, as he sat alone in his room, it occurred to him that he might speedily solve the problem of living at the *Gaillard-Bois,* where he breakfasted on the simplest dishes, thinking that he was economizing. He asked for his account, saying that he proposed to change his quarters, and found that he owed about a hundred francs.

The next day he went to the Latin Quarter, which David had recommended to him for cheapness. After looking about a long while, he finally found, on Rue de Cluny, near the Sorbonne, a wretched, furnished hotel, where he hired a room for the price he wanted to pay. He returned to the *Gaillard-Bois*, paid his bill there, and took up his abode on Rue de Cluny during the day. His change of quarters cost him only one cab fare.

After he had taken possession of his poor room, he put all Madame de Bargeton's letters together, tied them in a little bundle, placed it on the table, and, before writing to her, thought over the events of that fatal week. He did not reflect that he himself had been the first to deny his love, when he did not know what would become of his Louise in Paris; he did not realize his own offence against her, he simply saw his present situation, for which he blamed Madame de Bargeton: instead of assisting him, she had ruined him. He flew into a rage, the rage of wounded pride, and wrote the following letter in the paroxysm of his wrath:

"What would you say, madame, of a woman who had been attracted by some poor, timid child, full of those noble beliefs which, later in life, men call illusions, and who had exerted the fascinations of coquetry, all the resources of her wit and the most seductive pretence of maternal love to lead that child astray? Neither the most flattering promises, nor the card-houses which aroused his wondering admiration, cost her anything; she leads him away, she takes possession of him, she scolds him for his lack of confidence and flatters him turn and turn about; when the child deserts his family and follows her blindly, she leads him to the shore of a vast sea, smilingly launches him upon it in a frail skiff and forces him to meet its storms, alone and without resource; then, from the cliff where she stands, she laughs at him and wishes him good luck. You are that woman; I am that child. In that child's hands is a souvenir which might betray the crimes of your benevolence and the blessing of your desertion. You might have to blush when you see the child struggling with the waves, if you should remember that you had held him upon your bosom. When you read this letter, you will have that souvenir in your hands. You are free to forget everything. After the radiant hopes that your finger pointed out to me in the sky, I see the reality of poverty in the gutters of Paris. While you, brilliant and adored, journey through the grandeurs of that world to whose threshold you led me by the hand, I shall shiver with cold in the miserable garret to which you have banished me. But perhaps remorse will lay hold of you amid your festivities and your pleasures; perhaps you will think of the child you have cast into an abyss. If so, madame, think of him without remorse! From the depths of his misery that child offers you the only thing he has to offer, his forgiveness in one last glance. Yes, madame, thanks to you, I have nothing left. Nothing! But was not the world made from nothing? Genius should imitate God: I begin by imitating His clemency, uncertain whether I shall have His strength. You will have occasion to tremble only if I go to the bad: then you will be accessory to my sins. Alas! I pity you because you cannot now count for aught in the renown toward which my steps are tending under the guidance of hard work."

Having indited this emphatic epistle, full of the gloomy dignity which an artist of twenty-one often exaggerates, Lucien's thoughts turned to his family: he saw in his mind's eye the attractive apartments that David had fitted up for him, sacrificing a part

19

of his fortune for that purpose; he had a vision of the tranquil, modest, bourgeois pleasures that he had once enjoyed; the figures of his mother and sister and David gathered about him, he heard again the tears they shed at the time of his departure, and he wept himself, for he was alone in Paris, without friends, without protectors.

A few days later, he wrote as follows to his sister:

"MY DEAR EVE,

"Sisters enjoy the melancholy privilege of espousing more disappointments than pleasures when they share the existence of brothers devoted to art, and I begin to dread that I may become a heavy burden to you. Have I not already imposed upon you all, who have sacrificed yourselves for me? The memory of my past, replete with family joys, has helped me to bear my present solitude. With what great rapidity, like an eagle returning to his nest, have I traversed the distance that separates us, in order to find myself once more in the sphere of genuine affection, after experiencing the first miseries and the first disillusionment of Parisian society! Have your lights flickered? Have the firebrands on the hearth turned over? Have your ears burned? Has my mother said: 'Lucien is thinking of us?' Has David answered: 'He is fighting against men and things?' Dear Eve, I am writing this letter to you alone. To you alone should I dare to confide the good and the evil that may fall to my lot, blushing equally for either, for the good is as rare as the evil ought to be. I can tell you much in a few words: Madame de Bargeton was ashamed of me, denied me, dismissed me, repudiated me the ninth day after my arrival. When she saw me, she turned her head; and I, in order to follow her into the social set to which she proposed to introduce me, had spent seventeen hundred and sixty francs out

of the two thousand I brought from Angoulême, after all the
difficulty we had in obtaining them!—'Spent for what?' you
will say. Ah! my poor sister, Paris is a terrible gulf: you
can dine here for eighteen sous, and the simplest dinner at a
fashionable *restaurât* costs fifty francs ; there are waistcoats
and trousers for four francs and for forty sous; the fashionable tailors won't make them for less than a hundred francs.
It costs a sou to cross the gutters in the street, when it rains.
The very lowest cab fare is thirty-two sous. After living for
a while in the best quarter of the city, I am now at the Hôtel
de *Cluny*, Rue de Cluny, one of the meanest and darkest
little streets in Paris, cooped up between three churches and
the old buildings of the Sorbonne. I have a furnished room
on the fourth floor, and although it is very bare and dirty, I
pay fifteen francs a month for it. I breakfast on a two-sou
loaf and a sou's worth of milk, but I dine very comfortably
for twenty-two sous at the *restaurât* of one Flicoteaux, right
on the Place de la Sorbonne. Until winter comes, my expenses won't exceed sixty francs a month, everything included—at least I hope so. So my two hundred and forty
francs will be enough for the first four months. Between now
and then I have no doubt I shall sell the *Archer de Charles IX.*
and the *Marguerites.* So don't be at all alarmed on my account. Although the present is cold and bare and shabby, the
future is blue and rich and splendid. Most great men have
known the vicissitudes which disturb but do not crush me.
Plautus, a great comic poet, was a mill hand. Machiavelli
wrote *The Prince* in the evenings, after working with his
hands, on equal terms with other mechanics, during the day.
And the great Cervantes, too, who lost his arm in the battle
of Lepanto while contributing to that world-famous victory,
who was called *an old one-armed wretch* by the scribblers of his
day, allowed ten years to elapse between the first and second
parts of his Don Quixote, for lack of a publisher. We are
beyond that to-day. Disappointment and want fall to the lot
of none but unknown talents; but, when they have forced
themselves into the light, authors become rich, and I shall be

rich. I am living in my thoughts too. I pass half the day at
the Bibliothèque Sainte-Geneviève, where I am acquiring such
information as I lack, without which I could make little progress. To-day, therefore, I am almost happy. Within a few
days I have joyously adapted my life to my circumstances. I
devote myself from daybreak to work that I love; my material wants are certainly provided for; I meditate much, I
study, I do not see how I can now be wounded, after renoun-
cing society, where my vanity might suffer at any moment.
The illustrious men of any age are bound to live by themselves. Are they not the birds of the forest? they sing, they
charm nature, and no one can see them. So will I do, provided that I can realize the ambitious projects I have formed.
I do not regret Madame de Bargeton. A woman who acts as
she acted, does not deserve to be remembered. Nor do I regret
having left Angoulême. That woman did well in casting me
loose in Paris and leaving me to my own resources. This is
the land of writers, of thinkers, of poets. Here only can the
seeds of glory be sown, and I know of fair crops that they
are producing to-day. Here only can writers find, in museums
and collections, the ever-living works of the geniuses of the
past, who kindle and stimulate the imagination. Here only
do enormous libraries, always accessible, afford the mind information and abundant pasturage. Lastly, there is in Paris,
in the air and in the most trifling details, a living inspiration
that leaves its mark upon literary productions. One can
learn more in conversation at the café or the theatre in half
an hour, than in the provinces in ten years. Here, in truth,
everything is spectacular, everything is comparison and in-
struction. Excessive cheapness and excessive dearness, that
is Paris in a nutshell, a place where every bee finds its cell,
where every mind assimilates whatever is adapted to it.
Therefore, although I suffer at this moment, I do not repent.
On the contrary, a glorious future is unfolding before me and
consoles my heart in this moment of sorrow. Adieu, my
dear sister. Do not expect letters from me regularly: one of
the peculiarities of Paris is that one never realizes how time

flies. Life moves at an alarming speed. I embrace my
mother, David and yourself more lovingly than ever."

Flicoteaux is a name inscribed in many memories.
There were few students who boarded in the Latin
Quarter during the first twelve years of the Restoration who did not resort to that temple of hunger
and want. The dinner, consisting of three courses,
cost eighteen sous with a quarter of a bottle of wine or
a bottle of beer; and twenty-two sous with a bottle of
wine. The thing that undoubtedly prevented this
friend of youth from making a colossal fortune was
an item of the bill of fare printed in great letters in
the advertisements of his rivals, and thus conceived: BREAD AT YOUR DISCRETION, that is to
say, to indiscretion. Many great reputations have
had Flicoteaux for foster-father. Certainly the
heart of more than one illustrious man must be joyfully conscious of innumerable pleasant recollections
as he sees the café front with little square windows
looking on Place de la Sorbonne and Rue Neuve-de-
Richelieu, which Flicoteaux II. or III. had left un-
touched, before the days of July, allowing it to
retain the dingy hue, the ancient and respectable
air which denoted profound contempt for the charlatanism of the outer world, a sort of advertisement
for the eyes at the expense of the stomach adopted
by almost all the *restaurateurs* of to-day. Instead
of the quantities of stuffed birds, not intended to be
cooked, instead of the impossible fishes which justify the clown's jest: "I have seen a fine carp and

I mean to buy it a week hence;" instead of the early fruit, which should be called *late fruit*, displayed in fallacious tiers for the pleasure of corporals and their sweethearts, honest Flicoteaux exhibited divers salad-bowls embellished with many a patch, wherein stewed prunes rejoiced the gaze of the customer, who was assured that the word *dessert*, which was too lavishly used in other advertisements, was not a delusion and a snare. The six-pound loaves, cut in four pieces, removed all doubt as to the unlimited supply of bread. Such were the luxurious surroundings of an establishment which, had it existed in his time, Molière would have made famous, so amusing is the epigram of the name. Flicoteaux still lives; he will live as long as students desire to live. They go there to eat, nothing less, nothing more; but they eat there as they work, with gloomy or joyous activity, according to their dispositions or the circumstances of their lives.

This celebrated establishment consisted at this time of two long, narrow, low rooms, at right angles to each other, one on Place de la Sorbonne, the other on Rue Neuve-de-Richelieu; both were supplied with tables from some abbey refectory, for their length was decidedly monastic, and they were always laid for one meal or another, with the napkins of the regular customers in numbered tin napkin-rings. Flicoteaux I. changed the table linen on Sundays only; but Flicoteaux II. changed it twice a week, so it was said, as soon as his supremacy

was threatened by his rivals. The restaurant is a
workshop with its tools rather than a banquet hall
with its luxury and its aids to enjoyment; everyone
leaves it as promptly as possible. Within, everything is swift movement. The waiters come and
go without sauntering, they are all busy, all necessary. The dishes show but little variety. The
potato is everlasting; if there were no potatoes in
Ireland, if the crop should fail everywhere else, you
would still find them at Flicoteaux's. They have
been served there for thirty years, of the blond hue
affected by Titian, surrounded by chopped herbs,
and they enjoy a privilege much desired by women:
as you found them in 1814, so you will find them in
1840. Mutton cutlets and filet of beef are to the
menu of that establishment what woodcock and filet
of sturgeon are to Véry's, special dishes which must
be ordered in the morning. The female of the ox
is the principal resource, and her son is much in
evidence in the most ingenious shapes. When the
whiting and mackerel make their appearance off
shore they bob up in Flicoteaux's larder. There
everything corresponds with the vicissitudes of
agriculture and the caprice of the French seasons.
You can learn there things that are not even suspected by the wealthy, the indolent and those who
are indifferent to nature's varying phases. The
student who is penned up in the Latin Quarter can
obtain there the most exact knowledge of the crops:
he knows when it is a good year for beans and peas,
when the market is overflowing with cabbage, what

material for salad is most abundant and whether the
beet-root has failed. An old calumny, revived
about the time Lucien first went there, consisted in
attributing the appearance of beefsteaks to some
epidemic among horses.

Few Parisian restaurants present such a fine
spectacle. There you find only youth and confidence, poverty cheerfully endured, although there
are not lacking ardent and sober faces and clouded
and anxious ones. The costumes are generally
careless. For that reason well-dressed customers
attract attention. Everyone knows that the un-
usual garb means: an appointment with a mistress,
a theatre party or a call in a higher sphere. It is
said that friendships have been cemented there between students who have subsequently become
famous, as we shall see in the course of this narrative. Nevertheless, except for the young men from
the same province grouped at one end of a table,
the diners, generally speaking, have a gravity of
demeanor which is not easily melted, perhaps because of the catholicity of the wine, which is not
calculated to cause a flow of spirits. Those who
have patronized Flicoteaux's will remember several
dark-browed mysterious personages, enveloped in
the mists of utter destitution, who dined there perhaps for two years and disappeared, without a ray
of light concerning these Parisian jack-o'-lanterns
having ever reached the eyes of the most inquisitive
habitués. The friendships begun at Flicoteaux's
are cemented in the neighboring cafés with the

flames of a glowing punch, or the heat of a small cup of coffee, laced with some fiery liqueur.

During the early days of his abode at the Hôtel de Cluny, Lucien, like all neophytes, was regular and modest in his habits. After the sad experience of fashionable life that had absorbed all his capital, he plunged into work with the initial ardor that is so quickly cooled by the obstacles and distractions which Paris presents to all lives, the most luxurious as well as the poorest, and which, in order to be overcome, demand the savage energy of real talent or the dogged persistence of ambition. Lucien would drop in at Flicoteaux's about half-past four, having discovered the advantage of being among the first to arrive; the dishes were then more varied, and one's favorite was not likely to be exhausted. Like all poetic minds, he had taken a fancy to a particular location, and his choice exhibited much discernment. On his first visit to the place, he had noticed, near the desk, a certain table at which the faces of the guests, as well as such snatches of their conversation as he could catch on the wing, betrayed comrades in the literary profession. Moreover, he instinctively guessed that by taking a seat near the desk, he would have an opportunity to talk with the proprietors. Sooner or later he would make their acquaintance, and then, if he should become embarrassed pecuniarily, doubtless he would be able to obtain such credit as he might need. He had taken his seat therefore at a small square table beside the desk, where he saw only two covers supplied with white napkins without rings, and intended probably for transient guests. Lucien's vis-à-vis was a thin, pale, young man, probably as poor as himself, whose handsome face, already pinched by want, announced that vanished hopes had fatigued his brow and left in his heart furrows wherein the seeds sown did not take root. Lucien felt impelled toward the stranger by these vestiges of a poetic nature and by an irresistible outflow of sympathy.

This young man, the first with whom the Angoulême poet succeeded in opening a conversation after a week of polite attentions, words and brief sentences exchanged, was named Etienne Lousteau. Some two years before, Etienne, like Lucien, had left his native province, Berri. His animated gestures, his gleaming eyes, his sometimes abrupt speech, indicated a bitter acquaintance with literary life. Etienne had come from Sancerre, his tragedy in his pocket, attracted by the same things that pointed the way to Lucien: glory, power, wealth. At first he dined at the restaurant several days in succession, but before long he appeared only at intervals. When Lucien met his poet again after five or six days' absence, he hoped to see him the next day as well, but the next day his place was taken by a stranger. When two young men have met and conversed yesterday, the flame of that day's conversation is reflected upon to-day's; but these long intervals compelled Lucien to break the ice anew every time, and retarded the progress of an intimacy that advanced but slowly during the first weeks. By dint of questioning the female at the desk, Lucien learned that his future friend was the manager of a small newspaper, for which he wrote reviews of new books and acted as critic at the Ambigu-Comique, the Gaieté and the Panorama-Dramatique. The young man suddenly became a personage in Lucien's eyes, who determined to be a little more personal in his next attempt at conversation, and to make some sacrifices in order to obtain a friendship so necessary to a beginner.

The journalist was absent a fortnight. Lucien did not as yet know that Etienne dined at Flicoteaux's only when he had no money, a circumstance that accounted for the gloomy, discontented expression, the coldness of manner, which Lucien met with flattering smiles and soft words. Nevertheless, this connection demanded mature reflection, for this obscure journalist seemed to lead an extravagant life, a succession of *petits verres*, cups of coffee, bowls of punch, plays and supper-parties. Now, during the early days of his sojourn in the quarter, Lucien's conduct was that of a poor child bewildered by his first experience of Parisian life. And so, after he had studied the price of the different articles of food and weighed his purse, Lucien did not dare adopt Etienne's ways, dreading to begin again the blunders that he still repented. Still under the yoke of provincial customs, his two guardian angels, Eve and David, appeared before him at the least evil thought, and reminded him of the hopes reposed in him, his responsibility for his old mother's happiness, and all the promises of his genius.   He passed his mornings at the Bibliothèque Sainte-Geneviève studying history.   His first researches had shown him horrible errors in his *Archer de Charles IX.* When the library closed, he returned to his damp, cold room to correct his work, rearrange it, suppress whole chapters.   After dining at Flicoteaux's, he went down to the Passage du Commerce, to Blosse's bookstall, and read the recent publications, the newspapers, the reviews and the new poems, in order to keep abreast of the intellectual movement of the time, and returned to his wretched hotel about midnight, having used no fuel or light.   All this reading wrought such a change in his ideas, that he reviewed his collection of sonnets upon flowers, his cherished *Marguerites,* and worked them over so thoroughly that not a hundred lines were retained.

Thus Lucien at first led the pure and innocent life of poor boys from the provinces, who find the Flicoteaux fare luxurious when compared with the paternal table, whose recreation consists in slow promenades through the paths at the Luxembourg, casting sheep's eyes at the pretty women while the blood beats madly in their veins, who never leave the quarter and who devote themselves religiously to hard work, thinking of their future. But Lucien, a born poet, often the victim of most intense longings, was powerless against the seductions of the theatre posters.   The Théâtre-Français, the Vaudeville, the Variétés, the Opéra-Comique, where he sat in the pit, relieved him of about sixty francs. What student could resist the joy of seeing Talma in the rôles he has made famous? The theatre, the first love of all poetic minds, fascinated Lucien. The actors and actresses seemed to him imposing personages; he did not believe in the possibility of passing the footlights and knowing them familiarly. The authors of his pleasure were to him marvelous beings whom the newspapers treated like important affairs of state. To be a dramatic author, to see one's works performed—what a fondly cherished dream! Some audacious mortals, like Casimir Delavigne, had seen that dream come true! These pregnant thoughts, these moments of faith in himself, followed by despair, acted powerfully upon Lucien, and kept him in the blessed path of work and economy, despite the sullen grumbling of more than one frenzied desire. With excessive prudence he made it his rule never to enter the Palais-Royal, that abode of perdition, where, in a single day, he had spent fifty francs at Véry's and nearly five hundred francs in clothes. And so, when he yielded to the temptation to see Talma, the two Baptistes, Fleury or Michot, he went no farther than the dark gallery where people stood in line from half-past five and where belated ones were obliged to pay ten sous a place in the line near the office. Often the words: *There are no more tickets!* rang in the ears of more than one disappointed student, who had stood there more than two hours.

After the play, Lucien would return home, with downcast eyes, paying no heed to the scenes in the streets, which were well supplied with living seductions. Perhaps some of those adventures may have happened to him, which, though exceedingly simple, occupy an enormous place in young and timorous imaginations. Alarmed by the rapid diminution of his capital, one day when he was counting over his remaining stock, Lucien had a cold shiver at the thought that he must make inquiries for a publisher and seek work for which he would be paid. The young journalist, who was the only friend he had made, no longer came to Flicoteaux's. Lucien awaited some lucky chance which did not turn up. At Paris there is no such thing as chance except for people who have a very wide circle of acquaintance; the chances of success in every direction increase in proportion to the number of one's relations, and chance too is on the side of the larger battalions. Like a man in whom the proverbial forehandedness of provincials was not yet extinct, Lucien did not choose to wait until he had only a crown or two left; he determined to confront the publishers.

*

One sharp morning in the month of September, he walked down Rue de la Harpe, his two manuscripts under his arm. He went as far as Quai des Augustins and along the sidewalk there, looking alternately at the waters of the Seine and the bookshops, as if some kind spirit were advising him to plunge into the water rather than to plunge into literature. After much painful hesitation, after a profound scrutiny of the faces, more or less amiable, attractive, repellent, cheerful or dejected, which he saw through the windows or standing in the doorways, he pitched upon a house in front of which several clerks were busily engaged packing books. Business was very brisk; the walls were covered with placards:

FOR SALE:

LE SOLITAIRE, *by Monsieur le Vicomte d'Arlincourt, 3d edition.*

LEONIDE, *by Victor Ducange, 5 volumes, 12mo, printed on superfine paper. Price, 12 francs.*

INDUCTIONS MORALES, *by Kératry.*

"Those men are fortunate!" cried Lucien.

The poster, a new and original creation of the famous Ladvocat, had recently made its first appearance on the walls. Paris was soon bespangled by

(303)

advertisements of this sort, one of the sources of public revenue. At last, his heart swollen with excitement and anxiety, Lucien, lately such a great man in Angoulême and now so small in Paris, glided along by the intervening houses and mustered up courage to enter the shop, which was crowded with clerks, customers and booksellers. "And perhaps with authors!" thought Lucien.

"I would like to speak with Monsieur Vidal or Monsieur Porchon," he said to a clerk.

He had read in great letters on the sign:

VIDAL AND PORCHON,

Booksellers on Commission for France and Foreign Countries.

"Both those gentlemen are engaged," said the clerk.

"I will wait."

They left the poet in the shop examining the books; he passed nearly two hours looking at titles, opening books, reading a page here and there. At last he rested his shoulder against a glass door with little green curtains, behind which he suspected that either Vidal or Porchon was, and overheard the following conversation:

"Will you take five hundred copies? In that case, I will let you have them at five francs and give you the double thirteenth."

"What price does that make them?"

"Sixteen sous less."

"Four francs four sous," said either Vidal or Porchon to the man who was offering his books.

"Yes," the vender replied.

"On credit?" queried the purchaser.

"You old rascal! and you would settle with me eighteen months hence with notes to run a year, eh?"

"No, to be adjusted at once," replied Vidal or Porchon.

"On what time? Nine months?" inquired the author or publisher who seemed to have a book to sell.

"No, my dear man, a year," replied that one of the commission merchants with whom he was talking.

There was silence for a moment.

"You have me by the throat!" cried the unknown.

"But do you suppose we shall have disposed of five hundred copies of *Léonide* in a year?" retorted the commission merchant to Victor Ducange's publisher. "If books sold as publishers would like to have them, we should all be millionaires, my dear master; but they sell to suit the public. Walter Scott's novels are sold at eighteen sous the volume, three francs twelve the whole work, and do you suppose I can sell your trash at a higher price? If you want me to push your story for you, make it an object for me.—Vidal!"

A fat man left the desk and approached, with a pen behind his ear.

20

"In your last trip, how many copies of Ducange's books did you sell?" Porchon asked him.

"I sold two hundred of the *Petit Vieillard de Calais;* but in order to do it I had to cry down two other works on which we didn't get such good commissions, and which afterwards became very pretty *rossignols.*"

Later Lucien learned that this sobriquet of *rossignol*—literally, *nightingale,*—was given by booksellers to works which remained stowed away upon shelves in the dark depths of their shops.

"You know, too," added Vidal, "that Picard has novels in press. They promise us twenty per cent commission on the regular bookseller's price, in order to give them a successful start."

"Well, let it be for a year then," replied the publisher piteously, crushed by this last confidential remark of Vidal to Porchon.

"Is it agreed?" Porchon asked him abruptly.

"Yes."

The publisher took his leave, and Lucien heard Porchon say to Vidal:

"We have three hundred copies ordered; we'll postpone his settlement, we'll sell the *Léonide* at a hundred sous a copy, we'll make the purchasers settle in six months, and—"

"And there are fifteen hundred francs in our pockets," rejoined Vidal.

"Oh! I saw that he was very hard up."

"He's in trouble up to his ears! he pays Ducange four thousand francs for two thousand copies."

Lucien stopped Vidal as he came out through the little door of the cage.

"Messieurs," he said to the partners, "I have the honor to salute you."

The commission merchants hardly returned his salutation.

"I am the author of a historical romance after the style of Walter Scott, entitled *L'Archer de Charles IX.* I should be very glad if you would purchase it."

Porchon glanced coldly at Lucien and laid his pen on his desk. Vidal looked at the poet with a brutal expression and replied:

"Monsieur, we are not publishers, we are commission merchants. When we print a book on our own account, it is an undertaking that we enter into only with *well-known names.* Furthermore, we purchase none but serious books, histories, summaries."

"But my book is very serious; it is an attempt to depict in its true light the struggle between the Catholics who adhered to the absolute monarchy, and the Protestants who wished to establish a republic."

"Monsieur Vidal!" cried a clerk.

Vidal disappeared.

"I don't undertake to say, monsieur, that your book may not be a masterpiece," Porchon continued, with a decidedly discourteous gesture, "but we deal only in books that are already printed. Go and see the men who buy manuscripts: Père

Doguereau, Rue du Coq, near the Louvre; he's one of those who go in for novels. If you had spoken sooner, you might have seen Pollet, the rival of Doguereau and of the booksellers of the wooden galleries."

"Monsieur, I have a collection of poems—"

"Monsieur Porchon!" some one called.

"Poetry!" cried Porchon angrily. "What do you take me for, eh?" he added, laughing in his face, as he disappeared in his back shop.

Lucien crossed Pont Neuf, buried in thought. The little that he had understood of this commercial jargon led him to believe that, in the eyes of those dealers, books were what cotton nightcaps are to capmakers,—simply an article of merchandise to be bought cheap and sold dear.

"I have made a mistake," he said, impressed nevertheless by the brutal and material aspect his late experience imparted to literature.

He spied on Rue du Coq a modest shop which he had already passed, bearing these words in yellow letters on a green background: DOGUEREAU, BOOK-SELLER. He remembered that he had seen those words at the foot of the title page in several of the novels he had glanced over at Blosse's bookstall. He entered, not without that internal trepidation which the certainty of a conflict causes in all men of imagination. He found in the shop an old man of curious appearance, one of the original figures of the book trade under the Empire. Doguereau wore a black coat with enormous square skirts, whereas it

was the prevailing fashion to cut frockcoats in the
shape of a codfish's tail.   He had a waistcoat of
cheap material with squares of various colors, from
which hung, in the region of the fob, a steel chain and
a copper key, which dangled against his very full
black breeches. The watch must have been of the
size of an onion.   His costume was completed by iron-
gray milled stockings, and shoes embellished with
silver buckles.   The old man's bare head was
decorated with grizzly locks, poetically sparse in
quantity.

Père Doguereau, as Porchon called him, suggested
the professor of belles-letters by his coat, his
breeches and his shoes, and the tradesman by his
waistcoat, his watch and his stockings.   His countenance did not contradict that strange combination:
he had the magisterial, dogmatic air, the wrinkled
face of the instructor in rhetoric, and the bright
eyes, the suspicious mouth, the vague restlessness
of the publisher.

"Monsieur Doguereau?" queried Lucien.

"I am the man, monsieur."

"I am the author of a novel," said Lucien.

"You are very young," replied the bookseller.

"But my age has nothing to do with the matter,
monsieur."

"True," said the old man taking the manuscript.
"Ah! deuce take me! *L'Archer de Charles IX.!* a
good title.   Come, young man, tell me your subject in two words."

"It is a historical work, monsieur, after the

style of Walter Scott, in which the struggle between the Protestants and Catholics is presented as a conflict between two systems of government, in which the throne was seriously threatened. I have taken sides with the Catholics."

"An original idea, young man, on my word! Well, I will read your book, I promise you. I should have preferred a novel after the style of Madame Radcliffe; but if you are a worker, if you have a little style, originality, ideas, and the art of giving them the proper stage-setting, I ask nothing better than to be of service to you. What do we need?— good manuscripts."

"When may I come again?"

"I am going to the country this evening and shall return the day after to-morrow; I shall have read your work meanwhile, and if it suits me, we can come to terms that same day."

Lucien, finding him such an agreeable old fellow, conceived the fatal idea of producing the manuscript of *Les Marguerites*.

"I have also written a number of poems, monsieur—"

"Ah! you're a poet! I want nothing to do with your novel then," said the old man, handing him the manuscript. "Rhymesters make a mess of it when they try to write prose. In prose, there's no poetic license, you must really say something."

"But, monsieur, Walter Scott wrote verses too—"

"So he did," said Doguereau, and he softened his tone, guessed at the young man's penurious condition and kept the manuscript. "Where do you live? I will come and see you."

Lucien gave his address without the least suspicion of any hidden motive on the old man's part; he did not recognize in him the publisher of the old school, a survivor of the days when publishers strove to keep Voltaire and Montesquieu under lock and key in an attic, dying of hunger.

"I have just this moment come through the Latin Quarter," said the old man after he had read the address.

"What a fine fellow!" thought Lucien as he took leave of the bookseller. "I have fallen in with a friend of young men, a connoisseur who knows something. Talk to me! It's just as I told David, true talent makes its way easily enough in Paris."

Lucien returned home happy and light of heart; he was dreaming of glory. Forgetting the words of sinister import that had fallen upon his ear in Vidal and Porchon's counting-room, he fancied himself already in possession of twelve hundred francs. Twelve hundred francs represented a year's stay in Paris, a year, during which he would produce new works. How many projects did he build upon that hope! How many sweet dreams did he dream, when he saw his livelihood fairly established upon hard work! He arranged his rooms to the best advantage, and was very near making some purchases. He allayed his impatience only by reading incessantly at Blosse's bookstall. Two days later old Doguereau, surprised at the style displayed by

Lucien in his first work, enchanted by the exaggeration of the characters, quite permissible in dealing with the epoch in which the scene of the romance was laid, and impressed by the imaginative ardor with which a young author sketches his first plot— Père Doguereau was not spoiled!—came to the hotel where his Walter Scott in germ had his abode. He had decided to pay a thousand francs outright for the manuscript of *L'Archer de Charles IX.*, and to bind Lucien by an agreement for several works to be produced. When he saw the hotel, the old fox revised his decision.

"A young man who lives in such a place as that has only modest tastes; he loves study and hard work; I need give him only eight hundred francs."

The landlady, when he inquired for Monsieur Lucien de Rubempré, replied:

"Fourth floor."

The bookseller looked up and saw nothing but the sky above the fourth floor.

"This young man," he thought, "is a pretty fellow, indeed he's very handsome; if he should earn too much money, he would plunge into dissipation and wouldn't work. In our common interest, I will offer him six hundred francs; but in cash, not notes."

He ascended the stairs and knocked thrice on Lucien's door, which was opened by Lucien himself. The room was desperately bare. There was a bowl of milk and a two-sou roll on the table. Goodman

L'ARCHER DE CHARLES IX.

When he saw the hotel, the old fox revised his decision.

"A young man who lives in such a place as that has only modest tastes ; he loves study and hard work ; I need give him only eight hundred francs."

*   *   *   *   *   *   *   *   *

He ascended the stairs and knocked thrice on Lucien's door, which was opened by Lucien himself. The room was desperately bare.

Copyrighted 1897 by G. B. & Son

Xavier Le Sueur sc.

ADRIEN MOREAU

Doguereau was deeply impressed to find genius in such destitute circumstances.

"Let him preserve these simple manners," he thought, "this frugality, these modest needs.—It gives me pleasure to see you," he said to Lucien. "This, monsieur, is the way Jean-Jacques lived, whose career yours is likely to resemble in more ways than one. In such lodgings as these, the fire of genius burns and great works are produced. This is how men of letters ought to live, instead of gormandizing in cafés and restaurants, and wasting their time and talent and our money there."

He sat down.

"Young man, your novel is not bad. I have been a professor of rhetoric and I know the history of France; there are some excellent things in it. In fact, you have a future."

"Ah! monsieur."

"I tell you, we can afford to do business together. I will buy your novel—"

Lucien's heart expanded, he breathed freely; he was about to enter the world of literature, his work would be printed at last.

"I will buy it of you for four hundred francs," said Doguereau sweetly, glancing at Lucien with an expression that seemed to proclaim a great exhibition of generosity.

"Four hundred francs the volume?" queried Lucien.

"The whole novel," said Doguereau, betraying no astonishment at Lucien's surprise. "But," he

added, "it will be cash down.   You will undertake
to write two novels a year for me for six years.
If the first is exhausted in six months, I will pay
you six hundred francs for those that come after.
Thus, by writing two a year, you will have a
hundred francs a month, your living will be assured
and you will be very fortunate.   I have some authors
to whom I pay only three hundred francs a novel.   I
give two hundred francs for a translation from the
English.   Formerly this price would have been
considered exorbitant."

"We cannot make a bargain, monsieur; I beg
you to return my manuscript," said Lucien, in a
freezing tone.

"There you are," said the old bookseller.   "You
know nothing about business, monsieur.   In publishing an author's first novel, a publisher has to
risk sixteen hundred francs for the paper and printing.   It's easier to write a novel than to find such
a sum of money as that.   I have the manuscripts of
a hundred novels at my shop, and I haven't a hundred and sixty thousand francs in my cash-box.
Alas!   I haven't made as much as that in the twenty
years I've been in the business.   Fortunes are not
to be made at the trade of publishing novels.   Vidal
and Porchon won't take them from us except on
conditions that become every day more burdensome
to us.   Where you risk only your time, I have to
put out two thousand francs.   If we make a mistake—for *habent sua fata libelli*—I lose two thousand francs, while you have simply to dash off an

ode on the subject of public stupidity. After you have meditated upon what I have the honor to say to you, you will come and see me again.—You will come to me again," the bookseller repeated authoritatively, in reply to a gesture of superb disdain on Lucien's part. "Far from finding a publisher who will risk two thousand francs for a young and unknown man, you won't find a clerk who will take the trouble to read your scrawl. I, who have read it, can point out several errors in your French. You have put *observer* for *faire observer*, and you say *malgré que: Malgré* takes a direct object."

Lucien seemed humiliated.

"When I see you again, you will have lost a hundred francs," added Doguereau, "for then I will give you only three hundred."

He rose and bowed, but on the threshold he stopped and said:

"If you had not talent and a future, if I were not interested in studious young men, I would not have proposed such advantageous terms. A hundred francs a month! Think of it. After all, a novel in a drawer isn't like a horse in the stable, it doesn't eat any food. Upon my word, they don't give as much for them now!"

Lucien took his manuscript and threw it on the floor, crying:

"I would rather burn it, monsieur!"

"You have a poet's head," said the old man.

Lucien devoured his roll, swallowed his milk and went downstairs. His room was not large enough;

he could do nothing there but pace back and forth like a lion in its cage at the Jardin des Plantes. At the Bibliothèque Sainte-Geneviève, whither he purposed going, he had often noticed, always in the same corner, a young man of about twenty-five years, working with that sustained application which nothing distracts or disturbs, and by which genuine literary workmen can always be recognized. Evidently the young man had long been a frequenter of the library, for the attendants and the librarian himself were most obliging to him; the librarian allowed him to take away books which Lucien saw the studious stranger bring back the next morning. He recognized in him a brother in poverty and hope.   Short, slender and pale, this persistent toiler concealed a fine forehead beneath a mass of unkempt black hair; he had shapely hands, he attracted the notice of the indifferent by a vague resemblance to the engraving of the portrait of Bonaparte by Robert Lefebvre.   The engraving in question is in itself a whole poem of glowing melancholy, of restrained ambition, of concealed activity. Examine it carefully; you will find therein genius and discretion, tact and grandeur.   The eyes are as bright as a woman's.   The glance is greedy of space and longs for difficulties to overcome.   Even if Bonaparte's name were not written beneath it, you would gaze as long upon it.

The young man whose face so resembled that face, ordinarily wore trousers made with feet like stocking feet, in thick-soled shoes, a frockcoat of

very ordinary material, a black cravat, a gray
and white mixed waistcoat buttoned to the neck,
and a cheap hat. His contempt for everything useless in the way of dress was perceptible. Lucien
found this mysterious stranger, marked with the seal
that genius stamps upon the brows of its slaves,
the most regular of all the habitués of Flicoteaux's;
he ate there to live, heedless of the various dishes
with which he seemed familiar, and he drank nothing but water. At Flicoteaux's, as at the library,
he displayed a sort of dignity, due without doubt
to the consciousness of a life intent upon something
great, which made him unassailable. His expression was pensive. Meditation dwelt upon his nobly-
proportioned, handsome forehead. His bright black
eyes, which saw clearly and quickly, denoted a
habit of going to the bottom of things. Simple in
his bearing, he had a grave and thoughtful face.
Lucien had an involuntary feeling of respect for
him. Several times already, they had looked at
each other as if on the point of speaking, as they
went in or out of the library or restaurant, but
neither had thus far ventured. The silent young
man sat at the farther end of the room, in the part
that ran at right angles to Place de la Sorbonne;
Lucien therefore had been unable to form an acquaintance with him, although he felt drawn toward
him, for his whole appearance exhibited unmistak-
able symptoms of superiority. As they came to
realize later, they were two untried, inexperienced,
retiring natures, subject to all the apprehensions

whose emotions amuse solitary men. Had it not been for their sudden meeting at the moment of Lucien's disastrous experience, perhaps they would never have become acquainted. But, as he turned into Rue des Grès, Lucien saw the young stranger coming from Sainte-Geneviève.

"The library is closed, monsieur, I don't know why," he said.

At that moment Lucien had tears in his eyes; he thanked the unknown with one of those gestures which are more eloquent than speech, and which, as between young man and young man, open hearts at once. They walked together down Rue des Grès toward Rue de la Harpe.

"Then I will go and walk in the Luxembourg garden," said Lucien. "When one has once come out, it is hard to return and work."

"One is no longer in the current of necessary ideas," observed the stranger. "You seem unhappy, monsieur?"

"I have just had a singular experience," said Lucien.

He described his visit to the quay, then to the old bookseller and the proposition he had made; he told his name and said a few words as to his situation. In about a month, he had spent sixty francs for board, thirty francs at the hotel, twenty francs at the theatre, ten francs at the bookstall—in all a hundred and twenty francs,—and he had only a hundred and twenty francs left.

"Monsieur," said the stranger, "your story is

identical with my own and with those of a thousand
to twelve hundred young men who come to Paris
every year from the provinces. We are not the
most unfortunate men in the world. Do you see
that theatre?" he said, pointing to the turrets of
the Odéon. "One day a man of talent who had
wallowed in the slough of absolute destitution, took
up his abode in one of the houses on the square;
married to a woman he loved—a refinement of
misery by which neither of us is as yet oppressed;
poor or rich, as you choose, in the possession of
two children; over head and ears in debt, but with
full confidence in his pen. He offers at the Odéon
a comedy in five acts, it is accepted, it has a favorable reception, the actors rehearse it and the manager hurries forward the rehearsals. These five
pieces of good fortune constitute five dramas even
more difficult of realization than the task of writing
five acts. The poor author, living in an attic that
you can see from here, exhausts his last remaining
resources in order to live during the preparations
for the performance of his play, his wife carries his
clothes to the Mont-de-Piété, the family eats nothing but bread. On the day of the last rehearsal,
the eve of the first performance, they owed fifty
francs in the quarter, to the baker, the milkwoman
and the concierge. The poet had retained what
was absolutely necessary, a coat, shirt, waistcoat,
trousers and boots. Sure of success, he embraces
his wife and tells her that the end of their misery
is at hand. 'Indeed there is no longer a chance

against us!' he cries.—'There is fire,' says the
wife; 'look, the Odéon is burning!' Monsieur,
the Odéon *was* burning. So don't complain. You
have clothes, you have no wife or children, you
have luck to the amount of a hundred and twenty
francs in your pocket and you owe nothing to anybody. The play was finally performed a hundred
and fifty times at the Théâtre Louvois. The king
bestowed a pension on the author. As Buffon has
said, genius is patience. Patience is, in truth, that
quality in man which most nearly resembles the
process that nature employs in her creations.
What is art, monsieur? it is nature in a concen-
trated form."

The two young men were by this time at the
Luxembourg. Lucien learned the name, since become famous, of the person who strove to comfort
him. The young man was Daniel d'Arthez, to-day
one of the most illustrious writers of our age, and
one of those rare beings, who, as a poet has so finely
said, present "the perfect union of a noble character and noble talent."

"One cannot be a great man for nothing," said
Daniel in his soothing voice. "Genius waters her
works with her tears. Talent is a moral being,
which has, like all beings, a childhood subject to
childish maladies. Society spurns incomplete
talents, as nature makes way with feeble or ill-
developed creatures. The man who would soar
above his fellows must make ready for a struggle,
recoil at no obstacle. A great writer is a martyr

who will not die, that's the whole of it. You have on your forehead the stamp of genius," said D'Arthez to Lucien, with a glance that enveloped him from head to foot; "if you have not her strong will in your heart, if you have not her angelic patience, if, however far from your goal you may be driven by the caprice of destiny, you do not constantly resume the road to your infinitude of glory, as the tortoise, in whatever country he may be, resumes the road to his beloved Ocean,—then do you renounce the pursuit to-day."

"Do you too expect suffering, pray, monsieur?" said Lucien.

"Trials of every sort; slander, treachery, injustice on the part of my rivals; the insults, the cunning, the sharp dealing of tradesmen," the young man replied in a resigned voice. "If your work is worthy, what matters a loss at first?"

"Will you read mine and pass judgment on it?" said Lucien.

"I will," said D'Arthez. "I live on Rue des Quatre-Vents, in a house where one of the most illustrious men, one of the greatest geniuses of our day, a phenomenon in science, Desplein, the greatest surgeon ever known, suffered his first martyrdom, struggling with the initial difficulties of life and glory in Paris. That remembrance gives me every night the dose of courage of which I stand in need every morning. I am in the room where he, like Rousseau, has so often eaten bread and cherries, but without Thérèse. Come in an hour; I will be there."

21

The two poets parted, pressing each other's hands with an indescribable effusion of melancholy emotion. Lucien went to get his manuscript. Daniel d'Arthez went to the Mont-de-Piété to pawn his watch and buy a couple of bundles of wood, so that his new friend should find a fire in his room, for it was quite cold.

Lucien was punctual to his appointment; first of all, he saw a house of less respectable aspect than his own hotel; a house with a dark passage, at the end of which he could distinguish an ill-lighted staircase. Daniel d'Arthez's room, on the fifth floor, had two wretched windows between which stood a bookcase blackened by time and use and filled with ticketed boxes. A poor cot-bed of painted wood, not unlike those seen in college rooms, a night-table purchased at second hand and two horse-hair covered armchairs stood in the back part of the room, the walls of which were covered with a Scotch paper varnished by smoke and by time. A long table covered with papers stood between the fireplace and the two windows. Opposite the fireplace was a dilapidated mahogany commode. A second-hand carpet entirely covered the floor. That necessary luxury saved fuel. In front of the table was a common desk-chair covered with red sheepskin worn white by long use, which with six other common chairs completed the furnishing of the room. Lucien noticed an old metal candlestick with a screen, provided with four wax candles. When he asked for an explanation of the wax candles, detecting on all sides symptoms of extreme poverty, D'Arthez replied that it was absolutely impossible for him to endure the odor of a tallow-dip. This circumstance indicated a most delicate sense of smell, the sure indication of exquisite sensitiveness.

The reading lasted seven hours. Daniel listened religiously, without making a remark of any sort, one of the rarest proofs of refined taste that an auditor can give.

"Well?" said Lucien, placing the manuscript on the mantelpiece.

"You have started upon a noble and glorious road," said the young man gravely; "but your work must be rewritten. If you don't want to be Walter Scott's mimic and nothing else, you must form a different style, for you have palpably imitated him. You begin, as he does, with long conversations to explain the position of your characters; when they have had their talk, you begin the description and action. That antagonism which is essential to every dramatic work comes in last of all. Reverse the terms of the problem. Replace these diffuse conversations, which are magnificent in Scott's hands but colorless in yours, with descriptive passages, to which our language is so well adapted. Let the dialogue in your case be the natural consequence that crowns your preparations. Enter upon the action of the drama first of all. Take your subject sometimes around the body, sometimes by the tail; in a word, vary your plots so that you may never be twice the same. You will do a new thing

in adapting to the history of France the form of the
Scotchman's dramatic dialogue.   Walter Scott is
entirely without passion; he knows nothing of it,
or perhaps it is forbidden him by the hypocritical
customs of his country.   In his view, woman is
duty incarnate.   With rare exceptions, his heroines
are absolutely the same; he had but one sketch for
them all, as painters say.   They are all based upon
Clarissa Harlowe; as he refers them all to one idea,
he could do no more than make many copies of the
same type, varied by the more or less vivid coloring.   Woman sows discord in society through passion.   Passion has an infinite number of accidents.
Depict the passions then; you will have vast stores
to draw upon, of which that great genius deprived
himself in order that he might be read in all the
families of prudish England.   In France, you will
find fascinating peccadilloes, and manners and customs glowing with Catholicism to contrast with the
sombre figures of Calvinism during the most impassioned period of our history.   Each authenticated
reign, from Charlemagne down, will require at
least one work, and some will require four or five,
as those of Louis XIV., Henri IV. and François I.
Thus you will write a picturesque history of
France, in which you will depict the costumes, the
furniture, the houses, without and within, and the
details of private life, at the same time imparting
to your work the spirit of the time of which it
treats, instead of laboriously working over known
facts.   You have a means of being original by

sweeping away the popular errors that disfigure the
memories of most of our kings. Dare, in your first
work, to rehabilitate the grand and magnificent
figure of Catherine, whom you have sacrificed to
the prejudices that are still hovering over her.
Lastly, paint Charles IX. as he was, not as Protes-
tant writers have made him. After ten years of
persistent toil, you will attain glory and fortune."
   It was then nine o'clock. Lucien imitated the
secret action of his future friend by asking him to
dine with him at Edon's, where he spent twelve
francs. During the dinner, Daniel confided the
secret of his hopes and his labors to Lucien.
D'Arthez would not admit the possibility of any
extraordinary talent without profound knowledge of
metaphysics. He was engaged at that moment in
despoiling ancient and modern times of all their
treasures of philosophy, in order to assimilate them
to one another. He desired, like Molière, to be a
profound philosopher before writing comedies.
He studied the written world and the living
world, thought and deed. He had for friends,
learned naturalists, young doctors, political writers
and artists, a society of studious, serious-minded
men with brilliant futures. He made his living by
conscientious and poorly paid articles, written for
biographical dictionaries, encyclopædias or dictionaries of the natural sciences; he wrote neither more
nor less than it was necessary for him to do in order
to live and to be able to follow out his thought. He
had an imaginative work, undertaken solely for the

purpose of studying the resources of the language. This book, still unfinished, taken up and laid aside capriciously, he kept for days of great distress. It was a psychological work of lofty purpose under the form of a novel.

Although Daniel displayed his talent modestly, he assumed gigantic proportions in Lucien's eyes. When they left the restaurant, at eleven o'clock, Lucien had conceived a strong friendship for this unobtrusive virtue, for this unconsciously sublime nature. The poet did not discuss Daniel's advice, he followed it to the letter. His eminent talent, already matured by thought and by a single, unpublished criticism, made for his own benefit, not for another's, had suddenly opened before him the doors of the most magnificent palaces of the imagination. The provincial's lips had been touched by a glowing coal and the words of the hard-working Parisian found the soil all prepared in the brain of the poet of Angoulême. Lucien set about recasting his work.

*

Overjoyed to have met in the Parisian desert a heart overflowing with generous sentiments in harmony with his own, the provincial great man did what all young men do who are hungering for affection: he clung to D'Arthez like a chronic disease, he called for him to go to the library, he walked with him at the Luxembourg when the weather was fine, he went with him every evening to his poor room, after dining with him at Flicoteaux's,—in short, he pressed close to his side as the troops pressed close to one another in the frozen plains of Russia.

During the early days of his acquaintance with Daniel, Lucien noticed with pain that his presence caused a certain amount of embarrassment when his new friend and his chosen intimates were together. The conversation of those superior beings, of whom D'Arthez spoke to him with heartfelt enthusiasm, was confined within the limits of a reserve quite out of harmony with their demonstrations of warm friendships. Lucien would discreetly take his leave at such times, conscious of something like grief at the ostracism to which he was subjected, and at the interest aroused in him by these unknown personages; for they all called one another by their Christian names. All, like D'Arthez, bore upon their foreheads the hall-mark of genius. After some secret opposition, which Daniel, unknown to Lucien, exerted himself to overcome, he was deemed worthy to enter this brotherhood of great minds. He was thus enabled to make the acquaintance of these men, who were bound together by the keenest sympathy, by the seriousness of their intellectual existence, and who met almost every evening at D'Arthez's room. One and all felt that he was to be a great writer; they had looked upon him as their leader since they had lost one of the most exceptional minds of the age, their first leader, a mystical genius who, for reasons which it would be useless to give, had returned to his province, and whom Lucien had often heard spoken of by the name of Louis. One will readily understand to how great an extent these men were likely to arouse the interest and curiosity of a poet, if we give the names of those who, like D'Arthez, have since won renown; for several of them succumbed.

Among those who are still living was Horace Bianchon, at that time a house-surgeon at the Hôtel-Dieu, who has since become one of the brilliant lights of the Parisian school of medicine, and who is now so well known that it is unnecessary to describe his personal appearance or to discuss his character and the nature of his mind.

Then there was Léon Giraud, that profound philosopher, that bold theorist who dissects all systems, passes judgment on them, expresses them by new formulæ and drags them at the feet of his idol, HUMANITY; always great, even in his errors, ennobled by his perfect good faith. This intrepid worker, this conscientious scholar, has become the leader of a school of politics and morals upon the merits of which time alone can pronounce. Although his convictions have cast his lines in regions far removed from those in which his comrades have followed their destinies, he has none the less remained their faithful friend. Art was represented by Joseph Bridau, one of the best painters of the younger school. Except for the unavowed misfortunes to which his too impressionable nature condemns him, Joseph, whose last word has not yet been said, by the way, might have proved a worthy successor of the great masters of the Italian school; he has the Roman skill in drawing and the Venetian genius for color; but love kills him and does not pierce his heart alone: love shoots his arrows into his brain, disturbs the current of his life and makes his work strangely uneven. When his ephemeral mistress makes him either too happy or too wretched, Joseph will sometimes send to the Exposition sketches in which the colors are laid on so thick as to mar the outlines, or, it may be, a picture which he has tried to finish while laboring under the burden of imaginary sorrows, and in which he has paid such close attention to the outlines that the coloring, in which he is a master, is entirely forgotten. He constantly disappoints both the public and his friends. Hoffman would have adored him for his bold advances in the field of art, for his caprices, for his imagination. When he is

at his best, he arouses admiration; he relishes it,
and loses his head when he fails to receive praise
for abortive works, in which the eyes of his soul
see all that is not apparent to the eyes of the public.
Capricious to the last degree, his friends have
sometimes seen him destroy a completed picture
which it seemed to him that he had elaborated too
much.

"There's too much work in it," he would say;
"it's too much like a student."

Original always and sometimes sublime, he has
all the drawbacks and all the advantages of nervous
organizations, in which perfection changes to
disease. His mind is a twin-brother to Sterne's,
but without the taste for literary toil. His witty
remarks, his flashes of thought, are indescribably
delicious. He is eloquent and knows how to love,
with due allowance for his caprices, which he carries into affairs of the heart as well as into his
work. He was dear to the club by reason of those
very qualities which bourgeois society would have
called his failings. Lastly, there was Fulgence
Ridal, one of the authors of our day who possess
the greatest genius for humor, a poet indifferent to
fame, who tosses to the stage only his most commonplace productions, and retains the most attractive scenes in the seraglio of his brain, for himself
and his friends; who seeks from the public only
so much money as is essential to his independence,
and, when he has obtained it, no longer chooses to
work. Slothful and prolific as Rossini, obliged,

like all great comic poets, like Molière and Rabelais, to look at everything from every point of view, he was a confirmed sceptic, he could and did laugh at everything. Fulgence Ridal is a great practical philosopher. His knowledge of the world, his genius for observation, his contempt for renown, which he calls ostentation, have not withered his heart. As active in behalf of others as he is indifferent to his own interests, if he takes a step forward, it is for a friend. In order not to belie his truly Rabelaisian mask, he does not despise good cheer nor does he seek it; he is at once sad and joyous. His friends call him *the dog of the regiment*, and nothing could describe him better than that sobriquet.

Three others there were, at least as superior in mental endowment as the four friends whose profiles we have painted, who fell by the roadside one after another. First, Meyraux, who died after setting in motion the celebrated dispute between Cuvier and Geoffroy Saint-Hilaire,—a great question which was destined to divide the scientific world into partisans of one or the other of those two men of equal genius, a few months before the death of him who maintained the superiority of a narrow, analytical science against the pantheist, who still lives and whom Germany reveres. Meyraux was the friend of that Louis who was soon to be snatched away from the intellectual world by a premature death which he had foreseen. To these two men, both marked as victims by death, both unknown to-day

despite the immense extent of their learning and
their genius, we must add Michel Chrestien, a republican of lofty aims who dreamed of the federation of Europe, and who counted for much in the
moral movement of the Saint-Simonists in 1830. A
politician of the force of Danton or Saint-Just, but
as simple and gentle as a girl, full of illusions and
of love, endowed with a melodious voice that would
have enraptured Mozart, Weber or Rossini and with
which he sang certain of Béranger's ballads in a
way to make the heart drunk with poesy, with love
or with hope, Michel Chrestien, poor like Lucien,
like Daniel, like all the rest, earned his living with
Diogenes-like recklessness. He made indexes for
great works, prospectuses for publishers, and was
as mute concerning his own doctrines as a tomb is
mute concerning the secrets of its dead. This joyous intellectual Bohemian, this great statesman,
who might perhaps have changed the face of the
world, died in the cloister of Saint-Merri like a
common soldier. Some tradesman's bullet there
laid low one of the noblest creatures who trod the
soil of France. Michel Chrestien died for other
doctrines than his own. His contemplated federation was a much greater menace than the republican
propaganda to European aristocracy; it was more
rational and less insane than the shocking ideas of
indefinite freedom proclaimed by the young madmen who put themselves forward as heirs of the
Convention. The noble plebeian was mourned by
all who knew him; there is not one of them who

does not to this day think often of that great, unknown politician.

These nine persons composed a club in which esteem and friendship kept the peace between the most contradictory ideas and doctrines. Daniel d'Arthez, a Picardian of gentle birth, adhered to the monarchy with a depth of conviction equal to that with which Michel Chrestien clung to his idea of European federalism. Fulgence Ridal laughed at the philosophical doctrines of Léon Giraud, who, in turn, predicted to D'Arthez the end of Christianity and of the family. Michel Chrestien, who believed in the religion of Christ, the divine artisan of the law of equality, defended the immortality of the soul against the scalpel of Bianchon, the analyst *par excellence.* They all discussed without disputing. They had no vanity, each having only the others for auditors. They told one another of their works, and consulted one another with the adorable good faith of youth. If any serious matter came up, any one of them would lay aside his own opinion in order to enter into the ideas of his friend, the more apt to assist him because he was impartial in relation to a cause or a work outside of his own ideas. Almost all of them showed a yielding, tolerant spirit, two qualities which demonstrated their superiority. Envy, that ghastly treasure of our disappointed hopes, our abortive talents, our failures, our wounded self-esteem, was unknown to them. Moreover, all of them were walking in different paths. Thus, they who, like Lucien, were admitted to their companionship, felt perfectly at ease.

True talent is always kindly and sincere, frank and not stiff and formal; its epigrams give pleasure to the mind and do not seek to wound the self-esteem. When the first emotion caused by involuntary respect had passed away, one experienced infinite delight in the company of these choice spirits. Familiarity did not lessen each one's consciousness of his own worth, and each felt a profound respect for his neighbor; lastly, as each was conscious of his ability to be in his turn benefactor or beneficiary, they all accepted favors without ceremony. Their conversation, always delightful to listen to and never tiresome, embraced the most varied range of subjects. The shafts of wit, as light as arrows, always went straight and swift to the mark. The great external misery and the splendor of intellectual riches produced a strange contrast. No one thought of the realities of life except as a source of friendly jesting.

One day when the cold season gave premature warning of its approach, five of D'Arthez's friends made their appearance, each with a parcel of wood under his cloak, one and all having had the same thought; as if at a picnic where every guest was expected to bring refreshment, every one should contribute a pie. Being all endowed with that moral beauty that reacts upon form and, no less than midnight toil, gilds youthful faces with a divine shade, they presented those somewhat irregular features to which a pure life and the fire of thought impart regularity and purity. Their foreheads were remarkable for their poetic amplitude. Their bright, sparkling eyes bore witness to their spotless lives. The sufferings of poverty, when they made themselves felt, were endured so cheerfully, shared with such eagerness by all, that they did not mar the serenity peculiar to the faces of young men still free from serious faults, who have not demeaned themselves by the base paltering with vice induced by poverty endured with ill grace, by the longing to succeed without choice of means and by the readiness with which men of letters accept or forgive treachery.

The thing that makes friendships indissoluble and increases their charm twofold is a feeling that is lacking in love—certainty. These young men were sure of themselves; the enemy of one became the enemy of all, and they would have sacrificed their most pressing interests to maintain the holy union of their hearts unbroken. All being incapable of a base act, they could meet every accusation with a peremptory denial and defend one another with perfect security. Equally noble in heart and equally strong in matters of sentiment, they could think and say to one another whatever they chose, within the domain of knowledge and intelligence; hence the innocence of their intercourse, the lightheartedness of their speech. Certain of understanding one another, their minds wandered at will; they were entirely unceremonious in their dealings, they confided their sorrows and joys to one another, and thought and suffered without concealment. The exquisite delicacy that makes the fable of the *Two Friends* a treasury for great minds, was habitual among them. Their strictness in the matter of admitting a new dweller to their sphere can be imagined; they were too conscious of their greatness and their happiness to disturb the latter by opening the door to new and unknown elements.

This federation of sentiments and interests endured without clash or misunderstanding for twenty years. Death alone, which removed Louis Lambert, Meyraux and Michel Chrestien from the circle, could diminish the number of stars in that noble constellation. When the last named fell, in 1832, Horace Bianchon, Daniel d'Arthez, Léon Giraud, Joseph Bridau and Fulgence Ridal, heedless of the dangers of the undertaking, went to Saint-Merri to recover his body in order to pay it the last earthly honors, although the political furnace was white hot. They escorted the cherished remains to the cemetery of Père-Lachaise during the night. Horace Bianchon was daunted by no obstacle and surmounted them all; he made a personal application to the ministers, avowing to them his long and enduring friendship for the deceased federalist. It was a touching scene, engraved forever in the memory of the few friends who assisted the five famous men. As you walk through the beautiful cemetery, you will notice a lot, purchased in perpetuity, in the centre of which rises a turf-covered mound surmounted by a cross of black wood upon which this name is carved in red letters: MICHEL CHRESTIEN. It is the only monument of that description. The five friends thought it fitting to do homage to that simple-minded man in this simple way.

Thus the fairest dreams of sentiment were realized in that cold attic. There a band of brothers, all equally strong in different branches of knowledge, mutually enlightened one another with perfect good faith, telling one another everything, even their unworthy thoughts; all were men of great learning and all had been tried in the crucible of poverty. Having once been admitted among these chosen mortals and accepted as their equal, Lucien represented poetry and beauty there. He read sonnets which were much admired. They asked him for a sonnet as he asked Michel Chrestien to sing him a *chanson*. Thus Lucien found in Rue des Quatre-Vents, an oasis in the Parisian desert.

In the early days of October, Lucien, having expended what remained of his money for a little wood, was left penniless while he was engaged most intently upon the recasting of his book. Daniel d'Arthez burned peat and endured poverty, he was as prudent as an old maid, and resembled a miser, so methodical was he in his habits. His courage spurred on Lucien's, who, being a newcomer in the club, felt an invincible repugnance to speak of his destitution. One morning he went to the Rue du Coq to sell *L'Archer de Charles IX.* to

22

Doguereau, but did not find him.   He did not realize
how indulgent great minds are.   Each one of his
friends could imagine the weaknesses peculiar to
men of poetic nature, the depression that follows
the efforts of the mind overexcited by the contem-
plation of that nature which it is their mission to
reproduce.   Those men, so strong in the face of
their own misfortunes, were moved by Lucien's
sufferings.   They understood his lack of money.
So it was that the club supplemented the evenings
passed in pleasant conversation, in profound meditation, in listening to poetry, in exchanging confidences, in soaring on unfettered wings through the
realms of the intellect, through the future of nations,
through the vast domains of history, by a proceeding that shows how little Lucien understood his
new friends.

"Lucien, my friend," said Daniel, "you didn't
come to Flicoteaux's to dinner yesterday, and we
know why."

Lucien could not restrain the tears that rolled
down his cheeks.

"You lacked confidence in us," said Michel
Chrestien; "we will make a cross on the mantelpiece, and when we have reached ten—"

"We have all had some extra work to do," said
Bianchon; "I have been looking after a rich patient
for Desplein; D'Arthez has written an article for
the *Révue Encyclopédique;* Chrestien undertook to
sing one evening in the Champs-Elysées with a
handkerchief and four candles; but he found a

pamphlet to write for a man who wants to become
a statesman, and he gave him six hundred francs'
worth of Machiavelli; Léon Giraud has borrowed
fifty francs from his publisher, Joseph has sold some
sketches, and Fulgence had his play given on Sunday to a full house."

"Here are two hundred francs," said Daniel;
"take them and see that you don't get caught
again."

"Upon my word, if he isn't going to kiss us, as
if we had done something extraordinary!" said
Chrestien.

To convey an idea of the pleasure Lucien enjoyed
in the midst of that living encyclopædia of angelic
spirits, of young men instinct with the varied forms
of originality that each of them derived from the
branch of learning which he cultivated, it will be
sufficient to quote the replies Lucien received, on
the following day, to a letter written to his family,
a masterpiece of affection and wounded sensitiveness, a pitiful cry torn from him by his distress:

DAVID SÉCHARD TO LUCIEN.

" MY DEAR LUCIEN:

" You will find enclosed a ninety days' draft, to your order,
for two hundred francs. You can negotiate it at our correspondent's, Monsieur Métivier, dealer in paper, Rue Ser-
pente. My dear Lucien, we have absolutely nothing. My
wife has undertaken to manage the printing office and acquits
herself of the task with a devotion, patience and zeal that
make me bless God for having given me such an angel for a

wife. Even she realizes how impossible it is for us to send you the slightest assistance. But my dear boy, I believe you to be embarked upon such a promising career, accompanied by such great and noble hearts, that you cannot fail to fulfil your glorious destiny, assisted by the almost divine intellects of Messieurs Daniel d'Arthez, Michel Chrestien and Léon Giraud, and advised by Messieurs Meyraux, Bianchon and Ridal, whom we know through your dear letter. I have made this draft, therefore, without Eve's knowledge, and I will find some way to pay it when it is due. Do not turn aside from the path you have chosen : it is rough, but it will be glorious. I would rather suffer untold ills than know that you had fallen into some slough in Paris, where I have seen so many. Have the courage to avoid, as you are doing, bad places and bad men, light-headed fools and men of letters of a certain type whom I learned to appraise at their real value during my stay in Paris. In short, be the worthy emulator of those celestial minds whom your letter has made dear to us. Your conduct will soon be rewarded. Adieu, my beloved brother ; you have rejoiced my heart, for I did not anticipate so much courage on your part.

" DAVID."

EVE SÉCHARD TO LUCIEN.

"MY DEAR BROTHER :

" Your letter has made us all weep. May the noble hearts to whom your good angel has guided you, know that a mother and a poor young wife will pray to God morning and evening for them ; and if the most fervent prayers ascend as far as His throne, they will obtain some blessings for you all. Yes, my brother, their names are written on my heart. Ah ! I shall see them some day. Even though I have to make the journey on foot, I will go and thank them for their friendship for you, for it has spread a balm upon my open wounds. Here, my dear, we are working like poor mechanics.

My husband, that great, unappreciated man whom I love more every day as I discover from moment to moment fresh treasures in his heart, has abandoned his printing office, and I can guess why: your poverty, ours and our mother's, are killing him. Our adored David is devoured like Prometheus by a vulture, a ghastly, sharp-beaked sorrow. As for him, the noble-hearted man, he hardly heeds it. He is engrossed by the hope of a fortune in store. He passes all his time experimenting in paper-making ; he has asked me to attend to the business in his place and he assists me as much as his preoccupation permits. Alas! I am *enceinte*. This fact, which would under certain circumstances have overwhelmed me with joy, makes me very sad in our present situation. My poor mother has become young again, she has recovered all her old strength for her fatiguing occupation of nurse. If it were not for anxiety about money, we should be very happy. Old Père Séchard will not give his son a liard ; David has been to see him to borrow a few sous to send you, for your letter drove him to despair. ' I know Lucien, he will lose his head and do something foolish,' he said. I scolded him. ' My brother, fail to do what he ought, whatever happens! ' I replied. ' Lucien knows that I should die of grief if he did.' Mother and I have pawned some little things, but David has no suspicion of it; mother will redeem them as soon as she gets a little money. In that way, we have obtained a hundred francs which I am sending you by express. Don't think ill of me for not answering your first letter, my dear. We were in a position where we had to drudge at night, and I was working like a man. Ah! I didn't know I had so much strength. Madame de Bargeton is a heartless, soulless woman ; even if she had ceased to love you, she owed it to herself to protect you and help you after tearing you from our arms to cast you into that horrible Parisian ocean, where one needs a special blessing from God to fall in with true friends amid those seas of men and interests. She is not to be regretted. I did wish that you had some devoted woman with you, a second myself; but now that I know you

have friends who have the same feelings for you that we
have, my mind is at rest. Spread your wings, my noble, beloved genius! You will be our glory as you already are our
love.

"EVE."

" MY DARLING CHILD:

" After what your sister has written, I can only give you
my blessing and assure you that my prayers and my thoughts
are full of you alone, alas! to the detriment of those I have
before my eyes; for there are hearts in which the absent are
always right, and so it is with the heart of

"YOUR MOTHER."

Thus, two days later, Lucien was able to repay
his friends the loan they had offered him with such
delicacy. Never perhaps had life seemed fairer to
him, but the impulsive movement of his self-esteem
did not escape the profound gaze of his friends or
their delicate perception.

"One would say you were afraid to owe us anything," cried Fulgence.

"Oh! the pleasure he manifests is a very serious
thing in my eyes," said Chrestien; "it confirms
my observations; Lucien is vain."

"He is a poet," said D'Arthez.

"Do you bear me ill-will for a feeling as natural
as mine?"

"We must give him credit for not concealing from
us what he felt," said Léon Giraud, "he is still
frank; but I'm afraid that he will suspect us sooner
or later."

"Why, pray?" Lucien asked.

"We can read your heart," replied Joseph Bridau.

"You have within you," said Michel Chrestien, "a diabolic wit with which you will justify in your own eyes, things that are most opposed to our principles: instead of being a sophist in ideas, you will be a sophist in action."

"Yes, I am afraid of it," said D'Arthez. "Lucien, you will have admirable discussions with yourself, in which you will be great, but which will lead to blameworthy acts. You will never be in accord with yourself."

"Upon what do you base your diagnosis, pray?" queried Lucien.

"Your vanity is so great, my dear poet, that you show it even in your friendship!" cried Fulgence. "All vanity of that sort indicates deplorable egotism, and egotism is the bane of friendship."

"Great God!" cried Lucien, "is it possible that you don't know how dearly I love you?"

"If you loved us as we love each other, would you have shown so much eagerness and emphasis in returning what it gave us such pleasure to give you?"

"We don't lend one another anything here, we give," said Joseph Bridau bluntly.

"Don't think us rough, my dear child," said Michel Chrestien, "we look ahead. We are afraid of seeing you some day prefer the pleasure of petty revenge to the pleasure of our pure friendship. Read Goethe's *Tasso*, the greatest work of that great genius, and you will learn there that the poet loves bright-colored stuffs, festivals, triumphs, parade; be Tasso without his folly. Do society and its pleasures beckon to you? Remain here. Transport to the region of ideas, all that you ask of your vanity. Folly for folly, be virtuous in act and vicious in thought, instead of thinking worthy thoughts and behaving ill, as D'Arthez said."

Lucien hung his head: his friends were right.

"I confess that I am not so strong as you are," he said looking up at them with a winning expression. "I haven't the loins and the shoulders with which to sustain the weight of Paris or to struggle courageously. Nature has given us temperaments and faculties of a different order, and you know better than anyone, the reverse side of virtue and vice. I am already tired out, I tell you in confidence."

"We will sustain you," said D'Arthez; "that is just what faithful friends are good for."

"The help I have just received cannot be depended upon, and we are all equally poor; I shall soon be pursued again by want. Chrestien, who is at the beck and call of the first comer, can do nothing with publishers. Bianchon's pursuits lie in an entirely different direction. D'Arthez knows only the publishers of scientific works or specialties, who have no influence with the publishers of novelties. Horace, Fulgence, Ridal and Bridau work on lines that take them a hundred leagues from bookshops. I must make up my mind to something."

"Make up your mind to do as we do, suffer!" said Bianchon; "suffer with a brave heart and trust to hard work!"

"But that which is only suffering to you is death to me," said Lucien earnestly.

"Before the cock crows thrice," said Léon Giraud with a smile, "this man will have betrayed the cause of hard work for that of sloth and the vices of Paris."

"To what has hard work brought you?" laughed Lucien.

"When one leaves Paris for Italy, one doesn't find Rome half way," said Joseph Bridau. "You would have peas grow all dressed with butter."

"They don't grow that way for anybody except the eldest sons of peers of France," said Chrestien. "But we poor fellows plant them and water them, and we relish them all the more."

The conversation took a jocose turn and the subject was changed. Those far-seeing minds, those kindly hearts, tried to make Lucien forget this little quarrel, but he understood thenceforth how hard it was to deceive them. He soon reached a despairing frame of mind which he carefully concealed from his friends, deeming them implacable mentors. His southern nature, which ran so readily over the whole keyboard of emotions, led him to form the most contrary resolutions.

Several times he spoke of trying his hand at writing for the newspapers, and his friends invariably said:

"Do nothing of the kind!"

"It would be the tomb of the comely, the gentle Lucien whom we know and love," said D'Arthez.

"You would not resist the constant conflict between work and pleasure that is found in the lives of journalists; and resistance is the corner-stone of virtue. You would be so enchanted with the exercise of power, with the right of life and death over works of the mind, that you would be a journalist in two months. To be a journalist is to become proconsul in the republic of letters. He who can say whatever he chooses soon reaches the point of doing whatever he chooses! That is a maxim of Napoléon's and is easy to understand."

"Would you not be with me?" said Lucien.

"We should not be there," cried Fulgence. "As a journalist, you would no more think of us than the brilliant, courted dancer at the Opéra, in her silk-lined carriage, thinks of her native village, her cows and her wooden shoes. You have the qualities of the journalist, brilliancy and promptness of thought, in only too great measure. You would never deny yourself the pleasure of letting fly a shaft of wit, though it should make your friend weep. I see journalists in the theatre lobbies, and they make me shudder. Journalism is a hell, a pit of iniquity, falsehood, treachery, which one cannot pass through, and from which one can emerge unscathed only when protected, as Dante was, by Virgil's divine laurel-wreath."

The more the club argued with Lucien against

that course, the more his longing to become acquainted with the danger impelled him to take the
risk and he began to question himself: was it not
absurd to allow himself to be surprised again by
want without having taken any steps to avert it?
In view of the failure of his attempts to find a purchaser for his first novel, Lucien felt but slightly
tempted to write a second. Moreover, what could
he live on while he was writing it? He had exhausted his stock of patience during a month of pri-
vation. Why should not he do nobly what journalists
did in a conscienceless, undignified way? His
friends insulted him with their suspicions and he
would prove to them his strength of mind. Perhaps he would assist them some day and be the
herald of their renown!

"After all, what does friendship amount to that
draws back at the idea of becoming an accomplice?"
he asked Michel Chrestien one evening, when he
and Léon Giraud had walked home with him.

"We draw back at nothing," replied Chrestien.
"If you were unfortunate enough to kill your mistress,
I would help you to conceal your crime and might
perhaps esteem you still; but if you should become
a spy, I would shun you with horror, for then you
would be an infamous coward with premeditation.
That is journalism in two words. Friendship par-
dons the misstep, the irreflective impulse of passion; but it must be implacable to one who has
deliberately resolved to barter his soul and mind
and thought."

"May I not become a journalist in order to sell my collection of poems and my novel, and then abandon the trade at once?"

"Machiavelli might act so, but not Lucien de Rubempré," said Léon Giraud.

"Very well," cried Lucien, "I will show you that I am the equal of Machiavelli."

"Ah!" cried Michel, pressing Léon's hand, "you have destroyed him. —Lucien," he continued, "you have three hundred francs and that is enough to live on comfortably for three months; very good, set to work and write another novel; D'Arthez and Fulgence will help you with the plot; you will improve, you will become a genuine novelist. I will find my way into one of those *lupanars* of thought, I will be a journalist for three months, I will sell your books for you to some bookseller whose publications I will attack, I will write articles and will have others written for you; we will make the book a great success, you will be a great man, and you will still be our Lucien."

"You must have a very low opinion of me, if you think that I would succumb where you would be safe," said the poet.

"O *mon Dieu*, forgive him, for he is a mere child!" cried Michel Chrestien.

Having polished up his mind during the evenings passed with D'Arthez and his friends, Lucien began to study the articles, humorous and otherwise, in the less important newspapers. Confident that he could prove himself at least the equal of their

cleverest editors, he tried his hand secretly at that
gymnastic form of thought and went out one morning with the brilliant idea of going to some colonel
of those light horse of the press and asking for employment. He arrayed himself in his most distinguished costume and as he crossed the bridges, he
thought that authors, journalists, writers, his future
brethren in short, would show a little more consideration and unselfishness than the two varieties of
publisher with whom his hopes had come in contact. He would surely meet with sympathy,
perhaps with true, comforting affection like that he
had found in the club on Rue des Quartre-Vents.
A prey to the emotion aroused by a presentiment
listened to but resisted—a form of emotion to which
men of imagination are much addicted—he reached
Rue Saint-Fiacre, near Boulevard Montmartre, and
halted in front of a building containing the offices
of a small newspaper, a building whose outward
appearance caused his heart to beat fast like that
of a young man about to enter an evil place.
Nevertheless, he went up to the offices, which were
located in the entresol. In the first room, which
was divided into two equal parts by a partition
reaching to the ceiling consisting in part of boards
and in part of an iron grating, he found a one-armed
veteran who was holding several reams of paper
steady on his head with his only hand, and had between his teeth the certificate required by the
Stamp Office. This poor man, whose face was of
a yellowish hue and studded with red protuberances,

to which he owed his sobriquet, *Coloquinte,* pointed
out to him the Cerberus of the paper behind the
grating. He was an old officer, decorated with the
Cross, his nose enveloped in gray moustaches, a
black silk cap on his head, and buried in a blue
frockcoat of ample proportions like a turtle under its
shell.

"With what number does monsieur wish his subscription to begin?" asked the officer of the Empire.

"I didn't come to subscribe," Lucien replied.

As he spoke, he glanced at a sign on the door opposite that by which he had entered and read these
words: EDITORIAL OFFICE; and beneath them:
The public is not admitted.

"A claim then, no doubt?" rejoined Napoléon's
former trooper. "We were a little hard on Mariette,
I admit. But what do you expect! I don't even
know why it was as yet. But if you demand satisfaction, I am ready," he added, glancing at a collection of foils and pistols, the modern stand of arms,
heaped together in a corner.

"Still less do I come for that, monsieur. I desire
to speak with the editor in chief."

"There's never anyone here before four o'clock."

"Here, my old Giroudeau, I make it eleven
columns, which at a hundred sous each, comes to
fifty-five francs; I have had forty, so, you see, you
still owe me fifteen francs as I said."

These words came from a little pinched face,
transparent as the half-cooked white of an egg,
pierced by a pair of eyes of a soft shade of blue

but with a horribly malignant expression—a face that belonged to a thin young man who was hidden behind the old soldier's opaque body. The voice made Lucien's blood run cold; it was half way between the mewing of a cat and the hoarse asthmatic howl of the hyena.

"Very true, my little warrior," said the retired trooper, "but you count titles and blank spaces; my orders from Finot are to take the whole number of lines and divide by the number of lines in a column. If you perform that compressing operation upon your article, you will make it three columns less."

"What! he doesn't pay for blank spaces, the Turk! but he reckons them when he settles with his partner for all the editorial articles in bulk. I'm going to see Etienne Lousteau, Vernou—"

"I can't go behind my orders, my boy," said the officer. "What! for fifteen francs will you turn against your nurse, when you can write articles as easily as I smoke a cigar! Why! you can just pay for one bowl less of punch for your friends, or win an extra game of billiards, and you're all right."

"Finot is saving money by means that will cost him very dear," said the editor, as he rose and left the room.

"Wouldn't one think he was Voltaire or Rousseau?" said the cashier to himself, glancing at the provincial poet.

"I will call again about four o'clock, monsieur," said Lucien.

During the discussion he had noticed on the walls, portraits of Benjamin Constant, General Foy and the seventeen illustrious orators of the liberal party, mingled with caricatures against the government. He had looked with especial interest at the door of the sanctuary whence the clever sheet was issued that amused him every day and that enjoyed the right of casting ridicule upon kings, upon the most important events—the right, in short, of dismissing the most solemn subjects with a jest. He went out and strolled along the boulevards, a novel form of entertainment to him, and so attractive that the hands of the clocks in the watchmaker's windows pointed to four o'clock before he realized that he had not breakfasted. He hurried back to Rue Saint-Fiacre, climbed the stairs, did not find the old officer, but saw the veteran sitting on his pile of stamped paper, eating a crust of bread and doing his sentry duty with a resigned air, worn as naturally in the service of the paper as in the old days of extra picket duty, and with as little comprehension of what he was doing as he formerly had of the reasons for the Emperor's rapid marches.

Lucien conceived the audacious idea of deceiving this redoubtable official; he pulled his hat down over his eyes and opened the door of the sanctum just as if he belonged to the establishment.

The editorial office presented to his greedy eyes a round table covered with a green cloth, and six chairs of cherry wood covered with straw seats that were still fresh and new. The floor of the room, painted in colors, had not been polished, but it was clean—a fact indicating that callers were few. On the mantelpiece were a mirror, a grocer's clock covered with dust, two candlesticks in which two tallow-dips were carelessly stuck, and a few visiting cards. On the table some old newspapers lay about an inkstand in which the ink had dried up and resembled lacquer; it was supplied with quills twisted into curious shapes. He read several articles written in an almost illegible, hieroglyphic handwriting upon stray bits of paper, and torn at the top by the compositors at the printing office, who use that method of marking articles that are in type. Here and there he saw and admired caricatures drawn upon colored paper with much skill, by men who had evidently been trying to kill time and keep their hand in by killing something or somebody.

Pinned to the wall-paper of a watery green color were nine caricatures drawn with the pen during office hours, all referring to the *Solitaire*, a book which was then enjoying unheard-of popularity in Europe and had probably became a bore to newspaper men:—"The *Solitaire*, appearing in the provinces, astonishes the ladies."—"Effect of reading the *Solitaire* in a chateau."—"Effect of the *Solitaire* upon domestic animals."—"The *Solitaire*, having been explained to savage tribes, achieves a most brilliant triumph."—"The *Solitaire* translated into Chinese, and presented by the author to the Emperor at Pekin."—"Elodie ravished by Mont

23

Sauvage.''—This caricature seemed very immodest
to Lucien, but it made him laugh.—''The *Solitaire*
carried in procession by the newspapers under a
canopy.''—''The *Solitaire*, causing a press to burst,
wounds the bears.''—''The *Solitaire* read backward
astonishes the academicians by its superior beau-
ties.''—Lucien discovered on the wrapper of a newspaper, a drawing representing an editor holding out
his hat, and beneath it the words: *Finot, my hundred francs!* signed by a name that has since become famous but will never be illustrious.   Between
the mantelpiece and the window were a secretaire,
a mahogany armchair, a waste-paper basket and an
oblong hearth rug, the whole covered with a thick
layer of dust.   There were only draw-curtains at
the windows.   On top of the desk there were about
twenty works that had been placed there during the
day, engravings, music, snuff-boxes *à la Charte*,
a copy of the ninth edition of the *Solitaire*, still the
great joke of the moment, and ten or twelve sealed
letters.

When Lucien had made an inventory of this extraordinary furniture and had thought and thought
until his head swam, five o'clock having struck, he
returned to the veteran to question him.   Coloquinte
had finished his crust and was awaiting with the
patience of a soldier on sentry-go the return of his
decorated superior, who was walking on the boulevard perhaps.   At that moment a woman appeared
in the doorway, having given notice of her approach
by the rustle of her dress on the stairway and the

light feminine step so easily recognized. She was quite pretty.

"Monsieur," she said to Lucien, "I know why you puff up Mademoiselle Virginie's hats so, and I have come, first of all, to subscribe for a year; but tell me the terms—"

"I am not employed on the paper, madame."

"Ah!"

"Do you want your subscription to begin with the month of October?" the veteran asked.

"What is madame's business?" inquired the old officer, entering at that moment.

He held a conference with the fair milliner. When Lucien, tired of waiting, returned to the outer room, he heard these concluding words: "Why, I shall be delighted, monsieur. Mademoiselle Florentine may come to my shop and choose whatever she wants. I keep ribbons. So it's all agreed; you won't have anything more to say about Virginie, a bungler, incapable of inventing a style, while I invent all mine!"

Lucien heard the chinking sound of a number of coins falling into the cash-box. Then the officer began to make up his daily account.

"Monsieur, I have been here an hour," said the poet, with some irritation.

"Haven't *they* come?" said the Napoléonic veteran, showing some interest as a matter of courtesy. "I'm not surprised. It's some time since I've seen *them*. It's the middle of the month, you see! Those fellows only come around on pay-day, the twenty-ninth or thirtieth."

"And Monsieur Finot?" queried Lucien, who had remembered the manager's name.

"He's at home, Rue Feydeau. Coloquinte, old boy, take him everything that has come to-day, as you carry the paper to the printing office.

"Where in the deuce is the paper made up?" said Lucien, speaking to himself.

"The paper?" said the clerk, as Coloquinte handed him the change from the Stamp Office; "the paper?—*broum! broum!*—Be at the printing office at six o'clock to-morrow morning, old fellow, to keep the carriers up to their work.—The paper, monsieur, is made up in the street, at the authors' homes, at the printing office, between eleven o'clock and midnight. In the Emperor's day, monsieur, these shops for scribbling on paper weren't known. Ah! he would have shaken them up with four men and a corporal, and not have let himself be hoodwinked by fine phrases as these other people are. But enough said. If my nephew finds it profitable and if he writes for *the other's* son, why, after all—*broum! broum!*—there's no harm done. Well, well! subscribers don't seem to be coming in in regiments, and I think I'll leave the guard-house."

"You seem to be well posted on the subject of editing a newspaper, monsieur," said Lucien.

"On the financial side, *broum! broum!*" said the officer, noisily clearing his throat. "A hundred sous or three francs, according to the talent displayed,— for a column of fifty lines of forty letters each, not counting blank spaces—that's the rule. As for the editors, they're a curious lot, young fellows I wouldn't have for camp followers, and, just because they make fly tracks on white paper, they seem to look down on an old captain of dragoons of the Garde Impériale, retired with the rank of major, who entered every capital in Europe with Napoléon—"

Lucien, finding that he was being edged toward the door by the ex-trooper, who was brushing his blue coat and manifested an intention of leaving the office, had the courage to stand firm.

"I came here to be employed as an editor," he said, "and I promise you that I am filled with respect for one of the captains of the Garde Impériale, those men of bronze—"

"Well said, my little *pékin*," rejoined the officer. "But which class of editors do you want to enter?" he added, passing over Lucien's body, so to speak, and descending the stairs.

He stopped at the porter's lodge to light his cigar.

"If any subscriptions come in, Mère Chollet," he said, "take them and make a note of them.—Always subscriptions, I think of nothing but subscriptions," he continued, turning to Lucien, who had followed him. "Finot is my nephew, the only one of my family who has done anything to make my position more comfortable. So whoever seeks a quarrel with Finot, finds old Giroudeau, captain in the dragoons of the guard, who began as a common soldier in the army of Sambre-et-Meuse, was five years master-at-arms in the First Hussars, in the army of Italy!

One, two, and it's all up with the fault-finder!" he
added, making a pass with an imaginary sword.
"Now then, my boy, we have different classes of
editors: there's the editor who edits and gets his
pay, the editor who edits and gets nothing—him
we call a volunteer; lastly, there's the editor who
edits nothing and who isn't the biggest fool of the
lot, for he makes no mistakes; he passes for a
writer, he belongs to the paper, he pays for our
dinner, he loiters about the theatres, he keeps an
actress, he's very fortunate. Which do you want
to be?"

"Why, an editor who works hard and, on that
account, is well paid."

"Yes, you're just like all raw recruits, wanting
to be marshals of France! Take old Giroudeau's
advice,—file left, slow time,—and go and pick up
nails in the gutter like yonder youth who has been
in the service, you can tell by his carriage.—Isn't
it an outrage that an old soldier, who has marched
up to the cannon's mouth a thousand times, should
be picking up nails in Paris? *Dieu de Dieu,* you're
a rascal, you didn't support the Emperor!—Look
you, my boy, that man you saw this morning has
earned forty francs this month. Could you do any
better? And, according to Finot, he's the brightest
of all his editors."

"When you joined the Sambre-et-Meuse, didn't
they tell you there was danger ahead?"

"*Parbleu!* yes."

"Very good."

"Well, go and see my nephew Finot, a good fellow, the squarest man you will ever meet, if you can succeed in meeting him; for he wriggles about like a fish. In his trade, you see, he doesn't write himself, but keeps others writing. It seems that his parishioners prefer amusing themselves with actresses to soiling paper. Oh! they're a queer lot! Farewell, until I have the honor of meeting you again."

The cashier began to twirl his redoubtable leaded cane, one of *Germanicus's* protectors, and left Lucien standing on the boulevard, as perplexed by this sketch of the editorial function as he had been by the definitive results of his literary venture with Porchon and Vidal. Ten times Lucien called on Andoche Finot, manager of the paper, at his house on Rue Feydeau, without finding him. Early in the morning, Finot had not returned home. At noon, Finot was out: breakfasting, they said, at some café. Lucien went to that café, and, surmounting an invincible repugnance, inquired for Finot of the proprietress; Finot had just gone. At last Lucien, thoroughly weary of his quest, came to look upon Finot as an apocryphal, fabulous personage, and he decided that it was a simpler matter to keep watch upon Etienne Lousteau at Flicoteaux's. That young journalist would doubtless explain the mystery that surrounded the existence of the paper with which he was connected.

LIST OF ETCHINGS

―――

VOLUME XXX